Routledge Revivals

Theophrastus and the Greek Physiological Psychology Before Aristotle

First published in 1917, *Theophrastus and the Greek Physiological Psychology Before Aristotle* is on the history of ancient Greek physiological psychology. It includes the author's essays on Theophrastus and his writings on sense perception; the original Greek text and his own translation of *On the Senses*, which had not previously been translated in full into English. This book will be of interest to students of medicine, psychology and philosophy.

Theophrastus and the Greek Physiological Psychology Before Aristotle

George Malcolm Stratton

First published in 1917
By George Allen & Unwin Ltd

This edition first published in 2024 by Routledge
4 Park Square, Milton Park, Abingdon, Oxon, OX14 4RN

and by Routledge
605 Third Avenue, New York, NY 10017

Routledge is an imprint of the Taylor & Francis Group, an informa business

© George Allen & Unwin 1917

All rights reserved. No part of this book may be reprinted or reproduced or utilised in any form or by any electronic, mechanical, or other means, now known or hereafter invented, including photocopying and recording, or in any information storage or retrieval system, without permission in writing from the publishers.

Publisher's Note
The publisher has gone to great lengths to ensure the quality of this reprint but points out that some imperfections in the original copies may be apparent.

Disclaimer
The publisher has made every effort to trace copyright holders and welcomes correspondence from those they have been unable to contact.

A Library of Congress record exists under LCCN: 18003252

ISBN: 978-1-032-74871-9 (hbk)
ISBN: 978-1-003-47137-0 (ebk)
ISBN: 978-1-032-74885-6 (pbk)

Book DOI 10.4324/9781003471370

THEOPHRASTUS *and the* GREEK PHYSIOLOGICAL PSYCHOLOGY BEFORE ARISTOTLE

By GEORGE MALCOLM STRATTON

PROFESSOR OF PSYCHOLOGY IN THE UNIVERSITY OF CALIFORNIA

LONDON: GEORGE ALLEN & UNWIN LTD.
NEW YORK: THE MACMILLAN COMPANY

First published in 1917

(All rights reserved)

PREFACE

STRANGE to say, there exists in English no complete translation of Theophrastus's small but exceedingly valuable writing *On the Senses*. And this must be my excuse for undertaking a work that could have been so much better done by many another hand. An understanding of Greek physiological psychology before Plato and after Aristotle requires that one know his Theophrastus; and having studied this fragment long myself, in the attempt to learn more of the history of psychology, it seemed but a neighbourly act to lighten, if one could, the labour of other psychologists until some abler help should come.

For while Theophrastus's account of the views of others is for the most part available in English, scattered here a sentence and there a paragraph through the works of men like Burnet and Beare, yet the canny judgments by Theophrastus himself, which in extent are nearly one-half of his *De Sensibus*, are usually either given in briefest summary or else omitted. And so one receives no feeling, which the connected whole would give, of the state of critical psychology in the later day. With the thought, then, that there will be readers interested in this later work and especially in Theophrastus's own psychology, and who will be unwilling to use him merely as a reporter of his predecessors, I have attempted to gather from the *De Sensibus* and his other writings the substance of his

Preface

own convictions regarding sense perception and the particular senses and in regard to pleasure and pain, and have offered this by way of introduction. It will I hope be found useful by those who wish—not an exhaustive account of the man's views of these subjects; for this I do not pretend to give—but something far fuller than is to be had in the well-known histories by Zeller, Chaignet, and Siebeck.

The Greek text of the *De Sensibus* used and here reproduced is substantially that of Diels in his *Doxographi Graeci*, with such changes as he himself has made in those portions of it included in his *Fragmente der Vorsokratiker*. Departures from the readings of Diels I have tried faithfully to indicate; but to a very few minor changes in punctuation I have thought it unnecessary to draw attention. Nor in the translation have I carried through in stubborn consistency my general purpose to indicate by angular brackets, < >, those English expressions that have no corresponding words in the Greek. I have omitted these marks when I felt that the occasion was very slight for troubling in this way the reader's eye.

To publications in English my indebtedness is greatest to Beare's *Greek Theories of Elementary Cognition from Alcmaeon to Aristotle*. No one who has not gone over this book almost line by line and word by word and compared it with the sources can sufficiently appreciate the scholarly care and expository judgment that have entered into it. In the pages following, from a sin that seems ever to beset the academic mind, my moments of dissent from his judgment will doubtless stand forth; but I should not wish these to obscure the larger agreement and admiration which I really feel.

In a more personal way I am under obligations to my colleagues in the University of California, Professor Clapp

Preface

and Professor Linforth of the Greek Department, who have read the translation of the *De Sensibus*, coming to my frequent relief with corrections and suggestions of importance, and helping me over many a troublesome place. The full degree of my debt to Professor A. E. Taylor of the University of St. Andrews it will be difficult for me to make the reader know. With extraordinary kindness and generosity, he also has examined this translation and many of the notes, and out of his own rich fund of Aristotelian knowledge has written me a running comment and criticism on the whole. The quotations from his manuscript, which he has permitted me to make, will give some imperfect idea of the character of his assistance; but in numberless ways, impossible to indicate, my own work has profited by his ample scholarship in this region of Greek learning. But since in some cases I have ventured to maintain what he would have otherwise, the reader must not hold him nor any but myself responsible for the errors which with all patience and endeavour doubtless still remain.

G. M. S.

BERKELEY, *March* 1917.

CONTENTS

I

THEOPHRASTUS AS PSYCHOLOGIST OF SENSE PERCEPTION, AND AS REPORTER AND CRITIC OF OTHER PSYCHOLOGISTS . . . 15

1. THE GENERAL VALUE OF HIS WRITING *ON THE SENSES* 15

2. THEOPHRASTUS'S OWN DOCTRINE UPON THE MAIN TOPICS OF THE *DE SENSIBUS* . . 18
    - Sense Perception in General . . 18
    - Vision 27
    - Hearing 33
    - Smell 36
    - Taste 43
    - Touch 46
    - Pleasure and Pain . . . 48

3. THEOPHRASTUS'S GENERAL METHOD OF EXPOSITION AND OF CRITICISM IN THE *DE SENSIBUS* 51

II

THE TEXT AND TRANSLATION OF THE FRAGMENT *ON THE SENSES* 65

III

NOTES UPON THE TRANSLATION AND TEXT OF THEOPHRASTUS'S *DE SENSIBUS* . . 153

INDEX 223

ABBREVIATIONS USED IN CITATION

A. and E. P.: Aristotle and the Earlier Peripatetics; being a translation from Zeller's 'Philosophy of the Greeks', by Costelloe and Muirhead. London, 1897.
A. E. T.: Manuscript notes by Professor A. E. Taylor of the University of St. Andrews, Scotland.
Beare: Greek Theories of Elementary Cognition from Alcmaeon to Aristotle, by John I. Beare. Oxford, 1906.
Burnet: Early Greek Philosophy, by John Burnet. Second Edition, London, 1908.
De Caus. Pl.: Theophrasti de Causis Plantarum. (ΠΕΡΙ ΦΥΤΩΝ ΑΙΤΙΩΝ.)
De Igne: Theophrasti Libellus de Igne. (ΠΕΡΙ ΠΥΡΟΣ.)
De Odor.: Theophrasti Libellus de Odoribus. (ΠΕΡΙ ΟΣΜΩΝ.)
De Sens.: Theophrasti Fragmentum de Sensibus. (ΠΕΡΙ ΑΙΣΘΗΣΕΩΝ.)
Dox.: Doxographi Graeci: Collegit . . . Hermannus Diels. Berolini MDCCCLXXIX.
Hist. Pl.: Theophrasti Historia Plantarum. (ΠΕΡΙ ΦΥΤΩΝ ΙΣΤΟΡΙΑΣ.)
Ph. d. Gr.: Die Philosophie der Griechen, von Eduard Zeller. Erster Theil, Fünfte Auflage, Leipzig, 1892.
Philippson: ΥΛΗ ΑΝΘΡΩΠΙΝΗ, scripsit et edidit Ludovicus Philippson. Berolini, 1831.
Prantl: Aristoteles über die Farben: Erläutert durch eine Uebersicht der Farbenlehre der Alten, von Dr. Carl Prantl. München, 1849.
Prisc.: Prisciani Lydi quae Extant: Metaphrasis in Theophrastum et Solutionem ad Chosroem Liber: edidit I. Bywater. Berolini, MDCCCLXXXVI.
Vorsokr.: Die Fragmente der Vorsokratiker: griechisch und deutsch von Hermann Diels. Dritte Auflage, Berlin, 1912.
Wim.: Theophrasti Eresii Opera, quae supersunt, Omnia . . . recensuit . . . Fredericus Wimmer. Parisiis, MDCCCLXVI.

I

THEOPHRASTUS AS PSYCHOLOGIST OF SENSE PERCEPTION, AND AS REPORTER AND CRITIC OF OTHER PSYCHOLOGISTS

I

THE GENERAL VALUE OF HIS WRITING
ON THE SENSES

THEOPHRASTUS'S work *On the Senses,* or *On Sense Perception and the Sensory Objects*,[1] is the most important source of our knowledge of the earlier Greek physiological psychology. Those interested primarily in the theory of the soul will ascribe to the historical portions of Aristotle's *De Anima* a higher value for the knowledge of his predecessors than to Theophrastus's account. But for an acquaintance with what these earlier investigators knew and thought of the observable processes of the mind—the processes by which we gain our impressions of the outer world and reproduce and elaborate these impressions; the processes of pleasure and pain; and the connection which all these and emotion and purpose and temperament have with the different parts or states of the body—of all these matters that are so important for modern psychology Theophrastus

---

[1] The title Περὶ αἰσθήσεων has the higher manuscript authority. But Περὶ αἰσθήσεως also appears; and this with the addition of καὶ περὶ αἰσθητῶν better describes the whole composition, and has often been adopted (v. Philippson, 85 n.; *Dox.* 499 n.). Yet even this enlargement does not indicate the real scope of the writing, which includes such topics as intelligence, pleasure and pain, temperament, and talent. That Theophrastus himself was deliberately including an account of the intellectual powers is shown by his words at the close of § 58.

gives in this fragment a report far fuller than we find in Aristotle's *De Anima*, even when this is supplemented by the historical material in the other works of Aristotle. And one may in perfect justice go even farther and say that for a knowledge of Greek psychology before Plato,—apart from the question as to the nature of the soul, which Theophrastus in this writing almost wholly ignores,—we are indebted to Theophrastus for more than to all the other ancient authorities combined.[2] The *De Sensibus* is thus more than an account of the psychology of sense perception; it is rather an account of all that field, distinct from Rational Psychology, which later came to be known as Empirical Psychology and is now designated simply as Psychology.

But Theophrastus's work is more than a report of what his predecessors observed and thought. After a passionless and undistorted account of another's theories, there comes in almost every case a criticism, with a severity of logic that permits one better to know the kind of scrutiny to which these early psychological doctrines were subjected in the later Athenian universities. "Absurd" or "childish", Theophrastus does not hesitate to declare them, with marshalled evidence for his condemnation. Yet he keeps admirably clear the distinction between reporter and judge, and the reader is usually at no loss to know when the one and when the other is speaking.

But while, both as reporter and as judge, he seems studiously to hold back his own more positive conviction upon the topic under discussion, yet he does not wholly

---

[2] This statement, which may to some seem extravagant, is made only after a careful collation of the material in the *De Sensibus*, in the case of each of the authors there treated, with the material upon these men from other sources, as collected by Diels. And in such a comparison one is impressed not merely with the amount, but with the high accuracy in general of Theophrastus's report.

The Value of the *De Sensibus*

succeed in this restraint. In his very criticism one catches something of his view of the truth, some principle by which he judges, some observation of fact. And these chance utterances may now be gathered and supplemented by scattered statements in his other writings, that from these we may know something of his way of regarding those mental processes the history of whose psychology he is in the *De Sensibus* attempting to present.

II

THEOPHRASTUS'S OWN DOCTRINE UPON THE MAIN TOPICS OF THE *DE SENSIBUS*

SENSE PERCEPTION IN GENERAL

FOR Theophrastus, sense perception[1] is the 'principle' of conviction,[2] although our senses must in truth refer problems to our understanding.[3] Yet sense perception and understanding stand in the same relation to the same need in the individual[4]—the need, we may believe, of acquaintance with fact. He argues against the thought that the senses are busied merely with deceptive appearance; when properly functioning, they lead to truth. Instead of holding that one perception is as good as another, and that because some of our sense reports are patently false, all must be

---

[1] Accounts of certain phases of perception in Theophrastus will be found in *A. and E. P.*, II, 396 ff.; Siebeck, *Geschichte der Psychologie*, I, 2, 184 ff.; Chaignet, *Histoire de la Psychologie des Grecs*, I, 267 ff.; Poppelreuter, *Zur Psychologie des Aristoteles, Theophrast, Strato*, 35 ff.; Prantl, *Aristoteles über die Farben*, 181 ff. The account by Chaignet is, in my judgment, the best of these.

[2] Fragment XIII (Wim. 417); and cf. Fragment XVIII (Wim. 418), and *De Caus. Pl.* 2, 3, 5.

[3] Fragment XII (Wim. 414).

[4] *De Sens.* 32.

Theophrastus's Own Doctrine

counted worthless, he believes that we must not hesitate to distinguish between those that are better and those that are worse, between the perceptions of the well and of the sick, perceptions that are "in accord with the reality of things" and perceptions whose natural intent is somehow defeated.[5] In the usual course of things perception is "in accord with nature"; like the knowledge process generally, it is naturally aligned with what is better, working to our advantage, rather than to our confusion and loss.[6] For Nature is ever pressing on toward what is Best.[7]

And because we have in perception a process that is in harmony with nature, rather than at variance with her, it is unreasonable to suppose that perception normally brings pain; on the contrary, processes in accord with nature bring pleasure. Often, it is true, perception is painful; for example, when the sensory stimulation is too intense or too persistent. But as for the contention that perception is invariably painful, as Anaxagoras had held—this is to fly in the face not only of clear reason but of the clear observation that usually there is no pain in our perception and sometimes there actually is pleasure. If perception were to be linked fixedly with either, we should expect it to be with pleasure; but actually it is connected inseparably with neither. For there seems here to be a variable connection, like that which we observe in the case of thought; for both sense perception and thought would be impossible were they unceasingly attended either by pleasure or by pain.[8]

Perception when at its best, as has just been said, reaches out to external fact; our senses are not, as Democritus had urged, avenues that lie in darkness and lead to no truth. And since Theophrastus thus requires

---

[5] *De Sens.* 70.
[6] *De Sens.* 31, 32.
[7] *De Caus. Pl.* I, 16, 11; cf. *De Sens.* 32.
[8] *De Sens.* 17, 31, 32, 33.

us to recognize truth and reality in the objects of perception,[9] a theory of perception is insufficient, he holds, if it describes merely the affections in ourselves and fails to reveal the reality that acts upon our senses, fails to make clear why this reality produces its peculiar effects in us.[10] If perception reveals heat and cold,—and these, which have been regarded as the primal source of things, probably have an existence independent of our senses;— if it reveals heat and cold, hard and soft, heavy and light, and if these be due to some independent reality, it seems reasonable to believe that the objects of our other senses also have a character that is 'objective' and not existent merely in the sensory act itself.[11]

A theory of perception that confines itself to describing states in us is therefore insufficient. But equally insufficient is an explanation that neglects these states, that describes merely the external object and its inner constitution, and says nothing of the peculiar character of the sensory organs and of the sensory process in us. The passive factor, the recipient of the action, has a part in the total process and demands our attention, quite as much as does the agent in perception. The very fact that the same stimulus can have a variable effect according to the condition in which it finds our organs, convinces one that the scientist's attention must be directed beyond the stimulus, the 'object', the active feature in perception. The 'diathesis' of the perceptive organ must never be neglected.[12] An adequate account of taste, for example, must tell whether the stimulus is composed of what is like or of what is unlike the substance of the sense organ,

---

[9] *De Sens.* 70.
[10] *De Sens.* 89.
[11] *De Sens.* 71.
[12] *De Caus. Pl.* 6, 2, 1 ff.; cf. *ibid.* 6, 5, 4, where the 'diathesis' again is spoken of, but not specifically of the sense organ.

Theophrastus's Own Doctrine

and how the change in the sensuous faculty comes to pass.[13]

How then does the object act upon the sense organ; what lies in the character of organ and object and in their mutual relation that produces sense perception?

Theophrastus believes that the action of the object cannot normally be by means of material emanations; and for this he offers several reasons: among others, that such effluences would not explain our perceptions by means of touch and taste, and in smell they would imply a wasting away of certain odorous bodies which in fact are most enduring.[14] Nor will he admit that the sensory object comes into very contact with the organ or faculty of sense: nothing from the object actually penetrates to the sensitive organ and causes motion in it.[15] Theophrastus seems here to adopt without reserve the thought of Aristotle,[16] that all sensory objects act upon our senses through media and never by their presence direct.

He rejects the idea that our sensations are due to the action of substances that fit into the 'pores' of our sense organs: how could we in any such way perceive the rough and the smooth?[17] He also rejects the idea that the sense organs are pure and unmixed of composition; he holds, the rather, that there is always a mixed condition in the sense organs: warmth is present in them all, and moisture joins with other components in some of the organs of perception. Indeed it would be but reasonable to suppose that a mixture would offer a more favourable condition of perception than would a state of purity. For this would seem more nearly to promise the one indispensable condition of all sense perception, namely that

---

[13] *De Sens.* 72.
[14] *De Sens.* 20.
[15] Prisc. I, 16 and 37 (Bywater, 7 and 17).
[16] *De Anima* 423^b; but cf. the opening of Bk. III, 424^b.
[17] *De Sens.* 20.

The Greek Physiological Psychology

there should be a suitable *relation* between our senses and their objects. The cause of perception does not lie in the state of certain elements, but in the state of the organ with reference to its object, in what we may call its 'proportion'.[18] The same thought is expressed in another way when Theophrastus declares that sense perception implies a certain correspondence and a composition suited to the object; and that from this we can readily understand why a deficient stimulation remains unperceived and an excessive one causes pain and is destructive.[19]

At first sight this might seem to place Theophrastus with those who ascribe perception to likeness rather than to difference. Yet in regard to that great dispute of ancient times, his sympathies evidently were stronger with the partisans of difference. There is a certain reasonableness, he says, in explaining sense perception by the interplay of opposites, for alteration is held to be caused, not by similars, but by opposites.[20] The like is never altered by the like, he more than once declares.[21] Likeness itself is something quite vague; and as a principle of explanation, fails us unmistakably in many of the senses. Sound is not discerned by sound, nor is smell by smell, nor are the other objects discerned by what is kindred to them; but rather, we may say, by their opposites.[22]

And yet while an alteration (ἀλλοίωσις) is thus due to opposition, he is ready to entertain a doubt whether the perceptive process really is an alteration, and whether an opposite is cognizant of its opposite.[23] There is certainly a process which must be designated as assimilation (ὁμοίωσις),—not a material assimilation, however, but of

---

[18] Prisc. I, 43-45 (Bywater, 20 f.)
[19] De Sens. 32.
[20] De Sens. 31.
[21] De Sens. 49, 23.
[22] De Sens. 19.
[23] De Sens. 31.

Theophrastus's Own Doctrine

form and of 'proportion'.[24] Yet an affinity of a more material sort is recognized by Theophrastus in the case of taste and hearing. Here the sense-organs—so runs his thought—have a kinship with the objects they perceive since the tongue perceives savours, which are moist, through its own moisture, and the ear perceives sound, which is a movement of the air, through the air which in its confinement is set in motion within the ear. Theophrastus is aware that this seems irreconcilable with his general principle that the like is unaffected by the like; and moreover that it is not the treatment he would accord to the other senses.[25] But how he resolved these difficulties, we do not know. We do know, however, that in speaking of the senses generally, and with specific mention of hearing, taste, and smell, he says that the perceptive organs must be in a passive or neutral state; that when we have a ringing in the ears, or a taste on the tongue, or a smell in the nostrils, these organs all become blunted; and the more so, the fuller they are of what is like them.[26] It would thus appear that while in some instances the sense organs are of the same substance as the 'object' with which they deal, yet the *state* of this substance must be different from that to which it is finally brought in the perceptive process; that the state to which it is brought by the presence of the object—when it is most 'like' that object—is really a condition distinctly unfavourable to perception. Thus a saving element of difference is maintained in the theory, in spite of his recognition of the element of likeness.[27] In another

---

[24] Prisc. I, 1 and 7 (Bywater, 1 and 3).
[25] Prisc. I, 34 (Bywater, 15).
[26] *De Sens.* 19.
[27] Cf. Aristotle's *De Anima* II, 5, where 'the like' and 'the unlike', upon which earlier theories had split, are both accepted and given a place. But Theophrastus's attempt to do justice to both these factors differs in many ways from

The Greek Physiological Psychology

way, also, the principle of opposition is maintained. The perception of opposites—of bitter and sweet, for example—takes place in such a way that the organ is affected in opposite ways; not that the one portion of the tongue, let us say, is affected in the one way, and another part in the opposite way, but that one and the same part is affected in opposite ways at once.[28]

As for the physiology of perception in general, we know that Theophrastus rejected the notion that it took place in the body as a whole:[29] or that we think with the blood; for many sensitive creatures are bloodless, and the perceptive organs in those that are not bloodless are the very parts of the body least supplied with blood.[30] He also casts doubt upon the idea that the size of the perceptive organ is of any decisive importance for its power; in some respects animals with small organs may well excel large animals in sensory acuteness; in other respects the smaller organ may be inferior. Not the size, then, but rather the state and composition of the organ is probably of prime importance.[31] He would also in other ways limit the importance of mere quantity in the perceptive act. In the first place we cannot reduce to mere differences of quantity the differences we observe within the limits of a single sensory field like that of sight or of hearing. There is, in addition to all distinctions in

---

Aristotle's, while bearing a general resemblance to the master's. Nor does he appear to me to be quite as impartially opposed to both 'likeness' and 'difference' as Zeller's account would lead one to believe. See *A. and E. P.* II, 397 and note.

[28] Prisc. I, 8 (Bywater, 3 f.).

[29] Poppelreuter (*Zur Psychologie des Aristoteles, Theophrast, Strato*, 35 ff.) would have it that Theophrastus did not believe in any central organ of perception. The evidence he adduces for such an interpretation, however, seems to me quite unconvincing.

[30] *De Sens.* 23.

[31] *De Sens.* 34 f.

Theophrastus's Own Doctrine

amount, a *qualitative* difference between colours as we experience them, even as there is between tones as we experience them. Two colours may be equal in amount and yet be sensibly different, just as two musical tones that harmonize may be quantitatively equal while still revealing a difference of quality.[32] And farther, the effect which a stimulus has upon our sense is not decided by the mere intensity of the stimulus itself, but often by its contrast with its surroundings.[33]

That the different senses are differently related to one another, some being closer and more kindred than are others, was recognized by Theophrastus. He seems to have acknowledged a special group of senses that operated by 'contact'—a group which perhaps included both taste and touch;[34] and yet again, smell and taste are regarded by him as kindred: the subjective effect, the 'pathos' of their two orders of stimulation, is almost the same;[35] they are 'neighbouring' senses, they receive from each other a certain assistance and pleasure, and possess a farther community of character inasmuch as no savour is odourless nor is any odour wholly without taste.[36] But again, the fact that the air is the common feature of hearing and of smell brings these senses into a kind of relationship which requires us to give the special modification which the air must undergo to explain the fact that we do not hear odours nor smell sounds.[37]

---

[32] Fragment LXXXIX, 3 ff. (Wim. 437 f.).

[33] Fragment LXXXIX, 9 (Wim. 438).

[34] *De Sens.* 72. His doctrine that each of the senses has a 'medium' and never comes into absolute contact with its object, implies that he was using 'contact' here in a relative sense. See p. 21.

[35] *De Caus. Pl.* 6, 1, 1.

[36] *De Odor.* 9; 67; and cf. the more detailed comparison and contrast of smell and taste on pp. 41 f.

[37] Prisc. I, 42 (Bywater, 19); I, 30 (Bywater, 14); and cf. *De Sens.* 46.

The Greek Physiological Psychology

Upon the important group of problems connected with the 'common sensibles' of Aristotle we have almost nothing from Theophrastus. He declared the insufficiency of the image-theory of vision to account for our perception of size, motion, and distance.[38] And as to Aristotle's view that movement, rest, shape, size, number, and unity are perceived in some way by motion or as modifications of motion,[39] Theophrastus found it difficult to accept the idea that shape is perceived by means of motion.[40]

His farther view of perception will best appear as we take up in turn the several special senses.

---

[38] *De Sens.* 36.
[39] *De Anima* 425ᵃ 13 ff.
[40] Prisc. I, 46 (Bywater, 21).

VISION

IN the fragments which have come to us of his account of vision[1] Theophrastus seems to have held with Aristotle that light is not itself a 'body', or a corpuscular emanation.[2] If we are to regard darkness as something visible,—although at this point he leaves it an open question whether it is a visible object,—then light is not the universal and indispensable condition of sight.[3] He does not doubt, however, that light is visible.[4]

And again 'the transparent', like light, is not a body, but rather a condition or effect produced in a body[5]—in air, water, aether, and certain solid bodies.[6] Yet instead of regarding light as the actuality of the transparent, as

---

[1] According to Diogenes Laertius (V, 49), there was among Theophrastus's writings a work, in four books, on Vision,—Περὶ ὄψεως.

[2] Prisc. I, 20 (Bywater, 9); cf. Aristotle, *De Anima* 418^b 14 f. And for the relation of light to fire, see Theophrastus, *De Igne* 3 ff. In *De Sens.* 20, Theophrastus uses against Empedocles the idea that an emanation comes only from fire, yet without explicitly adopting this idea.

[3] Prisc. I, 20 (Bywater, 10); cf. Aristotle, *De Anima* 419^a 1 ff., where light is held not to be a universal condition of vision.

[4] *De Sens.* 37.

[5] Prisc. I, 17 (Bywater, 8).

[6] Prisc. I, 17 (Bywater, 8); cf. *De Caus. Pl.* 6, 1, 1, where air and water are mentioned. In Aristotle, *De Anima* 418^b 6, the list is "air, water, and many solid bodies".

Aristotle had done,[7] Theophrastus entertains the thought that the relation might be reversed, and the transparent be called the actuality of light. But after all, he sagely adds, we need not trouble ourselves about the mere words; it is more important to understand the character of the facts themselves.[8]

Colour, for Theophrastus, is the cause of our seeing colours.[9] He rejects Plato's idea that colour is a flame; there is, he admits, a certain resemblance between white and flame, but black would seem to be flame's very opposite.[10] A simple colour does not differ from another simple colour merely in quantity; we can mix them in equal quantities, and take an equal 'number', say, of the white and of the black.[11] There is, then, a difference between black and white which we must recognize as qualitative.

As for a decision how many 'simple' colours there are, we know that he recognized the difficulty of determining what colours are simple and what compound.[12] Black and white had traditionally been regarded as the only primary colours, and from these all others had been thought to be derived; and the attempt on the part of Democritus to assume a larger number of primaries is viewed by Theophrastus with some suspicion.[13] He himself recognizes

---

[7] *De Anima* 418^b 9; cf. 419^a 11 where light is declared to be the ἐντελέχεια of the transparent.

[8] Prisc. I, 18 (Bywater, 8 f.).

[9] Prisc. I, 21 (Bywater, 10).

[10] *De Sens.* 91.

[11] Fragment LXXXIX, 4 (Wim. 437).

[12] *De Sens.* 82.

[13] *De Sens.* 79. Prantl (183) represents Theophrastus as deriving all other colours by mixture from black and white. But a careful examination of the passages cited by Prantl fails to convince me that such is Theophrastus's clear meaning. That he recognized the contrast of black and white is evident enough: see e.g. *De Sens.* 91. Nor can I agree with Prantl

Theophrastus's Own Doctrine

seven kinds of colour, or eight if dusky gray (τὸ φαιόν) is to be distinguished, he says, from black (τοῦ μέλανος),—although he does not say that these seven or eight colours are all 'primaries'.[14]

Of the particular colours as they occur in nature[15] he has much to say, without making their interrelation clear. White and black he seems to have regarded as alike lacking in light.[16] The air is by its very nature black. And smoke is black because it is composed of moisture dissolved in breath, or air, and earth. These will appear ruddy in so far as they have fire in them; white seen through black appears crimson (φοινικοῦν), as when the sun is seen through smoke or gloom.[17]

Passing now from the physics of vision to its physiology, we find Theophrastus rejecting the theory that vision is a function of the body as a whole.[18] He also makes a spirited attack on the idea that objects make an imprint on the air, and that this imprint comes to us and causes vision—for air, he holds, is not to be moulded in this way, like wax; indeed water would seem to be better suited to receive such imprints than is the air, yet we see not so well by its means.[19] And farther, he sees great

---

(181) that in *De Sens.* 81, where it is said πρῶτον τὸ λευκὸν τὴν φύσιν, this is to be set down as Theophrastus's own view. I take it rather to be what Theophrastus believes to be a logical implication of *Democritus's* doctrine.

[14] *De Caus. Pl.* 6, 4, 1.

[15] For farther details as to the physical occurrence of certain of the colours, see Prantl, 181 ff.

[16] *De Sens.* 37.

[17] *De Igne* 75. Aristotle, according to Beare (65), had declared air to be *white*. In *De Igne* 31 the importance of moisture for the ruddiness of flame is emphasized.

[18] *De Sens.* 54.

[19] *De Sens.* 51 ff. The passage in Prisc. I, 33 (Bywater, 15), where Theophrastus is reported to have said that in reflection there occurs in the air something like an impression of

The Greek Physiological Psychology

difficulty in the theory that vision is due to the tiny image or reflection in the eye, however this image may be produced. For in the first place the size of the image is not that of the objects seen; in the reflection there cannot be enough contrasting objects at one and the same time to explain the variety of the objects we simultaneously see; and a number of features besides size, which vision detects, e.g., the motion and the distance of objects, are not adequately represented in the ocular image. And moreover many animals that possess sight, have eyes that do not reflect things at all,—animals that have hard and horny eyes, and aquatic animals generally. Finally if reflection explains vision, why does not many a lifeless thing that reflects,—water, for example, and polished bronze—have vision?[20]

As for the positive character of the visual process, Theophrastus has left us much in doubt. He seems to have re-adopted to some extent the idea that in the visual act something issues from the eye—a long-standing idea which Aristotle had rejected.[21] For only in such a way does it seem possible to understand Theophrastus's explanation of the connection between vision and dizziness. We become dizzy in looking down from great heights, he says, because 'vision' (in which he seems to include something extended from the pupil of the eye, in a way familiar to us from Plato) now straining and stretching into the distance, trembles and quivers; and 'vision' thus quivering and set in motion, sets in motion and produces

---

the shape, would seem to soften his scoffing words about 'air prints', when it came to explaining the special visual fact of mirroring. In *De Sens.* 36 he speaks of the reflection from water and from metals, without, however, attempting to explain it. In *De Igne* 73 the physics of the matter is discussed more fully.

[20] *De Sens.* 36, cf. *ibid.* 54.
[21] See Beare, 84.

Theophrastus's Own Doctrine

disorder in the inner organs of the body. But when we look aloft no such effect is felt; for 'vision' does not now strain into the distance, but is cut off in the light.[22] The ancient belief, somewhat different, that upon occasion flashes of fire could be emitted from the human eye is said to have been held by Theophrastus.[23]

While admitting the rôle which the water of the eye may play,[24] he is not inclined to ascribe to it exclusively the visual function. Like Plato, and unlike Aristotle, he attributes an important place to the fire within the eye. The exceptional night-vision which some animals possess, he believes is probably due to an intense fire in their eyes, comparable to the inherent glow which certain objects display at night.[25] And from this we may infer that in day-vision also the fire of the eye, but now a weaker fire, was for him an important element,—a thought which seems also to be close to his explanation of the impossibility of gazing at the sun or at anything exceeding bright. For this is due, he says, to the fact that a stronger light extinguishes a weaker[26]—a relation and effect which elsewhere is asserted of fire;[27] and while he may not have meant that the sun when gazed at extinguished the inherent light, or fire, of the eye, yet in view of his theory of nocturnal vision, just described, such an interpretation would not seem strained. Finally we know that he had little patience with the thought that the size

---

[22] *De Vertigine* 8.
[23] Simplicius *De Caelo* 268ᵃ 27 f.; cf. *A. and E. P.* II, 378, 398.
[24] *Prisc.* I, 42 (Bywater, 19).
[25] *De Sens.* 18. Zeller (*A. and E. P.* II, 398 n.) would have it, that in the case of sight, hearing, and smell, the immediate organs of sense perception for Theophrastus were formed of water and air.
[26] *De Sens.* 18.
[27] *De Igne* 1 and 10-12; *De An. Defect.* 1.

The Greek Physiological Psychology

of the eye had any important bearing upon the general keenness of sight. Instead of any general superiority of vision in animals with large eyes, as Anaxagoras had held, Theophrastus questions whether small-eyed animals may not surpass them in visual power; yet in the end he leaves it undecided. On the whole, the composition or constitution of the organ, as of the body generally, he regards as of more importance than its mere size.[28]

---

[28] *De Sens.* 34 f.

HEARING

THE sense of hearing has a certain connection with that of smell, for both of these senses receive from the air their stimulation. But the air is not of itself a sufficient cause of the sensations aroused in smell and hearing; for were this so, we ought to hear odours as well as sounds, and smell sounds as well as odours, and obtain comparable perceptions also from the air in the throat or wind-pipe. The air, if it is to be perceived by hearing or by smell, must have a right relation to the particular sense; and that which gives it a right relation to the organ of hearing is of course different from that which gives it a suitable relation to the sense of smell.[1] In the case of smell there is some peculiar kind of mixture, and the air has suffered some kind of change; while for hearing, the air has been given a special form, or 'figure' ($\sigma\chi\eta\mu\alpha\tau\iota\zeta\delta\mu\epsilon\nu o\varsigma$).[2] He defends the Aristotelian thesis that sound is connected universally with 'solid' bodies,[3] even though there comes sound from wind and thunder.[4]

He holds that there are tonal differences that cannot be

---

[1] Prisc. I, 42 (Bywater, 19); and cf. *De Sens.* 46.
[2] Prisc. I, 30 (Bywater, 14); cf. the use of $\sigma\chi\tilde{\eta}\mu\alpha$ in describing tone, in Fragment LXXXIX, 10 (Wim. 438 f.).
[3] Cf. Aristotle *De Anima* 419^b 19; it must be kept in mind that Aristotle sets with or among 'solid' bodies, undispersed air; if one strike the air so suddenly that it cannot disperse, he says, it will give forth a sound (419^b 22).
[4] Prisc. I, 36 (Bywater, 16).

regarded as mere differences of quantity; high tones and low possess some intrinsic distinction which makes it possible for them to bring forth harmony. So far as amount is concerned, a harmonious combination may be of tones that are equal. High and low both have their peculiar character. A shrill tone is not necessarily of greater amount than a deep tone; each may have a like degree and amount of motion, but a motion of different character. The idea of 'figure' (σχῆμα), and not of mere amount, must be employed to explain the difference.[5] Theophrastus also observes that a ringing in the ears tends to blunt the organ's sensitivity—an observation which he turns against those who urge, as a principle, that like is perceived by like. Change and contrast, and not monotony, have the truly stimulating effect on our sense of hearing.[6]

In describing more particularly the bodily process of hearing, he speaks of heat as common to the ear and to the other sense organs.[7] But air is the material more especially composing the organ of hearing,[8]—air which elsewhere he describes as 'cut off' and set in motion. There is, therefore, a correspondence of inner and outer in the case of hearing,—the inner air in motion, is the means by which we perceive the motions of the outer air,—a correspondence which Theophrastus recognizes as being exceptional to his general position that perception moves by difference rather than by similarity.[9] With explicit reference to hearing, he rejects the thought that

---

[5] Fragment LXXXIX (Wim. 437 ff.). He is here combating, according to Zeller (*A. and E. P.* II, 379), the view of Heraclides that a tone of higher pitch consists of more parts; and on the other hand, that of Plato and Aristotle, that such a tone moves more swiftly.

[6] *De Sens.* 19.

[7] Prisc. I, 43 (Bywater, 20).

[8] Prisc. I, 42 (Bywater, 19).

[9] Prisc. I, 34 (Bywater, 15).

Theophrastus's Own Doctrine

perception is not a local bodily process but is a function of the body as a whole.[10]

Hearing is the sense that most deeply stirs our emotions.[11] Music he regarded as a movement of the soul by which we are freed of the evils that come of passion.[12] An enumeration is given by Theophrastus of the 'principia', or springs of music. They are pain, pleasure, and inspiration; any one of these may change the character of the voice so that it loses its customary form and becomes musical.[13]

---

[10] *De Sens.* 57.

[11] Fragment XCI (Wim. 440).

[12] Fragment LXXXIX, 14 (Wim. 439); cf. also Fragments LXXXVII and LXXXVIII (Wim. 436) for the application of music to disease.

[13] Fragment XC (Wim. 440).

SMELL

WE have seen, but a few pages back, how Theophrastus makes the air a common factor in the senses of hearing and of smell, while yet asserting that it is no sufficient cause of the sensations aroused in either of these senses. The air must be specially modified, must be given a proper form or 'schema', before it can affect our hearing; for our sense of smell the air must have undergone a peculiar mixture, it must have suffered some kind of change.[1] Let us now observe further the account he gives of smell.

It is generally agreed, he tells us, that some sort of emanation occurs in odour.[2] Yet he himself finds difficulty in this traditional belief. For any emanation seems necessarily to imply a loss of substance; and were odours to arise by emanation, it would follow that "those substances with the strongest odour would most rapidly perish. Now the fact is nearly the reverse: the most fragrant plants and other bodies that are most odorous are the most enduring."[3] And close to this objection, if not but another phase of it, is his refusal to accept the idea that volatile or light bodies most strongly affect the sense of smell. The mere lightness is not enough: there must be some specific *odour* present in what is light. "For air and

---

[1] See p. 33.
[2] *De Sens.* 90.
[3] *De Sens.* 20.

Theophrastus's Own Doctrine

fire are the very lightest of substances, and yet produce in us no sensation of odour."[4]

To this list of the inodorous substances, he elsewhere adds a third, and with it gives an explanation. Water, air, and fire have no odour, he says, because they are *simple*, and all simple substances, of which these are but examples, are inodorous; whereas earth either is the only substance that has odour or is the substance giving us odour in its most pronounced form, just because earth is the most mixed of substances.[5]

Mixture, then, is essential to odour; and if air, fire, or water seems to possess odour, this is because it is no longer pure. But along with the mixture to account for the odour, and apparently as a process differing from mixture, he speaks of an alteration, an 'alloiosis,' of the substance.[6] No clear outline of this alteration is given us;[7] but in regard to the character of the 'mixture' we are left with somewhat more detail. Odour, he tells us, consists of the dry ingredient in savour, present in what is transparent (ἐν τῷ διαφανεῖ), for this transparent factor is something common to air and water.[8] And in speaking more particularly of artificial preparations, he states the different ways in which the moist and the dry may be combined,

---

[4] *De Sens.* 22.

[5] *De Odor.* 1; cf. *De Caus. Pl.* 6, 3, 1.

[6] *De Caus. Pl.* 6, 3, 1 ff. In *De Odor.* 7, somewhat strangely, in the light of his clear and repeated statements to the contrary, Theophrastus says, Εἰσὶ μὲν οὖν καὶ τοῖς ἀμείκτοις ὀσμαί τινες. But he is now speaking of the artificial modification of tastes and odours, and would perhaps here merely remind us that when we are thinking of the manufactured products we must remember that odours are already present in substances that are *comparatively* simple.

[7] In *De Caus. Pl.* 6, 3, 3 he connects it with those spontaneous changes which take place when things improve or deteriorate (as in rotting).

[8] *De Caus. Pl.* 6, 1, 1.

The Greek Physiological Psychology

and the need of intelligent skill to bring about desirable combinations.[9] Yet the odour itself can at times be over-mixed, and will affect our senses more strongly if we can obtain it somewhat simplified. Thus certain flowers,—for example, violets,—are for us more fragrant at a distance because the grosser and more earthy effluvia are left behind.[10]

Theophrastus is less dismayed than were many of his predecessors at the great variety of odours. He will by no means admit the impossibility of finding in them any true differences of kind. Some odours, he grants, are impossible to classify.[11] But on the whole we may hope for success here quite as in the case of savours; for quite as do the savours, the different odours produce in us different organic effects, in addition to their differences in pleasure or unpleasantness, upon which Plato laid such stress.[12] He often finds it convenient to divide odorous substances into those that are fragrant and those that are offensive.[13] Within this broad division, the particular kinds have not received established designations. There are differences among sensations we call 'sweet', as there are amongst those we call 'sharp'; but one would not hesitate to include in the list 'pungent' (δριμεῖα), 'strong' (ἰσχυρά), 'soft' (μαλακή), 'sweet' (γλυκεῖα), and 'heavy' (βαρεῖα ὀδμή). Some of these classes are common to fragrant and to offensive odours. As for the offensive odours as a group, they are most intimately connected with decay, and to some extent there is a trace of this odour of decay in everything, whether it be plant or animal or sub-

---

[9] *De Odor.* 7 f.

[10] *De Caus. Pl.* 6, 17, 1; cf. *De Odor.* 39, where the odour of roots, in contrast with that from flowers, is described as more lasting because ἰσχυροτέρα καὶ σωματωδεστέρα.

[11] *De Odor.* 1.

[12] *De Sens.* 90.

[13] *De Odor.* 1; and cf. *ibid.* 2, 3, and 64.

Theophrastus's Own Doctrine

stance inorganic. Fragrance, on the other hand, is the quality in substances that are softened by heat and have become subtile and farthest removed from what is earthy; while the opposites of these are offensive. He recognizes the fact that qualities from more than one class may be present in a single odour, for the 'sweets' may reveal a certain 'sharpness', and odours may be 'heavy' that on the whole are pleasant.[14] Elsewhere, without saying what the classes are, he is attracted by the idea that they are properly *seven*, and this he says without suggesting, as he does for colour and for savour, that this number of the classes of odours could easily be enlarged to eight.[15]

Some of the external conditions that influence odour already have appeared. We may add that he finds, on the whole, that dryness is favourable to odour, and especially to the fragrant odours;[16] yet for the time of day and of the year this general rule that heat is a favourable condition must not be pressed too far; for the time of greatest fragrance of flowers is not at midsummer nor in the heat of noon.[17]

Passing now from the character of the stimulus to that of the sensory organ and of the processes that there occur, we find Theophrastus hesitant and in a measure inconsistent as to the connection between smell and breathing. It is generally agreed, he says, that in the olfactory process there is an inhalation (ἀνάπνευσις) of air.[18] And he himself would upon occasion accept this common belief; for he says that the very character of odour lies in inhalation (ἐν ἀναπνοῇ).[19] Yet when Empedocles says that smell is due to inhalation (τῇ

---

[14] *De Odor.* 2 f.
[15] *De Caus. Pl.* 6, 4, 1.
[16] *De Caus. Pl.* 6, 14, 8.
[17] *De Caus. Pl.* 6, 17, 2 f.
[18] *De Sens.* 90.
[19] *De Odor.* 3.

The Greek Physiological Psychology

ἀναπνοῇ),[20] Theophrastus attacks him roundly. Odd, says he, is such an account of smell, since some animals that do not breathe (ἀναπνέει) at all have a sense of smell. And after presenting a variety of arguments against special aspects of the 'breathing' theory, he closes with the words: "In all likelihood respiration (τὸ ἀναπνεῖν) is not of itself the cause of smell, but is connected with it incidentally."[21] It would seem therefore that Theophrastus changed his mind, perhaps under the extreme provocation of an opportunity to argue against a man of eminence.

But in any event, the organ of smell is not of some pure and unmixed substance, although air is unquestionably the more prominent or dominant constituent of this organ. Nor does this inner air merely of itself give assurance that the external object which is so closely bound with air will be perceived; as already has been pointed out, there must be some effective 'ratio' between organ and object.[22] And furthermore our sense of smell as well as the external odour is made ineffectual by cold.[23] And certain diseased or otherwise abnormal conditions of the organ may make the sense entirely incapable of sensation; or it may by the presence of one odour be made insensible to some other; or by sheer excess of stimulation be made incapable of perception.[24]

In general the human sense of smell is, we may say, the very worst; for many things that evidently have for animals a characteristic odour are for us inodorous.[25]

---

[20] *De Sens.* 9.

[21] *De Sens.* 21 f. That there is no *necessary*—but only an 'accidental'—connection between respiration and smell seems also to be implied in his question, ἀλλ' εἰ ἄνευ τῆς ἀναπνοῆς δυνατὸν ὀσφραίνεσθαι, τί κωλύει καὶ ἀκούειν ἄνευ τοῦ ἀέρος ; Prisc. I, 35 (Bywater, 16).

[22] Prisc. I, 42 f. (Bywater, 19 f.).

[23] *De Caus. Pl.* 6, 17, 5.

[24] *De Sens.* 19, 21 ; *De Odor.* 45 f.

[25] *De Odor.* 4.

Theophrastus's Own Doctrine

There is also this further difference between the sense of smell in man and in animals, that with few or none of the animals is odour sought for its own sake but only incidentally, because it indicates the presence of food; and this, and not the odour itself, is desired;[26] whereas with us, while certain odours are pleasant by such association, others are pleasant independently and of themselves.[27] With animals the closer connection between nutrition and the pleasantness of the odour also explains the noticeable repugnance which certain of them show to odours that to us are most delightful. The idea of opposition to nature, to which allusion already has been made, here is introduced as a conscious principle of explaining the varying responses connected with the sense of smell.[28]

The relation of smell to taste, of which we have here a glimpse, appears as most intimate in all Theophrastus's account. They are not merely neighbouring and mutually helpful senses, inasmuch as savours are aided by the fragrance of what we eat or drink; they are even kindred in many ways.[29] The subjective effect in the two cases shows a close resemblance, although the two processes do not occur in the same parts of the body.[30] The stimuli also are alike in being composite and not simple; they become adapted to our senses by mixture and alteration;[31] and both tastes and odours are often artificially improved by still farther mixing and blending, of which he gives the kinds and character.[32] Stimuli and senses are, in

---

[26] *De Caus. Pl.* 6, 5, 1.
[27] *De Odor.* 5.
[28] *De Odor.* 4; *De Caus. Pl.* 6, 5, 1.
[29] *De Odor.* 9; 67; *De Caus. Pl.* 6, 9, 1.
[30] *De Caus. Pl.* 6, 1, 1; cf. *De Sens.* 90. Theophrastus says, elliptically, οὐκ ἐν τοῖς αὐτοῖς, and I may be in error in supplying, as the meaning, "parts of the body"; but in the light of the context no other fair interpretation occurs to me.
[31] *De Caus. Pl.* 6, 3, 2.
[32] *De Odor.* 1 and 7 (but see p. 37 n.); *De Caus. Pl.* 6, 3, 1.

the two cases, similarly affected by cold.33 Moreover no odour is tasteless, nor is any savour odourless; 34 and in general a change of odour in any substance implies a change of taste.35 In odours and savours there are common qualities, like sweetness; and there are many designations —though by no means all 36—common to the classes in the two regions, whose natures really are not far apart.37

But while in general the classifications of odour and of savour run parallel, we find no precise and absolute correspondence. In plants the fermentative action (πέψις) by which savour is produced is not precisely the same as that which produces flavour.38 Savours exist which no one would think of calling odours.39 Furthermore in spite of the general connection between the odour and the nutritive character of a substance, the pleasures of taste and of smell do not go hand in hand: fragrant things are not always agreeable to the taste, and some things agreeable to taste have an offensive smell.40 But with this we may well take up in its own right Theophrastus's account of taste.

---

33 *De Caus. Pl.* 6, 17, 5.
34 *De Odor.* 67.
35 *De Odor.* 68.
36 *De Odor.* 1.
37 *De Caus. Pl.* 6, 14, 12.
38 *De Caus. Pl.* 6, 17, 4.
39 *De Caus. Pl.* 6, 9, 2.
40 *De Odor.* 5; in *De Caus. Pl.* 6, 9, 4 he even goes so far as to say that normally all *fragrant* substances are *bitter* to the taste, and that bitter is a certain guise of fragrance.

TASTE

IN what has just preceded, there have appeared many of the features which Theophrastus ascribed to the stimulus and to the physiological process of taste in common with that of smell, and these need not here be repeated. But speaking of taste as distinguished from smell,[1] he says that its external stimulus (χυμός) is a commingling of the dry and the earthy with the moist, or it is a filtration, or infusion, of the dry through the moist under the influence of heat—the two accounts perhaps amounting to the same thing.[2] In all the savours there is a common 'material' (ὕλη), namely moisture; and under the action of heat— either resident or coming from the sun—they change from kind to kind, from opposite into opposite.[3] Yet the different saps or liquids (χυλοί) connected with taste have a somewhat different relation to the moist and the dry, though these are present in them all: sour (ὀξύς) and harsh (αὐστηρός) are closer to the moist; whereas the pungent (δριμύς) and the sweet (γλυκύς) are closer to dryness.[4]

As to the classification of savours, we have from Theophrastus a variety of proposals. He casts doubt on a

---

[1] In the Catalogue of Theophrastus's works (Diog. Laert. V, 43) we find Περὶ χυμῶν, χροῶν, σαρκῶν α', and Περὶ χυλῶν α' β' γ' δ' ε'.
[2] *De Caus. Pl.* 6, 1, 1.
[3] *De Caus. Pl.* 6, 7, 1.
[4] *De Caus. Pl.* 6, 11, 1.

The Greek Physiological Psychology

fourfold classification which he attributes to Plato,[5] nor does he believe that there is an endless number of tastes as was held by Menestor and other ancient scientists. He prefers to be counted with those who hold that the number of tastes is limited, and that what appear as an endless number are derived from these by mixture.[6] At times he seems to entertain the thought of *two* primary savours, namely bitter (πικρόν) and sweet, and of all others as derivatives of these; but without committing himself clearly to such a doctrine.[7] In a certain sense, however, he evidently regards these savours as something like 'principles'. Bitter is the normal taste of all things that are fragrant; it is perhaps a certain form or phase of fragrance itself. And sweet is the primal source of all the pleasant savours;[8] under it he names as varieties, the flavour of honey, of wine, of milk, and of water.[9] At other times he finds no difficulty in giving a list of the savours (χυμοί), which are eight: sweet (γλυκύς), oily (λιπαρός), bitter (πικρός), harsh (αὐστηρός), pungent (δριμύς), sour (ὀξύς), astringent (στρυφνός), saline (ἁλμυρός).[10] This list he proposes to reduce to seven—a number which attracts him, he confesses, as most suitable and natural—by striking out 'saline' as perhaps not sufficiently distinct from 'bitter', and he prefers not to include in his list the vinous taste, since this is a blend of 'sweet', 'astringent', and 'harsh'.[11] Yet though he finds the making of the list an easy task,

---

[5] *De Sens.* 89. For the truth of this attribution see p. 219.
[6] *De Caus. Pl.* 6, 3, 5.
[7] *De Caus. Pl.* 6, 6, 10; and cf. *De Odor.* 64.
[8] *De Caus. Pl.* 6, 9, 4; cf. *ibid.* 6, 6, 9.
[9] *De Caus. Pl.* 6, 9, 2; cf. *ibid.* 6, 4, 1, where the taste of milk is set down as a kind of sweet.
[10] *De Caus. Pl.* 6, 4, 1; cf. *ibid.* 6, 1, 2.
[11] *De Caus. Pl.* 6, 4, 1 f.; cf. the threefold classification, on another basis, *ibid.* 6, 3, 3, and the list of χυλοί in *Hist. Pl.* I, 12, 1.

Theophrastus's Own Doctrine

he admits the difficulty of arriving at the very essence of each of these kinds of flavour.[12]

But taste is not to be explained by classifying and describing the mere stimulants of taste. The character of the recipient, the sensory, function is also to be heeded.[13] If plants are to produce savours, they must concoct or distil juices that are harmonious with our nature.[14] The tongue, by reason of moisture, perceives savours.[15] He seems to hold that it has the faculty of being affected by strongest contrasts, like that of bitter and sweet, at one and the same time, and these contrary effects, he states, are not to be understood as occurring, the one in one part of the tongue, and the other in another part, but both together in one and the same part.[16] Elsewhere he speaks of the different organic effects which the different savours cause in us,[17] as well as of the like effects which, in different persons, very different stimuli may exceptionally induce. Yet in spite of this difference of origin, he is confident that the experiences which we thus call the same are intrinsically the same in quality.[18] The region of taste, finally, is specifically mentioned as one of those in which there is need that the organ be 'neutral' beforehand in order adequately to perceive: a savour already there blunts the sense.[19]

---

[12] *De Caus. Pl.* 6, 1, 2.

[13] *De Caus. Pl.* 6, 2, 1 f. For farther details of the physiological process of taste, which need not here be repeated, the reader is referred to the comparison and contrast of smell and taste, on pp. 41 f.

[14] *De Caus. Pl.* 1, 16, 1.

[15] Prisc. I, 34 (Bywater, 15).

[16] Prisc. I, 8 (Bywater, 3 f.).

[17] *De Sens.* 90.

[18] *De Sens.* 70.

[19] *De Sens.* 19.

TOUCH

OF Theophrastus's doctrine of touch we are almost wholly ignorant, save in so far as it is implied in his general account of perception. We there saw that he perhaps grouped taste and touch together as senses which operate by 'touch'.[1] And holding as he did to the reality of objects independent of our sensory organs, it is not surprising to have him mention specifically heat and cold as probably possessing an objective reality, rather than an existence merely as effects in our senses.[2] Cold and heat by their very nature tend to move, respectively, upward and downward; lightness and heaviness are not, as Plato held, relative and dependent on locality; they have an existence that is absolute.[3] He is also familiar with the other common contrasts between tactual objects —namely, that of hard and soft, and of rough and smooth.[4] His general doctrine that sense perception always involves some intermediary between object and sensory organ does not seem to have been surrendered by Theophrastus, any more than by Aristotle, even in the case of touch;[5] although, as we have just seen, there were certain senses that operated by touch or contact, in the looser meaning of the term. The organic sensations

---

[1] *De Sens.* 72.
[2] *De Sens.* 71.
[3] *De Sens.* 88 f. ; *De Ventis* 22.
[4] *De Odor.* 64.
[5] Prisc. I, 16 and 37 (Bywater, 7 and 17).

Theophrastus's Own Doctrine

of dizziness, to which reference has already been made when speaking of Theophrastus's account of vision, were considered and an attempt was made at a physiological explanation.[6]

---

[6] *De Vertigine* (Wim. 401 ff.).

PLEASURE AND PAIN

For Theophrastus pleasure is the normal accompaniment of what is in accord with Nature. As a rule, therefore, we take *pleasure* in things, since the common course of our functions is inevitably 'natural' and not antagonistic to nature.[1] And any particular function, like perception or understanding, may also be regarded as more intimately conjoined with pleasure than with pain. Yet we must not press our principle too far, and hold that these functions never bring pain; for perception often is accompanied by pain. But with the idea that pain is somehow involved in every operation of our senses, Theophrastus has no patience; such a doctrine is unreasonable, he holds, and is refuted by the plain facts of observation.[2] But excessive stimulation, just because it disturbs the nice correspondence which perception normally presupposes between the sense-organs and their objects, is destructive and therefore causes pain.[3]

Since pleasure is thus the accompaniment and expression of what is in harmony with nature, there is implied, at least distantly, that all those other things that are in accord with nature—such as are better, or in health (to give his own examples)[4]—are also more closely allied with pleasure; and their opposites, with pain. But this mutual adjust-

---

[1] *De Sens.* 31 f.
[2] *De Sens.* 31–33 ; *ibid.* 17.
[3] *De Sens.* 32.
[4] *De Sens.* 70.

Theophrastus's Own Doctrine

ment also implies that pleasantness or unpleasantness, like sense perception, is not an absolute property in the object, but is due to the object's relation to the organism, is due to the effect it has upon the organic condition. Especially in the case of food, where the needs of life are so varied as we pass from creature to creature, may we expect an inconstancy or even a reversing of the pleasurable or painful accompaniment. What furthers the life and gives pleasure in one case, hinders life and is repugnant in another.[5] The lower animals in particular are commonly ruled in their attractions and aversions by the meaning of the object as food: few or none of them seek odour for its own sake, but only incidentally because it is the odour of something that is good as food;[6] those objects that promise nourishment to the animals have for them a pleasant odour, and those that in their nature are antagonistic are offensive to their smell.[7]

But with us this is not invariably the case. It is true that many an odour is pleasant to us, as to the animals, because it suggests what we desire as food. But we seek certain odours also for their own sake,—for example, the fragrance of flowers. And now we become aware of the complication of pleasure and of unpleasantness, since fragrant things may be distasteful, and savoury things may have an offensive smell.[8] This partial independence of smell from taste in our case, since odours may be sought for their own sake, reminds us of Theophrastus's similar judgment regarding the perceptive act: its exercise may be sought by us for its own sake, and quite apart from any desire we may have directly for the thing perceived.[9]

But since he asserts that corruption gives an offensive

---

[5] *De Caus. Pl.* 6, 4, 7.
[6] *De Caus. Pl.* 6, 5, 1.
[7] *De Odor.* 4.
[8] *De Odor.* 5.
[9] *De Sens.* 31.

The Greek Physiological Psychology

odour, and that there is in everything—whether it be plant or animal or lifeless substance—some faint odour of decay,[10] it would seem as though he must in consistency have held that no pleasure of smell is wholly unmixed with unpleasantness—a view that would have been in one sensory department not so remote from that more universal opinion of Anaxagoras which Theophrastus is at such pains to refute,—that perception, however pleasant, is always fraught with pain.[11] Such nearness of the pleasant to the unpleasant is also suggested by his doctrine that bitter,—whose opposite is sweet, the source of all the pleasant savours—is perhaps the guise under which all of fragrance is concealed; bitter is normally the taste of things that are pleasant to our smell.[12] But his detailed description of the contrasts of pleasure and unpleasantness in taste and smell, with his physical and physiological accounts of them, need not farther be repeated.[13]

Finally, among the varied connections of pleasure and pain, Theophrastus notes that these experiences when excessive produce changes in the humours of the body; and when, under the sway of pleasure and pain, these humours affect the seat of respiration, there may be a complete suspension of consciousness.[14] He also mentions pleasure and pain, along with inspiration, as 'principia' of music; for these can turn the voice from its habitual mode and lift it to the plane of beauty.[15] Finally, he rejects Plato's doctrine that some pleasures are false; on the contrary Theophrastus maintains that all are true,[16]—that is, that they really are *pleasures*, whatever in other respects may be our judgment regarding them.

---

[10] *De Odor.* 3.
[11] Cf. *De Sens.* 17 and 31–33.
[12] *De Caus. Pl.* 6, 9, 4; cf. *ibid.* 6, 6, 9.
[13] Cf. pp. 38 f. and 44.
[14] *De An. Defect.* 7 (Wim. 409).
[15] Fragment XC. (Wim. 440).
[16] Fragment LXXXV (Wim. 435); cf. *A. and E. P.* 404 n.

III

THEOPHRASTUS'S GENERAL METHOD OF EXPOSITION AND OF CRITICISM IN THE *DE SENSIBUS*

WE have thus in some measure seen how perception and the special senses and pleasure and pain appeared to Theophrastus. And this prepares us to observe more justly the method of exposition and of criticism in his writing *On the Senses;* we become aware of the atmosphere of knowledge and prejudgment through which this careful student must view the work of others.

He methodically divides his writing into two parts, of which the first[1] is on the sensory and physiological processes, while the second part[2] is on the objects and stimuli, the more physical aspects of sensation. The men to whom his attention is confined are eight in number: Parmenides, Empedocles, Alcmaeon, Anaxagoras, Clidemus, Diogenes of Apollonia, Democritus, and Plato. And these appear to him to possess unequal importance. Of the ninety-one sections into which the text of the fragment has been divided, he gives but one to Clidemus, and but two to Alcmaeon, and two to Parmenides. He presents another group—Diogenes, Anaxagoras, and Plato—to each of whom he gives about equal space, namely ten

---

[1] §§ 1–58.
[2] §§ 59–91.

The Greek Physiological Psychology

or eleven sections,—many times the space he assigns either to Parmenides or to Alcmaeon, and yet small in comparison with what still others receive. Empedocles, with eighteen sections, has a very important place; while to Democritus falls the lion's share of attention: the account of his work extends through thirty-four sections, more than a third of the entire work.

Yet in all, the space he uses is extremely small. One cannot but acknowledge Theophrastus's extraordinary skill in giving on so reduced a scale so full and faithful a picture of the doctrines of these men. We admit this skill even while he stirs our impatience by begrudging us an extra word where one would gladly have had, by a phrase, some besetting doubt dispelled. One also would gladly have had from him, now and then, a word of admiration. It would perhaps be too much to expect of him a judgment as noble and almost impassioned as that which even Aristotle cannot repress at the opening of his great Psychology; but there are occasions when he might have half revealed some quiet glow of pleasure in the truth struck out sharp and new in the doctrines he reports. We know, for example, that Theophrastus held that, not things that are alike, but only opposites, affect each other. Yet he gives never a word of greeting to this doctrine at the moment when he unbares it in another. And again we find him urging as of great significance the principle that pleasure is the sign and utterance of what is normal, or "in accord with nature". Yet he can report to us such a principle almost beginning its life in Diogenes of Apollonia[3] and more fully grown in Plato,[4] but gives it no mark of recognition. At times, however, we find faint praise, half lost in condemnation, as when, after calling it childish, he says of Diogenes' theory of vision, that it at least in a measure succeeds in refuting certain

---

[3] *De Sens.* 43.
[4] *De Sens.* 84.

Theophrastus's Method of Criticism

false proposals, although it does not itself attain the truth.[5]

It is not to Theophrastus's present treatise, then, that one will go for expressed appreciation, but rather for a dispassionate and marvellously impartial report of his man, at the close of which, Theophrastus suddenly changes from reporter into critic. He turns upon the one he has brought before us, raining upon him blows as of tempered steel. And it is difficult to find any personal element here entering. To those who are nearer to his own beliefs, his face is as grim as to the opposition. Thus we know that the dispute regarding perception, whether its operation was by similarity or by contrast, was regarded by him as of great importance; in the case of every one, Theophrastus is looking for his stand upon this question, and at the beginning of his writing he makes this the one great principle of classifying the men whose doctrines he describes. Moreover, his own sympathies, while divided, as we know,[6] were rather with the 'contrast' party. Yet he criticises Anaxagoras with great severity,—with perhaps almost as great severity as appears when he criticises Plato, whom he places with those who favour similarity. Yet with Plato he seems oftener to miss the point, oftener to fight over words, as though there were here some especial want of sympathy. But if twice as much space is given to refuting Empedocles' ideas as to their exposition, we cannot well attribute this to animus. It is clear that Empedocles and Democritus were more interesting to him, perhaps because their doctrines of perception were so picturable, so frankly mechanical, so contrary to his own ways of thought, and they offered such happy marks for his weapons of offence. There can be little

---

[5] *De Sens.* 47; cf. a "certain reasonableness", which he is willing to concede to Anaxagoras's explanation of perception by the interplay of opposites, *ibid.* 31.

[6] See pp. 22 ff.

doubt that Theophrastus relished his thrusts into the vitals of these men.

We therefore must take Theophrastus here as we find him,—a reviewer with the tribal marks: less sedulous in discovering the merits than in pointing to the defects of the men over whom his cold eye ranges. In much of his other work the interest is more constructive,[7] more single in the aim to let fact and truth speak for themselves, less controversial; but here he lends his support to a custom, —of which he was by no means the father nor the last child,—of approaching in the spirit of a disputant whatever is even distantly connected with philosophy. Of his present work, forty-one of the ninety-one sections are given to criticism; and the case of Empedocles already mentioned, where the criticism is about double the length of the exposition, is almost paralleled by his treatment of Anaxagoras. Yet we may be grateful not only that his eagerness for the fray led him so little to misrepresent his adversary,—but that even in his destructive criticism he showed on the whole so admirable a method, having such definite standards of measuring the work of his great forerunners. Some attempt to observe the principles which guided him in his skilful refutations may perhaps seem here appropriate.

He had, as I have already attempted to set forth, a definite 'point of view' in considering sense perception; we should perhaps rather speak of his 'points of view'.

---

[7] It must be remembered that if the judgment is right which takes our present Περὶ αἰσθήσεων to be but a fragment of the work in many books, Περὶ φυσικῶν δοξῶν, it is possible that Theophrastus wrote another work in a single book, Περὶ αἰσθήσεων, whose title is given in Diogenes Laertius (V, 42). If this was a separate work, he doubtless gave expression in it to his constructive ideas upon sense perception, and this would explain his silence upon many a point in the fragment we possess.

Theophrastus's Method of Criticism

For he had more than a single principle or dogma that seemed immovable under his feet,—various convictions upon perception, that need not all again be told. But to some which he used most commonly and with most effect in these criticisms, it will perhaps be pardonable briefly to refer; for we shall soon pass on.

An explanation of sense perception must for him make clear the nature of the object and of the stimulus as external and independent realities. Both Plato and Democritus in their account of the action of the senses fail to satisfy him in this respect.[8] Yet he is equally unsatisfied by a theory that describes merely the object and the stimulus. Explanation is rightly seen to be an intricate affair, and must state the character of the sense-organ and set forth its correspondence with its object.[9] If one would explain how we perceive the external world, he must set forth the *mutual relation between sense-organ and sense-object*, rather than the character of either of these two terms in isolation. Such is one portion of his plan of criticism. Farther he uses against the theory that perception is due to a kinship or similarity between the object and our senses,—against Empedocles in particular,[10] —the principle that '*like' is not affected by 'like' but only by its opposite*—a principle which had perhaps been implied in the thought of Democritus,[11] and which had been acutely discussed by his own great teacher Aristotle.[12]

In attacking Democritus's doctrine that one person's senses attain no more, nor less, truth than another's, he rests his case on the principle that better and worse are not in us alone, but are active in the arrangement of the world; that *certain events and conditions are in accord with*

---

[8] *De Sens.* 70, 71, 88, 89.
[9] *De Sens.* 32.
[10] *De Sens.* 19, 23.
[11] *De Sens.* 49.
[12] Cf., e.g., *De Anima* 410^a 23 ; 417^a 19.

The Greek Physiological Psychology

the nature of things, while others are discordant;[13] and this idea he employs also against Anaxagoras's contention that pain is present in every act of perception. What conforms to Nature tends toward what is good; and any explanation which implies that natural powers are aimless or move constantly toward what is harmful must be abandoned.[14] These latter are appeals to principles wider than any special doctrine of perception, as is also his appeal against Democritus's view that, in hearing, the sound is spread to every nook and cranny of the body. Theophrastus here urges that *the causal relation is not the same as that of concomitance*: "for if the rest of the body is somehow affected conjointly with the organ of hearing", he says, "it by no means follows that the perception depends upon the body as a whole".[15]

We have, in this, passed quite beyond his own special doctrine of perception, as a standard by which others' theories may be judged. And now, continuing in this wider region, we see prominent his demand that a theory shall internally be simple and consistent. He is troubled by what seems to him inconstancy in several of the earlier psychologists, and for this reason they suffer his condemnation. Democritus would in general explain the effect of a sensory stimulus by the shape of its constituent atoms; but, Theophrastus points out, he is also found explaining the effect by their size, or their position.[16] He ascribes a particular atomic shape to each of the colours save green, and this one colour he explains in quite another way.[17] He holds that the *kinship* with the organ of sight is of prime importance for vision, and yet illogically declares

---

[13] *De Sens.* 70.

[14] *De Sens.* 31 ff.

[15] *De Sens.* 57.

[16] *De Sens.* 68 and 79; cf. his criticism of Democritus in *De Caus. Pl.* 6, 1, 6, and 6, 2, 1 ff.

[17] *De Sens.* 82.

Theophrastus's Method of Criticism

that sight depends on colour-contrast, implying that colours of the eyes' own hue are not reflected in them.[18] And so of other Democritean explanations. The inconsistency of Empedocles, too, is shown,—that he holds to a sensuous effluence from bodies; yet this could not always have been in keeping with the operation of his principle of Love.[19] And similarly in Plato's case: if he adopts figure as a means of explaining heat, let him rely on figure, then, to explain cold;[20] if he adopts, to explain vision, the idea that certain particles fit into the sense-organ, or 'correspond' with it, let him use this idea for all the senses.[21]

Not far from this demand for inner harmony, yet passing somewhat beyond, Theophrastus employs a logical 'razor' and requires that *a theory display economy*; that it use no more principles of explanation than are strictly needed. Thus he condemns Empedocles for introducing the idea of likeness between organ and stimulus to explain perception, when he has already explained it by contrast.[22] And Democritus needlessly introduces the idea of wax-like impressions on the air to explain our sight of objects, when he has already supposed that there is an emanation from the object, which could convey the object's form.[23] Furthermore, if our sight of objects is due to an emanation from them, why all this care to explain the difference between white and black by the internal structure of the objects, by minute passages that in one case are straight and in the other case are zig-zag?[24] And to his more formal requirements of sound explanation might be added

---

[18] *De Sens.* 54.
[19] *De Sens.* 20.
[20] *De Sens.* 87.
[21] *De Sens.* 91.
[22] *De Sens.* 15.
[23] *De Sens.* 51.
[24] *De Sens.* 80.

his demand for *accurate classification and definition*,—the demand that *things that are distinct should not be confused in terms*—'white', for example, with 'transparent' or 'brilliant'[25]—as well as the obvious requirement that we should be able to understand what an author means.[26]

But a favourite mode of criticism with Theophrastus has regard less to mere form, and more to fact and observation—a mode with which the modern scientist would feel full sympathy. He refutes many of these ancient theories by showing that *their implications are contrary to fact.* Thus—to give but a few examples,—Empedocles' theory of perception, which assumes a close fitting of material particle to particle, would be satisfied by purely physical mixture, and all things that mix should accordingly perceive.[27] And if the presence of many elements in some part of our bodies makes for perception, then bone and hair should be sensitive, for in them too are all the elements.[28] Furthermore, were Anaxagoras correct in his view that sight is fully explained by the reflection in the eye, many a lifeless thing would see; for there is a reflected image in water, in bronze, and in many another thing.[29] The assumption of a due proportion between breath and odours, which Diogenes employed in the explanation of smell, would require that we perceive odour with the breath in our chest, and not solely with that in our nostrils.[30] Nor can the greater purity of the air that is breathed by man account for his intellectual superiority to the brutes; for then mountaineers would surpass plainsmen, and birds would surpass us all.[31]

---

[25] *De Sens.* 80, 82.
[26] *De Sens.* 81.
[27] *De Sens.* 12.
[28] *De Sens.* 23.
[29] *De Sens.* 36.
[30] *De Sens.* 46.
[31] *De Sens.* 48. Cf. also Theophrastus's refutation of Empedocles' doctrine that pleasure and perception have a

Theophrastus's Method of Criticism

But in many a case Theophrastus, in order to find a theory absurd, hardly feels it necessary to develop the theory's *implications* and compare these with the facts; he points out that *the theory contradicts the facts almost in its very statement*. The theory of Empedocles, for example, that keenness of smell goes directly with greater inhalation is plainly against the fact that in sickness or at hard labour, the mere amount of breathing is of no avail.[32] Nor is he right in attributing intelligence directly to the blood; for many animals are bloodless, and in others the sense-organs are often the least supplied with blood.[33] Anaxagoras's doctrine that perception is always accompanied by pain, is refuted by the patent fact that perception is often neutral and at times is clearly pleasurable.[34]

Finally in cataloguing the variety of directions from which Theophrastus makes his attack, examples should be given of those criticisms which point out not so much that the theory contradicts the facts, as *that it would leave obvious facts quite unexplained*. Empedocles' use of likeness and unlikeness, for example, does not account for the clear difference between thought and pleasure and perception, all of which, upon Empedocles' principle, are effects of 'likeness'; and between pain and ignorance, which are due to 'difference'.[35] And against Anaxagoras's theory that vision is due to the reflection in the eye, is the fact that in this reflection we find no adequate representation of size, motion, and distance, nor of the many contrasting objects we see at once.[36]

But now in taking leave of Theophrastus's method, let

---

common source (*ibid.* 16), and his theory that odour is due to emanation (*ibid.* 20).

[32] *De Sens.* 21.
[33] *De Sens.* 23.
[34] *De Sens.* 31.
[35] *De Sens.* 23.
[36] *De Sens.* 36.

us for a moment enquire as to the justice of these his skilful assaults.

In general his criticisms, as already has been said, are of a high order; they point out unerringly the failure in many an early essay at explanation, and remove from our minds any lingering sense that the futility, the childishness, of much of this scientific speculation was never felt until the dawn of modern science. Yet we must know that Theophrastus was not always of clearest judgment, and at times would make the better reason in his adversary appear worse, or would tilt for a mere word.

In illustration of these less creditable attempts, one might perhaps include his objection to Plato's definition of 'soft', as that which yields to our flesh. "But if whatever is yielding is soft", interposes Theophrastus, "evidently water and air and fire are soft. And since he says that any substance is yielding that has a small base, fire would be the softest of all. But none of these statements is widely accepted, nor in general is it held that a thing is soft that moves freely around and behind the entering body; but only what yields in 'depth' without free change of place." [37] Equally unprofitable in his remark regarding Plato that "it is incorrect to liken odour to vapour and mist, and to say that vapour and mist are identical. Nor does he himself seem actually so to regard them; for vapour is in transition from water to air, he says, while mist is in transition from air to water. And yet in regard to mist the very opposite is generally held to be the fact; for when mist arises water disappears." [38] And unpenetrating, too, is Theophrastus's observation regarding Plato, that in his theory of vision "he agrees in general with Empedocles, since his idea that particles are proportioned to the organ of sight amounts to the thought that certain elements fit into the passages of

---

[37] *De Sens.* 87.
[38] *De Sens.* 90.

Theophrastus's Method of Criticism

sense." [39] It is difficult to understand how Theophrastus, basing, as he did, his account of Plato almost wholly on the *Timaeus*, could have failed to see that the difference here between Plato and Empedocles exceeded by far their likeness. Theophrastus, like Aristotle, furthermore, fails to appreciate Plato's penetrating originality in regard to the conceptions ' heavy ' and ' light '. The idea of relativity here, which we should accept as facing in the right direction, is for Theophrastus, who would have things heavy and light *per se*, merely a blunder.[40]

Yet these misadventures are not confined to his criticism of Plato, though here they are most evident. He more than once fails in judgment regarding Democritus. Thus Theophrastus is rather a formal logician than a penetrating scientist when he criticises as redundant Democritus's use of both emanations and air-prints.[41] For are these not addressed, we might urge, to very different aspects of our vision: the wax-like air-print to explain how we see the form of things; the emanation to explain our perception of its colour? A seal-like impression, we should have to say to Theophrastus, does not convey the hue; neither does a mere effluence, as we know well in the case of odour, convey the shape. And again his words sound as of a mere logician rather than as coming from a sympathetic interpreter of science when he says of Democritus's account of taste, that "the one glaring inconsistency running through the whole account is, that he no sooner declares savours to be subjective effects in sense than he distinguishes them by their figures. . . . For the figure cannot possibly be a subjective effect." [42] It might well be that for Democritus this was a 'glaring inconsistency', but it was a failing that leaned to virtue's side; for tastes

---

[39] *De Sens.* 91.
[40] *De Sens.* 88 f.
[41] *De Sens.* 51.
[42] *De Sens.* 69.

The Greek Physiological Psychology

are at once sensuous effects in us and are definite external stimuli; and for Democritus to observe and in a measure to do justice to this double existence which they have was better than for him to follow blindly the leading of his theory.

Such were the less happy turns of Theophrastus's critical judgment. But in closing this portion of our work, our minds may better rest upon attempts more fortunate; and these are not difficult to discover.

Of clear excellence is his criticism of Anaxagoras's idea that larger sensory organs imply better sensory power. "When Anaxagoras says that larger animals have better powers of sense, and that sense perception varies in general with the size of the organs of sense, one of these propositions raises the question whether small animals or large animals have better powers of sense. For it would seem to be essential to keener sense perception that minute objects should not escape it. And we might reasonably suppose, too, that an animal with power to discern smaller objects could also discern the larger. Indeed it is held that, so far as certain of the senses are concerned, small animals are superior to large ones; and in so far, consequently, the perceptive power of the larger animals would be inferior. But on the other hand, if it appear that many objects actually do escape the senses of small animals, then the sense perception of larger animals is superior."[43]

Of equal excellence is his attack on Democritus's theory that the form of objects is conveyed to our eyes by seal-like impressions on the air. What merciless advance upon the foe, what cold dismemberment, what burial of the remains! "Now in the first place", begins our critic, "this imprint upon the air is an absurdity. For the substance receiving such an imprint must have a certain consistence and not be 'fragile'; even as Democritus

---

[43] *De Sens.* 34 f.

Theophrastus's Method of Criticism

himself, in illustrating the character of the impression, says that it is as if one were to take a mould in wax. In the second place, an object could make a better imprint upon water than upon air, since water is denser. While the theory would require us to see more distinctly an object in water, we actually see it less so."[44] But assuming that this absurdity be fact, "and the air is moulded like wax that is squeezed and pressed, how does the reflection in the eye come into existence, and what is its character? . . . When several objects are seen in one and the same place, how can so many imprints be made upon the self-same air? And again, how could we possibly see each other? For the imprints would inevitably clash, since each of them would be facing the person from whom it sprung. All of which gives us pause.

"Furthermore, why does not each person see himself? For the imprints from ourselves would be reflected in our own eyes quite as they are in the eyes of our companions, especially if these imprints directly face us and if the effect here is the same as with an echo,—since Democritus says that in the case of the echo the vocal sound is reflected back to him who utters it. Indeed the whole idea of imprints made on the air is extravagant. For we should be forced to believe, from what he says, that all bodies are producing imprints in the air, and that great numbers of them are sending their impressions across one another's path,—a state of things at once embarrassing to sight and improbable on other grounds. If the impression moreover endures, we ought to see bodies that are out of sight and remote,—if not by night, at all events by day. And yet it would be but fair to assume that these imprints would persist at night, since then the air is so much cooler.

"Possibly, however, the reflection in the eye is caused by the sun, in sending light in upon the visual sense in the form of rays—as Democritus seems to mean. For the

---

[44] *De Sens.* 51.

idea that the sun 'drives the air from itself, and, in thus repelling, condenses it' as he says,—this is indefensible; since the sun by its very nature disperses the air." [45]

Such are a few of his many just objections. And while we have lingered long before letting Theophrastus speak entirely for himself, yet the delay will not have been vain if we should have caught some glimpse of his manner and success of criticism and of his varied knowledge and prepossessions in regard to sense perception. For thus we should have some portion of the background against which he viewed the work of the founders of Greek empirical psychology and of those who added to the labour of these founders, down to the time of Aristotle.

---

[45] *De Sens.* 52 ff.

II

THEOPHRASTUS ON THE SENSES

ΘΕΟΦΡΑΣΤΟΥ ΠΕΡΙ ΑΙΣΘΗΣΕΩΝ

1   Περὶ δ' αἰσθήσεως αἱ μὲν πολλαὶ καὶ καθόλου δόξαι δύ' εἰσίν· οἱ μὲν γὰρ τῷ ὁμοίῳ ποιοῦσιν, οἱ δὲ τῷ ἐναντίῳ. Παρμενίδης μὲν καὶ Ἐμπεδοκλῆς καὶ Πλάτων τῷ ὁμοίῳ, οἱ δὲ περὶ Ἀναξαγόραν καὶ Ἡράκλειτον τῷ ἐναντίῳ. τὸ δὲ πιθανὸν ἔλαβον οἱ μὲν ὅτι τῶν ἄλλων τε τὰ πλεῖστα τῇ ὁμοιότητι θεωρεῖται καὶ ὅτι σύμφυτόν ἐστι πᾶσι τοῖς ζῴοις τὰ συγγενῆ γνωρίζειν, ἔτι δ' ὡς τὸ μὲν αἰσθάνεσθαι τῇ ἀπορροίᾳ γίνεται, τὸ δ' ὅμοιον φέρεται πρὸς
2   τὸ ὅμοιον.   οἱ δὲ τὴν αἴσθησιν ὑπολαμβάνοντες ἐν ἀλλοιώσει γίνεσθαι καὶ τὸ μὲν ὅμοιον ἀπαθὲς ὑπὸ τοῦ ὁμοίου, τὸ δ' ἐναντίον παθητικόν, τούτῳ προσέθεσαν τὴν γνώμην· ἐπιμαρτυρεῖν δὲ οἴονται καὶ τὸ περὶ τὴν ἁφὴν συμβαῖνον· τὸ γὰρ ὁμοίως τῇ σαρκὶ θερμὸν ἢ ψυχρὸν οὐ ποιεῖν αἴσθησιν. καθόλου μὲν οὖν περὶ αἰσθήσεως αὗται παραδέδονται δόξαι. περὶ ἑκάστης δὲ τῶν κατὰ μέρος οἱ μὲν ἄλλοι σχεδὸν ἀπολείπουσιν, Ἐμπεδοκλῆς δὲ πειρᾶται καὶ ταύτας

THEOPHRASTUS ON THE SENSES

[PART I. THE SENSORY PROCESS]

THE various opinions concerning sense perception,[1] when regarded broadly, fall into two groups. By some investigators it is ascribed to similarity, while by others it is ascribed to contrast: Parmenides, Empedocles, and Plato attribute it to similarity; Anaxagoras and Heraclitus[2] attribute it to contrast.[3]

The one party is persuaded by the thought that other things are, for the most part, best interpreted in the light of what is like them; that it is a native endowment of all creatures to know their kin; and furthermore, that sense perception takes place by means of an effluence, and like is borne toward like.

The rival party assumes that perception comes to pass by an alteration; that the like is unaffected by the like, whereas opposites are affected by each other. So they give their verdict for this ⟨idea of opposition⟩. And to their mind further evidence is given by what occurs in connection with touch, since a degree of heat or cold the same as that of our flesh arouses no sensation.

Such then are the teachings handed down to us with regard to the general character of sense perception. As for the various senses severally, they are almost wholly neglected by these authors[4]—save Empedocles, who tries to refer also the particular senses to similarity.

The Greek Physiological Psychology

3 ἀνάγειν εἰς τὴν ὁμοιότητα. [παρμενίδου] Παρμενίδης μὲν γὰρ ὅλως οὐδὲν ἀφώρικεν ἀλλὰ μόνον, ὅτι δυοῖν ὄντοιν στοιχείοιν κατὰ τὸ ὑπερβάλλον ἐστὶν ἡ γνῶσις. ἐὰν γὰρ ὑπεραίρῃ τὸ θερμὸν ἢ τὸ ψυχρόν, ἄλλην γίνεσθαι τὴν διάνοιαν, βελτίω δὲ καὶ καθαρωτέραν τὴν διὰ τὸ θερμόν· οὐ μὴν ἀλλὰ καὶ ταύτην δεῖσθαί τινος συμμετρίας·

ὡς γὰρ ἑκάστοτε—φησίν—ἔχει κρᾶσιν μελέων πολυπλάγκτων,
τὼς νόος ἀνθρώποισι παρέστηκεν· τὸ γὰρ αὐτό
ἔστιν ὅπερ φρονέει μελέων φύσις ἀνθρώποισι
καὶ πᾶσιν καὶ παντί· τὸ γὰρ πλέον ἐστὶ νόημα.

4 τὸ γὰρ αἰσθάνεσθαι καὶ τὸ φρονεῖν ὡς ταὐτὸ λέγει· διὸ καὶ τὴν μνήμην καὶ τὴν λήθην ἀπὸ τούτων γίνεσθαι διὰ τῆς κράσεως· ἂν δ' ἰσάζωσι τῇ μίξει, πότερον ἔσται φρονεῖν ἢ οὔ, καὶ τίς ἡ διάθεσις, οὐδὲν ἔτι διώρικεν. ὅτι δὲ καὶ τῷ ἐναντίῳ καθ' αὑτὸ ποιεῖ τὴν αἴσθησιν, φανερὸν ἐν οἷς φησι τὸν νεκρὸν φωτὸς μὲν καὶ θερμοῦ καὶ φωνῆς οὐκ αἰσθάνεσθαι διὰ τὴν ἔκλειψιν τοῦ πυρός, ψυχροῦ δὲ καὶ σιωπῆς καὶ τῶν ἐναντίων αἰσθάνεσθαι. καὶ ὅλως δὲ πᾶν τὸ ὂν ἔχειν τινὰ γνῶσιν. οὕτω μὲν οὖν αὐτὸς ἔοικεν ἀποτέμνεσθαι τῇ φάσει τὰ συμβαίνοντα δυσχερῆ διὰ τὴν ὑπόληψιν.

5 Πλάτων δὲ ἐπὶ πλέον μὲν ἧπται τῶν κατὰ μέρος, οὐ μὴν εἴρηκέ γε περὶ ἁπασῶν, ἀλλὰ μόνον περὶ ἀκοῆς καὶ ὄψεως. καὶ τὴν μὲν ὄψιν ποιεῖ πυρός (διὸ καὶ τὸ χρῶμα

Theophrastus on the Senses

Parmenides gives no definition whatsoever, saying 3 merely that there are two elements, and that our knowledge depends upon the excess of one or the other. For according as the hot or the cold predominates does the understanding vary, there being a better and purer understanding derived from the hot; yet even such knowledge requires a certain proportion.5

> " For ever as it finds the blend in their far-wandering members," he says, "so does mind come to men; for that which has intelligence in men each and all is the same,—the substance of their members; since what is there in greater measure is their thought." 6

For to perceive by the senses and to have intelli- 4 gence are treated by him as identical; 7 consequently both remembering and forgetting arise, by the mixture ⟨of the elements mentioned⟩.8 But if there should occur an exact equality in the mixture, he does not make it clear whether there would or would not be thought, nor what would be the general state 9 ⟨resulting⟩. But that he also attributes perception to the opposite ⟨element⟩ 10 in its own right is evident from the passage where he says that a dead man—since now the fire has left him—does not perceive light and warmth and sound, but does perceive cold and silence and the other contrasting qualities; and that absolutely all being possesses some power of knowing. Accordingly by this thesis he seems arbitrarily to preclude discussion of the difficulties attending his position.

Plato 11 gives greater heed to the senses severally, 5 yet he actually does not speak of them all, but only of hearing and sight.12

⟨The organ of⟩ vision 13 he makes to consist of fire; (and this is why he regards colour also as a flame given off from bodies, having particles commensurate with the

φλόγα τιν' ἀπὸ τῶν σωμάτων σύμμετρα μόρια τῇ ὄψει ἔχουσαν), ὡς ἀπορροῆς τε γινομένης καὶ δέον συναρμόττειν ἀλλήλοις ἐξιοῦσαν μέχρι τινὸς συμφύεσθαι τῇ ἀπορροῇ καὶ οὕτως ὁρᾶν ἡμᾶς· ὥσπερ ἂν εἰς τὸ μέσον τιθεὶς τὴν ἑαυτοῦ δόξαν τῶν τε φασκόντων προσπίπτειν τὴν ὄψιν καὶ τῶν
6 φέρεσθαι πρὸς αὐτὴν ἀπὸ τῶν ὁρατῶν.   ἀκοὴν δὲ διὰ τῆς φωνῆς ὁρίζεται· φωνὴν γὰρ εἶναι πληγὴν ὑπ' ἀέρος ἐγκεφάλου καὶ αἵματος δι' ὤτων μέχρι ψυχῆς, τὴν δ' ὑπὸ ταύτης κίνησιν ἀπὸ κεφαλῆς μέχρι ἥπατος ἀκοήν. περὶ δὲ ὀσφρήσεως καὶ γεύσεως καὶ ἁφῆς ὅλως οὐδὲν εἴρηκεν, οὐδὲ εἰ παρὰ ταύτας ἄλλαι τινές εἰσιν, ἀλλὰ μᾶλλον ἀκριβολογεῖται περὶ τῶν αἰσθητῶν.

7 Ἐμπεδοκλῆς δὲ περὶ ἁπασῶν ὁμοίως λέγει καί φησι τῷ ἐναρμόττειν εἰς τοὺς πόρους τοὺς ἑκάστης αἰσθάνεσθαι· διὸ καὶ οὐ δύνασθαι τὰ ἀλλήλων κρίνειν, ὅτι τῶν μὲν εὐρύτεροί πως, τῶν δὲ στενώτεροι τυγχάνουσιν οἱ πόροι πρὸς τὸ αἰσθητόν, ὡς τὰ μὲν οὐχ ἁπτόμενα διευτονεῖν τὰ δ' ὅλως εἰσελθεῖν οὐ δύνασθαι. πειρᾶται δὲ καὶ τὴν ὄψιν λέγειν, ποία τίς ἐστι· καί φησι τὸ μὲν ἐντὸς αὐτῆς εἶναι πῦρ, τὸ δὲ περὶ αὐτὸ γῆν καὶ ἀέρα δι' ὧν διιέναι λεπτὸν ὂν καθάπερ τὸ ἐν τοῖς λαμπτῆρσι φῶς. τοὺς δὲ πόρους ἐναλλὰξ κεῖσθαι τοῦ τε πυρὸς καὶ τοῦ ὕδατος, ὧν τοῖς μὲν τοῦ πυρὸς τὰ λευκά, τοῖς δὲ τοῦ ὕδατος τὰ μέλανα γνωρίζειν· ἐναρμόττειν γὰρ ἑκατέροις ἑκάτερα. φέρεσθαι δὲ τὰ χρώματα

organ of vision);[14] assuming then that there is this effluence and that ⟨effluence and organ⟩ must unite, he holds that the ⟨visual stream⟩ issues forth for some distance and coalesces with the effluence, and thus it is we see.[15] His view, consequently, may be said to lie midway between the theories of those who say that vision falls upon ⟨its object⟩[16] and of those who hold that something is borne from visible objects to the ⟨organ of sight⟩.[17]

Hearing he defines in terms of sound:[18] for sound is a blow given by the air to the brain and blood, through the ears, and transmitted to the soul; the motion caused by this blow and extending from the head to the liver is hearing.[19]

Of smell, taste, and touch[20] he tells us nothing whatever,[21] nor does he say whether there are any other senses than these ⟨five⟩. He undertakes a more accurate account, however, of the objects[22] of these senses.

Empedocles has a common method of treating all the senses: he says that perception occurs because something fits into the passages of the particular ⟨sense organ⟩. For this reason the senses cannot discern one another's objects, he holds, because the passages of some ⟨of the sense-organs⟩ are too wide for the object,[23] and those of others are too narrow. And consequently some ⟨of these objects⟩ hold their course through[24] without contact, while others are quite unable to enter.

Then he attempts to tell us the character of the organ of vision. Its interior, he says, is of fire; while round about this ⟨internal fire⟩ are earth and air,[25] through which the fire, by reason of its subtilty, passes like the light in lanterns.[26] The passages ⟨of the eye⟩ are arranged alternately of fire and of water: by the passages of fire we perceive white objects; by those of water, things black; for in each of these cases ⟨the

The Greek Physiological Psychology

8 πρὸς τὴν ὄψιν διὰ τὴν ἀπορροήν.   συγκεῖσθαι δ' οὐχ ὁμοίως * * * [τὰς δ'] ἐκ τῶν ἀντικειμένων, καὶ ταῖς μὲν ἐν μέσῳ, ταῖς δ' ἐκτὸς εἶναι τὸ πῦρ· διὸ καὶ τῶν ζῴων τὰ μὲν ἐν ἡμέρᾳ, τὰ δὲ νύκτωρ μᾶλλον ὀξυωπεῖν· ὅσα μὲν πυρὸς ἔλαττον ἔχει, μεθ' ἡμέραν· ἐπανισοῦσθαι γὰρ αὐτοῖς τὸ ἐντὸς φῶς ὑπὸ τοῦ ἐκτός· ὅσα δὲ τοῦ ἐναντίου, νύκτωρ· ἐπαναπληροῦσθαι γὰρ καὶ τούτοις τὸ ἐνδεές· ἐν δὲ τοῖς ἐναντίοις ⟨ἐναντίως⟩ ἑκάτερον. ἀμβλυωπεῖν μὲν γὰρ καὶ οἷς ὑπερέχει τὸ πῦρ· ἐπαυξηθὲν ⟨γὰρ⟩ ἔτι μεθ' ἡμέραν ἐπιπλάττειν καὶ καταλαμβάνειν τοὺς τοῦ ὕδατος πόρους· οἷς δὲ τὸ ὕδωρ, ταὐτὸ τοῦτο γίνεσθαι νύκτωρ· καταλαμβάνεσθαι γὰρ τὸ πῦρ ὑπὸ τοῦ ὕδατος. ⟨γίγνεσθαι δὲ ταῦτα⟩, ἕως ἂν τοῖς μὲν ὑπὸ τοῦ ἔξωθεν φωτὸς ἀποκριθῇ τὸ ὕδωρ, τοῖς δ' ὑπὸ τοῦ ἀέρος τὸ πῦρ. ἑκατέρων γὰρ ἴασιν εἶναι τὸ ἐναντίον. ἄριστα δὲ κεκρᾶσθαι καὶ βελτίστην εἶναι τὴν ἐξ ἀμφοῖν ἴσων συγκειμένην. καὶ περὶ μὲν ὄψεως σχεδὸν
9 ταῦτα λέγει.   τὴν δ' ἀκοὴν ἀπὸ τῶν ἔσωθεν γίνεσθαι ψόφων, ὅταν ὁ ἀὴρ ὑπὸ τῆς φωνῆς κινηθεὶς ἠχῇ ἐντός. ὥσπερ γὰρ εἶναι κώδωνα τῶν ἴσων [?] ἤχων τὴν ἀκοήν, ἣν προσαγορεύει σάρκινον ὄζον· κινουμένην δὲ παίειν τὸν ἀέρα πρὸς τὰ στερεὰ καὶ ποιεῖν ἦχον. ὄσφρησιν δὲ γίνεσθαι τῇ ἀναπνοῇ. διὸ καὶ μάλιστα ὀσφραίνεσθαι τούτους, οἷς σφοδροτάτη τοῦ ἄσθματος ἡ κίνησις· ὀσμὴν δὲ πλείστην ἀπὸ τῶν λεπτῶν καὶ τῶν κούφων ἀπορρεῖν. περὶ δὲ

objects⟩ fit into the given ⟨passages⟩. Colours are brought to our sight by an effluence.[27] Yet ⟨eyes, he holds,⟩ are not all of like construction from these opposing elements:[28] in some ⟨eyes⟩ the fire is at the centre, in others it lies more external.[29] Because of this, certain animals see better by day, others by night: by day those whose eyes contain less of fire ⟨have an advantage⟩;[30] for with them the light within is made equal ⟨to the water within the eye⟩ by the ⟨light⟩ without. But those whose eyes have less of the opposite ⟨element[31]—their vision excels⟩ by night; for with them, also, their lack is supplied ⟨from without⟩. But reverse the conditions, and the opposite is true: for now even the animals that have fire in excess are dim of sight ⟨by day⟩,[32] since the fire within—increased still further by the daylight — covers and occupies the passages of water. And the same thing happens by night to those with water ⟨in excess⟩, because the fire is now overtaken by the water. This goes on until for the one group the ⟨excessive⟩ water is cut off[33] by the outer light; and for the other, the ⟨excessive⟩ fire is cut off by the air.[34] Thus each finds its remedy in its opposite. But that ⟨eye⟩ is of happiest blend and is best which is composed of both ⟨these constituents⟩ in equal measure. This represents fairly well what he says of vision.

He says that hearing results from sounds within ⟨the head⟩,[35] whenever the air, set in motion by a voice, resounds within. For the organ of hearing, which he calls a "fleshy off-shoot", acts as the 'bell' of a trumpet, ringing with sounds like ⟨those it receives⟩.[36] When set in motion ⟨this organ⟩ drives the air against the solid parts and produces there a sound.

Smell, according to Empedocles, is due to the act of breathing. As a consequence, those have keenest smell in whom the movement of the breath is most vigorous. The intensest odour emanates from bodies that are subtile and light. Of taste and touch severally he offers no

The Greek Physiological Psychology

γεύσεως καὶ ἀφῆς οὐ διορίζεται καθ' ἑκατέραν οὔτε πῶς οὔτε δι' ἃ γίγνονται, πλὴν τὸ κοινὸν ὅτι τῷ ἐναρμόττειν τοῖς πόροις αἴσθησίς ἐστιν· ἥδεσθαι δὲ τοῖς ὁμοίοις κατά τε ⟨τὰ⟩ μόρια καὶ τὴν κρᾶσιν, λυπεῖσθαι δὲ τοῖς ἐναντίοις. ὡσαύτως δὲ λέγει καὶ περὶ φρονήσεως καὶ ἀγνοίας.
10 τὸ μὲν γὰρ φρονεῖν εἶναι τοῖς ὁμοίοις, τὸ δ' ἀγνοεῖν τοῖς ἀνομοίοις, ὡς ἢ ταὐτὸν ἢ παραπλήσιον ὂν τῇ αἰσθήσει τὴν φρόνησιν. διαριθμησάμενος γάρ, ὡς ἕκαστον ἑκάστῳ γνωρίζομεν, ἐπὶ τέλει προσέθηκεν ὡς

ἐκ τούτων ⟨γὰρ⟩ πάντα πεπήγασιν ἁρμοσθέντα
καὶ τούτοις φρονέουσι καὶ ἥδοντ' ἠδ' ἀνιῶνται.

διὸ καὶ τῷ αἵματι μάλιστα φρονεῖν· ἐν τούτῳ γὰρ μάλιστα
11 κεκρᾶσθαι [ἐστὶ] τὰ στοιχεῖα τῶν μερῶν. ὅσοις μὲν οὖν ἴσα καὶ παραπλήσια μέμεικται καὶ μὴ διὰ πολλοῦ μηδ' αὖ μικρὰ μηδ' ὑπερβάλλοντα τῷ μεγέθει, τούτους φρονιμωτάτους εἶναι καὶ κατὰ τὰς αἰσθήσεις ἀκριβεστάτους, κατὰ λόγον δὲ καὶ τοὺς ἐγγυτάτω τούτων, ὅσοις δ' ἐναντίως, ἀφρονεστάτους. καὶ ὧν μὲν μανὰ καὶ ἀραιὰ κεῖται τὰ στοιχεῖα, νωθροὺς καὶ ἐπιπόνους· ὧν δὲ πυκνὰ καὶ κατὰ μικρὰ τεθραυσμένα, τοὺς δὲ τοιούτους ὀξεῖς φερομένους καὶ πολλοῖς ἐπιβαλλομένους ὀλίγα ἐπιτελεῖν διὰ τὴν ὀξύτητα τῆς τοῦ αἵματος φορᾶς· οἷς δὲ καθ' ἕν τι μόριον ἡ μέση κρᾶσίς ἐστι, ταύτῃ σοφοὺς ἑκάστους εἶναι· διὸ τοὺς μὲν ῥήτορας ἀγαθούς, τοὺς δὲ τεχνίτας, ὡς τοῖς μὲν ἐν ταῖς

Theophrastus on the Senses

precise account, telling us neither the manner nor the means of their operation,—save the ⟨assertion he makes with regard to all the senses in⟩ common, that perception arises because emanations fit into the passages of sense. Pleasure is excited by things that are similar ⟨to our organs⟩, both in their constituent parts and in the manner of their composition; pain, by things opposed.

In a like strain he speaks also of understanding and of ignorance. The one is due to what is like; the other to what is unlike; since in his view thought is either identical with sense perception or very similar to it. For after enumerating the ways in which we recognize each element by its like, he finally adds: 10

> "For from these have all things been fittingly conjoined, and by their means do creatures think and have delight and suffer grief."[37]

Accordingly, we think chiefly with the blood;[38] for here the elements are more fully mingled than in any other of our members.

Those in whom these mingled elements are of the same or nearly the same ⟨amount⟩, being neither widely separated nor too small nor of excessive size,—such persons are most intelligent and keen of sense; and others are intelligent and keen of sense according as they approach to such a mixture; but those whose condition is the very reverse are the least intelligent. Again, persons in whom the elements lie loose and rare[39] are slow and laborious; while such as have them compact and divided fine are impulsively carried away; they throw themselves into many a project, and yet accomplish little, because of the impetuous coursing of their blood.[40] But when the composition in some single member lies in the mean, the person is accomplished in that part. For this reason some are clever orators, others artisans; for in the one case the happy 11

χερσί, τοῖς δὲ ἐν τῇ γλώττῃ τὴν κρᾶσιν οὖσαν· ὁμοίως δ ἔχειν καὶ κατὰ τὰς ἄλλας δυνάμεις.

12 Ἐμπεδοκλῆς μὲν οὖν οὕτως οἴεται καὶ τὴν αἴσθησιν γίνεσθαι καὶ τὸ φρονεῖν, ἀπορήσειε δ' ἄν τις ἐξ ὧν λέγει πρῶτον μέν, τί διοίσει τὰ ἔμψυχα πρὸς τὸ αἰσθάνεσθαι τῶν ἄλλων. ἐναρμόττει γὰρ καὶ τοῖς τῶν ἀψύχων πόροις· ὅλως γὰρ ποιεῖ τὴν μῖξιν τῇ συμμετρίᾳ τῶν πόρων· διόπερ ἔλαιον μὲν καὶ ὕδωρ οὐ μείγνυσθαι, τὰ δὲ ἄλλα ὑγρὰ καὶ περὶ ὅσων δὴ καταριθμεῖται τὰς ἰδίας κράσεις. ὥστε πάντα τε αἰσθήσεται καὶ ταὐτὸν ἔσται μῖξις καὶ αἴσθησις καὶ αὔξησις· πάντα γὰρ ποιεῖ τῇ συμμετρίᾳ τῶν πόρων, ἐὰν μὴ

13 προσθῇ τινα διαφοράν. ἔπειτα ἐν αὐτοῖς τοῖς ἐμψύχοις τί μᾶλλον αἰσθήσεται τὸ ἐν τῷ ζῴῳ πῦρ ἢ τὸ ἐκτός, εἴπερ ἐναρμόττουσιν ἀλλήλοις; ὑπάρχει γὰρ καὶ ἡ συμμετρία καὶ τὸ ὅμοιον. ἔτι δὲ ἀνάγκη διαφοράν τινα ἔχειν, εἴπερ αὐτὸ μὲν μὴ δύναται συμπληροῦν τοὺς πόρους, τὸ δ' ἔξωθεν ἐπεισιόν· ὥστ' εἰ ὅμοιον ἦν πάντῃ καὶ πάντως, οὐκ ἂν ἦν αἴσθησις. ἔτι δὲ πότερον οἱ πόροι κενοὶ ἢ πλήρεις; εἰ μὲν γὰρ κενοί, συμβαίνει διαφωνεῖν ἑαυτῷ· φησὶ γὰρ ὅλως οὐκ εἶναι κενόν· εἰ δὲ πλήρεις, ἀεὶ ἂν αἰσθάνοιτο τὰ ζῷα· δῆλον

14 γὰρ ὡς ἐναρμόττει, καθάπερ φησί, τὸ ὅμοιον. καίτοι κἂν αὐτὸ τοῦτό τις διαπορήσειεν, εἰ δυνατόν ἐστι τηλικαῦτα μεγέθη γενέσθαι τῶν ἑτερογενῶν, ὥστ' ἐναρμόττειν, ἄλλως

Theophrastus on the Senses

mixture is in the tongue, in the other it is in the hands. And the like holds true for all the other forms of ability.[41]

Such is Empedocles' theory of the process both of sense perception and of thought. Yet from his account we might well be at a loss to know, first, wherein animate[42] beings differ from[43] other kinds of being so far as sense perception is concerned; since particles fit into the minute passages in lifeless objects also. For universally he regards mixture as due to a correspondence with these passages. This explains why oil and water will not mix,— in contrast to other fluids and to certain farther substances of which he recounts the peculiar combinations. Wherefore all things would perceive; and mixture, sense perception, and growth would be identical (for he ascribes them one and all to a correspondence with the passages), unless he add some farther difference. 12

In the second place, with regard even to animate things, why should the fire within the living creature perceive, rather than the fire without, if each really fits into the other? for ⟨on both sides⟩ there is proportion and likeness. And further there must be some difference between the two if the ⟨fire within⟩ is unable to fill up the passages, while the ⟨fire⟩ entering from without ⟨has this power⟩. Consequently if ⟨this internal fire⟩ were absolutely and in every respect the same ⟨as the fire without⟩, there would be no perception. Furthermore, are these passages empty or full? If empty, Empedocles is inconsistent; for he says that there is absolutely no void. But if full, creatures would perceive perpetually; for it is evident that a ⟨substance⟩ similar ⟨to another⟩—to use his own expression—fits ⟨into that other⟩. 13

And yet doubt might be felt upon the very point,— whether it were possible for diverse elements to be of precisely a size to fit each other; especially if it be 14

τε κἂν συμβαίνῃ, καθάπερ φησί, τὰς ὄψεις ὧν ἀσύμμετρος ἡ κρᾶσις ὁτὲ μὲν ὑπὸ τοῦ πυρός, ὁτὲ δὲ ὑπὸ τοῦ ἀέρος ἐμπλαττομένων τῶν πόρων ἀμαυροῦσθαι. εἰ δ' οὖν ἐστι καὶ τούτων συμμετρία καὶ πλήρεις οἱ πόροι τῶν μὴ συγγενῶν, πῶς, ὅταν αἰσθάνηται, καὶ ποῦ ταῦτα ὑπεξέρχεται; δεῖ γάρ τινα ἀποδοῦναι μεταβολήν. ὥστε πάντως ἔχει δυσκολίαν· ἢ γὰρ κενὸν ἀνάγκη ποιεῖν, ἢ ἀεὶ τὰ ζῷα αἰσθάνεσθαι πάντων, ἢ τὸ μὴ συγγενὲς ἁρμόττειν οὐ ποιοῦν αἴσθησιν
15 οὐδ' ἔχον μεταβολὴν οἰκείαν τοῖς ἐμποιοῦσιν. ἔτι δέ, εἰ καὶ μὴ ἐναρμόττοι τὸ ὅμοιον, ἀλλὰ μόνον ἅπτοιτο, καθ' ὁτιοῦν εὔλογον αἴσθησιν γίνεσθαι· δυοῖν γὰρ τούτοιν ἀποδίδωσι τὴν γνῶσιν τῷ τε ὁμοίῳ καὶ τῇ ἁφῇ· διὸ καὶ τὸ ἁρμόττειν εἴρηκεν. ὥστ' εἰ τὸ ἔλαττον ἅψαιτο τῶν μειζόνων, εἴη ἂν αἴσθησις. ὅλως τε κατά γε ἐκεῖνον ἀφαιρεῖται καὶ τὸ ὅμοιον, ἀλλὰ ἡ συμμετρία μόνον ἱκανόν. διὰ τοῦτο γὰρ οὐκ αἰσθάνεσθαί φησιν ἀλλήλων, ὅτι τοὺς πόρους ἀσυμμέτρους ἔχουσιν· εἰ δ' ὅμοιον ἢ ἀνόμοιον τὸ ἀπορρέον, οὐδὲν ἔτι προσαφώρισεν. ὥστε ἢ οὐ τῷ ὁμοίῳ ἡ αἴσθησις, ἢ οὐ διά τινα ἀσυμμετρίαν οὐ κρίνουσιν ἁπάσας ⟨τ'⟩ ἀνάγκη τὰς αἰσθήσεις καὶ πάντα τὰ αἰσθητὰ τὴν αὐτὴν ἔχειν φύσιν.
16 ἀλλὰ μὴν οὐδὲ τὴν ἡδονὴν καὶ λύπην ὁμολογουμένως

true, as he says, that eyes with some disproportion in their mixture [44] become dim of sight by a clogging of their passages, now with fire and now with air. Granting, however, that there is even here a nice adjustment, and that the passages are filled by what is alien, yet how and where are these ⟨occluding particles⟩ to be expelled when perception occurs? Some change must be assigned. Thus there is a difficulty in any case: for it is necessary to assume either the existence of a void, or that creatures are uninterruptedly perceiving things; [45] or else that an alien substance can fit into ⟨the sensory passages⟩ without causing perception and without involving the change peculiar to the substances that do cause ⟨perception⟩.

But, further, were we to suppose that what is like 15 does not *fit* ⟨the passages⟩ but merely *touches* ⟨there⟩, perception might reasonably arise from any source whatever. For he attributes our recognition of things to two factors—namely, to likeness and to contact; and so he uses the expression "to fit". Accordingly if the smaller ⟨particle⟩ touched the larger ones, there would be perception.[46] And likeness also, speaking generally, is out of the question, at least according to him, and commensurateness alone suffices.[47] For he says that substances fail to perceive one another because their passages are not commensurate. But whether the emanation is like or unlike ⟨the sensory organ⟩ he leaves quite undetermined.[48] Consequently either perception is not dependent on similarity; or else the failure to detect an object cannot be attributed to want of spatial correspondence, and the senses without exception and all the objects they perceive must have one and the same essential nature.

Moreover, his explanation of pleasure and pain is 16

The Greek Physiological Psychology

ἀποδίδωσιν ἥδεσθαι μὲν ποιῶν τοῖς ὁμοίοις, λυπεῖσθαι δὲ τοῖς ἐναντίοις· 'ἐχθρὰ' γὰρ εἶναι, διότι

'πλεῖστον ἀπ' ἀλλήλων διέχουσι . . .
γέννῃ τε κράσει ⟨τε⟩ καὶ εἴδεσιν ἐκμακτοῖσιν.'

αἰσθήσεις γάρ τινας ἢ μετ' αἰσθήσεως ποιοῦσι τὴν ἡδονὴν καὶ τὴν λύπην, ὥστε οὐχ ἅπασι γίνεται τοῖς ὁμοίοις. ἔτι εἰ τὰ συγγενῆ μάλιστα ποιεῖ τὴν ἡδονὴν ἐν τῇ ἁφῇ, καθάπερ φησί, τὰ σύμφυτα μάλιστ' ἂν ἥδοιτο καὶ ὅλως αἰσθάνοιτο· διὰ τῶν αὐτῶν γὰρ ποιεῖ τὴν αἴσθησιν καὶ τὴν ἡδονήν.

17 καίτοι πολλάκις αἰσθανόμενοι λυπούμεθα κατ' αὐτὴν τὴν αἴσθησιν, ὡς ⟨δ'⟩ Ἀναξαγόρας φησίν, ἀεί· πᾶσαν γὰρ αἴσθησιν εἶναι μετὰ λύπης. ἔτι δ' ἐν ταῖς κατὰ μέρος· συμβαίνει γὰρ τῷ ὁμοίῳ γίνεσθαι τὴν γνῶσιν· τὴν γὰρ ὄψιν ὅταν ἐκ πυρὸς καὶ τοῦ ἐναντίου συστήσῃ, τὸ μὲν λευκὸν καὶ τὸ μέλαν δύναιτ' ἂν τοῖς ὁμοίοις γνωρίζειν, τὸ δὲ φαιὸν καὶ τἆλλα χρώματα τὰ μεικτὰ πῶς; οὔτε γὰρ τοῖς τοῦ πυρὸς οὔτε τοῖς τοῦ ὕδατος πόροις οὔτ' ἄλλοις ποιεῖ κοινοῖς ἐξ ἀμφοῖν· ὁρῶμεν δ' οὐδὲν ἧττον ταῦτα τῶν ἁπλῶν.

18 ἀτόπως δὲ καὶ ὅτι τὰ μὲν ἡμέρας, τὰ δὲ νύκτωρ μᾶλλον ὁρᾷ. τὸ γὰρ ἔλαττον πῦρ ὑπὸ τοῦ πλείονος φθείρεται, διὸ καὶ πρὸς τὸν ἥλιον καὶ ὅλως τὸ καθαρὸν οὐ δυνάμεθ' ἀντιβλέπειν. ὥστε ὅσοις ἐνδεέστερον τὸ φῶς, ἧττον ἐχρῆν

inconsistent,[49] for he ascribes pleasure to the action of similars, while pain he derives from opposites. For these, he says, are "hostile", since

"most distant they stand from one another . . . in source and composition and in their moulded forms." [50]

Pleasure and pain thus are regarded by them [51] as sense perceptions or as accompaniments of sense perception; consequently ⟨the perceptive process⟩ does not in every case arise from similarity. Again, if kindred things especially cause pleasure by their contact, as he says, things which coalesce in their growth [52] should have the keenest pleasure,—and, in general, the keenest perception ⟨of one another⟩, for he assigns the same causes for sense perception as for pleasure. And yet 17 when we are perceiving, we often suffer pain in the very act of perception,—indeed, Anaxagoras declares, we *always* do. For all perception, he says, is linked with pain.

A like difficulty appears in connection with the senses severally; for his position [53] is that cognition is due to likeness. Now since, for him, the eye is composed of fire and of its opposite, it might well recognize white and black by means of what is like them; but how could it become conscious of gray and the other compound colours? For he assigns ⟨their perception⟩ neither to the minute passages of fire nor to those of water nor to others composed of both these elements together. Yet we see the compound colours no whit less than we do the simple.

Odd, too, is ⟨his account of⟩ the fact that certain 18 animals see better by day, and others by night.[54] For a weaker fire is extinguished by a stronger; [55] and for this reason we find it impossible to gaze at the sun or at anything exceedingly bright. Accordingly animals with less of light in their eyes ought to have had poorer vision by day. Or if what is qualitatively

ὁρᾶν μεθ' ἡμέραν· ἢ εἴπερ τὸ ὅμοιον συναύξει, καθάπερ φησί, τὸ δὲ ἐναντίον φθείρει καὶ κωλύει, τὰ μὲν λευκὰ μᾶλλον ἐχρῆν ὁρᾶν ἅπαντας μεθ' ἡμέραν καὶ ὅσοις ἔλαττον καὶ ὅσοις πλεῖον τὸ φῶς, τὰ δὲ μέλανα νύκτωρ. νῦν δὲ πάντες ἅπαντα μεθ' ἡμέραν μᾶλλον ὁρῶσι πλὴν ὀλίγων ζῴων. τούτοις δ' εὔλογον τοῦτ' ἰσχύειν τὸ οἰκεῖον πῦρ, ὥσπερ ἔνια 19 καὶ τῇ χρόᾳ διαλάμπει μᾶλλον τῆς νυκτός.   ἔτι δ' οἷς ἡ κρᾶσις ἐξ ἴσων, ἀνάγκη συναύξεσθαι κατὰ μέρος ἑκάτερον· ὥστ' εἰ πλεονάζον κωλύει θάτερον ὁρᾶν, ἁπάντων ἂν εἴη παραπλησία πως ἡ διάθεσις. ἀλλὰ τὰ μὲν τῆς ὄψεως πάθη χαλεπώτερον ἔσται διελεῖν· τὰ δὲ περὶ τὰς ἄλλας αἰσθήσεις πῶς κρίνωμεν τῷ ὁμοίῳ; τὸ γὰρ ὅμοιον ἀόριστον. οὔτε γὰρ ψόφῳ τὸν ψόφον οὔτ' ὀσμῇ τὴν ὀσμὴν οὔτε τοῖς ἄλλοις τοῖς ὁμογενέσιν, ἀλλὰ μᾶλλον ὡς εἰπεῖν τοῖς ἐναντίοις. ἀπαθῆ γὰρ δεῖ τὴν αἴσθησιν προσάγειν· ἤχου δὲ ἐνόντος ἐν ὠσὶν ἢ χυλῶν ἐν γεύσει καὶ ὀσμῆς ἐν ὀσφρήσει κωφότεραι πᾶσαι γίνονται ⟨καὶ⟩ μᾶλλον ὅσῳ ἂν πλήρεις ὦσι τῶν ὁμοίων, εἰ μή τις λεχθείη περὶ τούτων διορισμός.
20 ἔτι δὲ τὸ περὶ τὴν ἀπορροήν, καίπερ οὐχ ἱκανῶς λεγόμενον περὶ μὲν τὰς ἄλλας ὅμως ἔστι πως ὑπολαβεῖν, περὶ δὲ τὴν ἁφὴν καὶ γεῦσιν οὐ ῥᾴδιον. πῶς γὰρ τῇ ἀπορροῇ κρίνωμεν ἢ πῶς ἐναρμόττον τοῖς πόροις τὸ τραχὺ καὶ τὸ λεῖον;

Theophrastus on the Senses

similar does in fact supplement, and what is qualitatively different tends to destroy and thwart, as he says, then all creatures—both those that had less light and those that had more—should have seen white things better by day; and black, by night.[56] Yet in fact all but a few animals see every manner of object better by day. And for these ⟨exceptional animals⟩, we may reasonably suppose, the fire inherent in their eyes is peculiarly intense;[57] just as some objects by their own colour[58] glow brighter in the night.[59]

In those cases, moreover, where the blend is in equal 19 measure,[60] each component would of necessity be supplemented in turn. And consequently if an excess of the one element prevented the other from seeing,[61] all creatures would to all intents and purposes be in a like condition.[62]

Although it is a fairly difficult task to explain the facts of vision, yet how could we by *likeness* discern the objects with which the other senses deal? For the word 'likeness' is quite vague. ⟨We do⟩ not ⟨discern⟩ sound by sound, nor smell by smell, nor other objects by what is kindred to them; but rather, we may say, by their opposites. To these objects it is necessary to offer the sense organ in a passive state. If we have a ringing in the ears, or a taste on the tongue, or a smell in the nostrils, these organs all become blunted; and the more so, the fuller they are of what is like them,—unless there be a further distinction of these terms.

Next, as to the effluences. While his account, in 20 the case of the other senses, is inadequate, yet it is, in a way, intelligible; but his thought is indeed difficult to follow when it comes to touch and taste. How can we discern their objects by an effluence; or discern the rough and the smooth as fitting into the sensory passages? For it would seem [63] that, of

μόνου γὰρ δοκεῖ τῶν στοιχείων τοῦ πυρὸς ἀπορρεῖν, ἀπὸ δὲ τῶν ἄλλων οὐδενός. ἔτι δ' εἰ ἡ φθίσις διὰ τὴν ἀπορροήν, ᾧπερ χρῆται κοινοτάτῳ σημείῳ, συμβαίνει δὲ καὶ τὰς ὀσμὰς ἀπορροῇ γίνεσθαι, τὰ πλείστην ἔχοντα ὀσμὴν τάχιστ' ἐχρῆν φθείρεσθαι. νῦν δὲ σχεδὸν ἐναντίως ἔχει· τὰ γὰρ ὀσμωδέστατα τῶν φυτῶν καὶ τῶν ἄλλων ἐστὶ χρονιώτατα. συμβαίνει δὲ καὶ ἐπὶ τῆς Φιλίας ὅλως μὴ εἶναι αἴσθησιν ἢ ἧττον διὰ τὸ συγκρίνεσθαι τότε καὶ μὴ ἀπορρεῖν.

21 ἀλλὰ περὶ μὲν τὴν ἀκοὴν ὅταν ἀποδῷ τοῖς ἔσωθεν γίνεσθαι ψόφοις, ἄτοπον τὸ οἴεσθαι δῆλον εἶναι πῶς ἀκούουσιν, ἔνδον ποιήσαντα ψόφον ὥσπερ κώδωνος. τῶν μὲν γὰρ ἔξω δι' ἐκεῖνον ἀκούομεν, ἐκείνου δὲ ψοφοῦντος διὰ τί; τοῦτο γὰρ αὐτὸ λείπεται ζητεῖν. ἀτόπως δὲ καὶ τὸ περὶ τὴν ὄσφρησιν εἴρηκεν. πρῶτον μὲν γὰρ οὐ κοινὴν αἰτίαν ἀπέδωκεν· ἔνια μὲν γὰρ ὅλως οὐδ' ἀναπνέει τῶν ὀσφραινομένων. ἔπειτα τὸ μάλιστα ὀσφραίνεσθαι τοὺς πλεῖστον ἐπισπωμένους εὔηθες· οὐδὲν γὰρ ὄφελος μὴ ὑγιαινούσης ἢ μὴ ἀνεῳγμένης πως τῆς αἰσθήσεως. πολλοῖς δὲ συμβαίνει πεπηρῶσθαι καὶ ὅλως μηδὲν αἰσθάνεσθαι. πρὸς δὲ τούτοις οἱ δύσπνοοι καὶ οἱ πονοῦντες καὶ οἱ καθεύδοντες μᾶλλον ἂν αἰσθάνοιντο τῶν ὀσμῶν· τὸν πλεῖστον γὰρ ἕλκουσιν
22 ἀέρα. νῦν δὲ συμβαίνει τοὐναντίον. οὐ γὰρ ἴσως καθ' αὑτὸ τὸ ἀναπνεῖν αἴτιον τῆς ὀσφρήσεως, ἀλλὰ κατὰ συμβεβηκός, ὡς ἔκ τε τῶν ἄλλων ζῴων μαρτυρεῖται καὶ

the various elements, there is an effluence only from fire, but not from any of the others. Also if effluence involves a loss of substance—and this he uses as a universal testimony ⟨for his theory⟩[64]—and if it be true, too, that odours arise through effluence, then those substances with the strongest odour would most rapidly perish. Now the fact is nearly the reverse: the most fragrant plants and other bodies that are most odorous are the most enduring. In all consistency, moreover, at the time of Love,[65] there should be no sensory perception at all, or at least less than usual;[66] because under such circumstances recomposition and not effluence would be taking place.

Again, with regard to hearing, it is strange of him 21 to imagine that he has really explained how creatures hear, when he has ascribed the process to internal sounds and assumed that the ear produces a sound within, like a bell. By means of this internal sound we might hear sounds without, but how should we hear this internal sound itself? The old problem would still confront us.

Odd, too, is the account he gives of smell. In the first place, he does not assign a cause which applies to all cases, since some animals that have a sense of smell do not breathe at all.[67] Secondly, it is silly to assert that those have the keenest sense of smell who inhale most; for if the organ is not in health or is, for any cause, not unobstructed, mere breathing is of no avail. It often happens that a man has suffered injury ⟨to the organ⟩ and has no sensation at all. Furthermore, persons 'short of breath' or at hard labour[68] or asleep —since they inhale most air—should be most sensitive to odours. Yet the reverse is the fact. For in all 22 likelihood respiration is not of itself the cause of smell, but is connected with it incidentally; as is shown in the case of other living creatures as well as by the

The Greek Physiological Psychology

διὰ τῶν εἰρημένων παθῶν· ὁ δ' ὡς ταύτης οὔσης τῆς αἰτίας καὶ ἐπὶ τέλει πάλιν εἴρηκεν ὥσπερ ἐπισημαινόμενος

ὧδε μὲν οὖν πνοιῆς τε λελόγχασι πάντα καὶ ὀσμῶν.

οὐκ ἀληθὲς ⟨δὲ⟩ οὐδὲ τὸ μάλιστα ὀσφραίνεσθαι τῶν κούφων, ἀλλὰ δεῖ καὶ ὀσμὴν ἐνυπάρχειν. ὁ γὰρ ἀὴρ καὶ τὸ πῦρ
23 κουφότατα μέν, οὐ ποιοῦσι δὲ αἴσθησιν ὀσμῆς. ὡσαύτως δ' ἄν τις καὶ περὶ τὴν φρόνησιν ἀπορήσειεν, εἰ γὰρ τῶν αὐτῶν ποιεῖ καὶ τὴν αἴσθησιν. καὶ γὰρ ἅπαντα μεθέξει τοῦ φρονεῖν. καὶ ἅμα πῶς ἐνδέχεται καὶ ἐν ἀλλοιώσει καὶ ὑπὸ τοῦ ὁμοίου γίνεσθαι τὸ φρονεῖν; τὸ γὰρ ὅμοιον οὐκ ἀλλοιοῦται τῷ ὁμοίῳ. τὸ δὲ δὴ τῷ αἵματι φρονεῖν καὶ παντελῶς ἄτοπον· πολλὰ γὰρ τῶν ζῴων ἄναιμα, τῶν δὲ ἐναίμων τὰ περὶ τὰς αἰσθήσεις ἀναιμότατα τῶν μερῶν. ἔτι καὶ ὀστοῦν καὶ θρὶξ αἰσθάνοιτ' ἄν, ἐπεὶ οὖν ἐξ ἁπάντων ἐστὶ τῶν στοιχείων. καὶ συμβαίνει ταὐτὸν εἶναι τὸ φρονεῖν καὶ αἰσθάνεσθαι καὶ ἥδεσθαι καὶ ⟨τὸ⟩ λυπεῖσθαι καὶ [τὸ] ἀγνοεῖν· ἄμφω γὰρ ποιεῖ τοῖς ἀνομοίοις. ὥσθ' ἅμα τῷ μὲν ἀγνοεῖν ἔδει γίνεσθαι λύπην, τῷ δὲ φρονεῖν
24 ἡδονήν. ἄτοπον δὲ καὶ τὸ τὰς δυνάμεις ἑκάστοις ἐγγίνεσθαι διὰ τὴν ἐν τοῖς μορίοις τοῦ αἵματος σύγκρασιν, ὡς ἢ τὴν γλῶτταν αἰτίαν τοῦ εὖ λέγειν ⟨οὖσαν ἢ⟩ τὰς χεῖρας τοῦ δημιουργεῖν, ἀλλ' οὐκ ὀργάνου τάξιν ἔχοντα.

facts just recounted. But as though setting his hand and seal to the thought that it is the cause, he says again in closing,

> "In this wise have they all received as their portion both breath and odours."

Nor is it true that light [69] bodies most strongly affect the sense of smell; nay ⟨in addition to the lightness⟩ there must actually be some odour resident ⟨in the bodies⟩. For air and fire are the very lightest of substances, and yet produce in us no sensation of odour.

One might likewise have serious misgivings over his doctrine of thought, if Empedocles actually regards thought as having the same constitution as sense; [70] for then all ⟨creatures⟩ [71] would share in thought. And how can the notion be entertained that thinking arises in a process of change, and at the same time arises by the agency of the like? since the like produces no change in the like. And it is indeed quite ridiculous to suppose that we think with the blood: for many animals are bloodless; and of those that have blood, the parts about the organs of sense are the most deficient in blood. Furthermore, according to his view, bone and hair ought to perceive, since they too are composed of all the elements.[72] In all consistency, moreover, to think and to perceive and to enjoy would be identical processes; and, on the other hand, to suffer pain and to be ignorant,—for these two he ascribes to unlikeness. Accordingly, pain ought to accompany ignorance; and pleasure, the act of thinking. 23

Again, his idea is odd that the special abilities of men are due to the composition of the blood in their particular members,—as if the tongue were the cause of eloquence; or the hands, of craftsmanship; and as if these members did not have the rank of mere in- 24

διὸ καὶ μᾶλλον ἄν τις ἀποδοίη τῇ μορφῇ τὴν αἰτίαν ἢ τῇ κράσει τοῦ αἵματος, ἢ χωρὶς διανοίας ἐστίν· οὕτως γὰρ ἔχει καὶ ἐπὶ τῶν ἄλλων ζῴων. Ἐμπεδοκλῆς μὲν οὖν ἔοικεν ἐν πολλοῖς διαμαρτάνειν.

25 Τῶν δὲ μὴ τῷ ὁμοίῳ ποιούντων τὴν αἴσθησιν Ἀλκμαίων μὲν πρῶτον ἀφορίζει τὴν πρὸς τὰ ζῷα διαφοράν. ἄνθρωπον γάρ φησι τῶν ἄλλων διαφέρειν ὅτι μόνος ξυνίησι, τὰ δ᾽ ἄλλα αἰσθάνεται μέν, οὐ ξυνίησι δέ, ὡς ἕτερον ὂν τὸ φρονεῖν καὶ αἰσθάνεσθαι, καὶ οὔ, καθάπερ Ἐμπεδοκλῆς, ταὐτόν. ἔπειτα περὶ ἑκάστης λέγει. ἀκούειν μὲν οὖν φησι τοῖς ὠσίν, διότι κενὸν ἐν αὐτοῖς ἐνυπάρχει· τοῦτο γὰρ ἠχεῖν. φθέγγεσθαι δὲ τῷ κοίλῳ, τὸν ἀέρα δ᾽ ἀντηχεῖν. ὀσφραίνεσθαι δὲ ῥισὶν ἅμα τῷ ἀναπνεῖν ἀνάγοντα τὸ πνεῦμα πρὸς τὸν ἐγκέφαλον. γλώττῃ δὲ τοὺς χυμοὺς κρίνειν· χλιαρὰν γὰρ οὖσαν καὶ μαλακὴν τήκειν τῇ θερμότητι· δέχεσθαι δὲ καὶ διαδιδόναι διὰ τὴν μανότητα καὶ
26 ἁπαλότητα. ὀφθαλμοὺς δὲ ὁρᾶν διὰ τοῦ πέριξ ὕδατος. ὅτι δ᾽ ἔχει πῦρ δῆλον εἶναι· πληγέντος γὰρ ἐκλάμπειν. ὁρᾶν δὲ τῷ στίλβοντι καὶ τῷ διαφανεῖ, ὅταν ἀντιφαίνῃ, καὶ ὅσον ἂν καθαρώτερον ᾖ, μᾶλλον. ἁπάσας δὲ τὰς αἰσθήσεις συνηρτῆσθαί πως πρὸς τὸν ἐγκέφαλον· διὸ καὶ πηροῦσθαι κινουμένου καὶ μεταλλάττοντος τὴν χώραν· ἐπιλαμβάνειν γὰρ τοὺς πόρους, δι᾽ ὧν αἱ αἰσθήσεις. περὶ

Theophrastus on the Senses

struments! Indeed one might better for this reason assign the shape of the organ as the cause ⟨of talent⟩;[73] rather than ascribe this to the composition of the blood ⟨in the organ⟩,—which really has nothing to do with understanding. For this is the case[74] certainly with animals other ⟨than man⟩. Empedocles thus seems to have gone astray at many a point.

Of those who ascribe perception to something other 25 than similarity, Alcmaeon states, to begin with, the difference between men and animals. For man, he says, differs from other creatures "inasmuch as he alone[75] has the power to understand. Other creatures perceive by sense but do not understand"; since to think and to perceive by sense are different processes and not, as Empedocles held, identical.

He next speaks of the senses severally. Hearing is by means of the ears, he says, because within them is an empty space, and this empty space resounds.[76] A kind of noise is produced by the cavity,[77] and the internal air re-echoes this sound. Smelling is by means of the nostrils in connection with the act of respiration when one draws up the breath to the brain. By the tongue we discern tastes. For since it is warm and soft, the tongue dissolves ⟨substances⟩ with its heat; and because of its loose and yielding texture it readily receives and transmits ⟨the savours⟩.

Eyes see through the water round about.[78] And the 26 eye obviously has fire within, for when one is struck ⟨this fire⟩ flashes out. Vision is due to the gleaming,— that is to say, the transparent—character[79] of that which ⟨in the eye⟩ reflects the object; and sight is the more perfect, the greater the purity of this substance.[80] All the senses are connected in some way with the brain; consequently they are incapable of action if ⟨the brain⟩ is disturbed or shifts its position, for ⟨this organ⟩ stops up the passages through which the senses

The Greek Physiological Psychology

δὲ ἁφῆς οὐκ εἴρηκεν οὔτε πῶς οὔτε τίνι γίνεται. [ἀλλ']
Ἀλκμαίων μὲν οὖν ἐπὶ τοσοῦτον ἀφώρικεν.

27 Ἀναξαγόρας δὲ γίνεσθαι μὲν τοῖς ἐναντίοις· τὸ γὰρ ὅμοιον ἀπαθὲς ὑπὸ τοῦ ὁμοίου. καθ' ἑκάστην δ' ἰδίᾳ πειρᾶται διαριθμεῖν. ὁρᾶν μὲν γὰρ τῇ ἐμφάσει τῆς κόρης, οὐκ ἐμφαίνεσθαι δὲ εἰς τὸ ὁμόχρων, ἀλλ' εἰς τὸ διάφορον. καὶ τοῖς μὲν πολλοῖς μεθ' ἡμέραν, ἐνίοις δὲ νύκτωρ εἶναι τὸ ἀλλόχρων· διὸ ὀξυωπεῖν τότε. ἁπλῶς δὲ τὴν νύκτα μᾶλλον ὁμόχρων εἶναι τοῖς ὀφθαλμοῖς. ἐμφαίνεσθαι δὲ μεθ' ἡμέραν, ὅτι τὸ φῶς συναίτιον τῆς ἐμφάσεως· τὴν δὲ χρόαν τὴν κρατοῦσαν μᾶλλον εἰς τὴν ἑτέραν ἐμφαίνεσθαι
28 ἀεί.   τὸν αὐτὸν δὲ τρόπον καὶ τὴν ἁφὴν καὶ τὴν γεῦσιν κρίνειν· τὸ γὰρ ὁμοίως θερμὸν καὶ ψυχρὸν οὔτε θερμαίνειν οὔτε ψύχειν πλησιάζον οὐδὲ δὴ τὸ γλυκὺ καὶ τὸ ὀξὺ δι' αὐτῶν γνωρίζειν, ἀλλὰ τῷ μὲν θερμῷ τὸ ψυχρόν, τῷ δ' ἁλμυρῷ τὸ πότιμον, τῷ δ' ὀξεῖ τὸ γλυκὺ κατὰ τὴν ἔλλειψιν τὴν ἑκάστου· πάντα γὰρ ἐνυπάρχειν φησὶν ἐν ἡμῖν. ὡσαύτως δὲ καὶ ὀσφραίνεσθαι καὶ ἀκούειν τὸ μὲν ἅμα τῇ ἀναπνοῇ, τὸ δὲ τῷ διικνεῖσθαι τὸν ψόφον ἄχρι τοῦ ἐγκεφάλου· τὸ γὰρ περιέχον ὀστοῦν εἶναι κοῖλον, εἰς ὃ ἐμπίπτειν τὸν ψόφον.
29 ἅπασαν δ' αἴσθησιν μετὰ λύπης, ὅπερ ἂν δόξειεν ἀκόλουθον εἶναι τῇ ὑποθέσει· πᾶν γὰρ τὸ ἀνόμοιον ἁπτόμενον πόνον

Theophrastus on the Senses

act. Of touch he tells us neither the manner nor the means of its operation. So far and no farther, then, does Alcmaeon's discussion carry us.

27 Anaxagoras holds that sense perception comes to pass by means of opposites, for the like is unaffected by the like.[81] He then essays to review each sense separately. Accordingly he maintains that seeing is due to the reflection [82] in the pupil, but that nothing is reflected in what is of like hue, but only in what is of a different hue.[83] Now with most ⟨creatures⟩ this contrast of hue ⟨with that of the pupil⟩ occurs by day, but with some by night, and this is why the latter are keen of vision by night. But, in general, night the rather is of the eye's own hue. Furthermore, there is reflection by day, he holds, because the light is a contributing cause of reflection, and because the stronger of two colours is regularly reflected better in the weaker.[84]

28 Touch and taste, according to Anaxagoras, perceive their objects after this same manner.[85] For what is of the same degree of warmth or of cold ⟨as another object⟩ does not warm or cool ⟨this other object⟩ upon approaching it; and certainly we do not become aware of the sweet and of the sour by means of these qualities themselves. On the contrary we come to know the cold by the hot, the fresh and fit to drink by the brackish, the sweet by the sour,—according as we are deficient in one or another of these; although, as he says, they are all present in us.

And similarly of smell and hearing: the former accompanies inhalation; the latter depends upon the penetration of sound to the brain, for the enveloping bone [86] which the sound penetrates is hollow.

29 All sense perception, he holds, is fraught with pain,[87]—which would seem in keeping with his general principle,[88] for the unlike when brought in contact ⟨with our organs⟩ always brings distress. This is illus-

παρέχει. φανερὸν δὲ τοῦτο τῷ τε τοῦ χρόνου πλήθει καὶ τῇ τῶν αἰσθητῶν ὑπερβολῇ. τά τε γὰρ λαμπρὰ χρώματα καὶ τοὺς ὑπερβάλλοντας ψόφους λύπην ἐμποιεῖν καὶ οὐ πολὺν χρόνον δύνασθαι τοῖς αὐτοῖς ἐπιμένειν. αἰσθητικώτερα δὲ τὰ μείζω ζῷα καὶ ἁπλῶς εἶναι κατὰ τὸ μέγεθος ⟨τῶν αἰσθητηρίων⟩ τὴν αἴσθησιν. ὅσα μὲν γὰρ μεγάλους καὶ καθαροὺς καὶ λαμπροὺς ὀφθαλμοὺς ἔχει, μεγάλα τε καὶ πόρρωθεν ὁρᾶν, ὅσα δὲ μικρος, ἐναντίως. ὁμοίως δὲ
30 καὶ ἐπὶ τῆς ἀκοῆς. τὰ μὲν γὰρ μεγάλα τῶν μεγάλων καὶ τῶν πόρρωθεν ἀκούειν, τὰ δ' ἐλάττω λανθάνειν, τὰ δὲ μικρὰ τῶν μικρῶν καὶ τῶν ἐγγύς. καὶ ἐπὶ τῆς ὀσφρήσεως ὁμοίως· ὄζειν μὲν γὰρ μᾶλλον τὸν λεπτὸν ἀέρα, θερμαινόμενον μὲν γὰρ καὶ μανούμενον ὄζειν. ἀναπνέον δὲ τὸ μὲν μέγα ζῷον ἅμα τῷ μανῷ καὶ τὸ πυκνὸν ἕλκειν, τὸ δὲ μικρὸν αὐτὸ τὸ μανόν, διὸ καὶ τὰ μεγάλα μᾶλλον αἰσθάνεσθαι. καὶ γὰρ τὴν ὀσμὴν ἐγγὺς εἶναι μᾶλλον ἢ πόρρω διὰ τὸ πυκνοτέραν εἶναι, σκεδαννυμένην δὲ ἀσθενῆ. σχεδὸν δὲ ὡς εἰπεῖν οὐκ αἰσθάνεσθαι τὰ μὲν μεγάλα τῆς λεπτῆς ὀσμῆς, τὰ δὲ μικρὰ τῆς πυκνῆς.

31 Τὸ μὲν οὖν τοῖς ἐναντίοις ποιεῖν τὴν αἴσθησιν ἔχει τινὰ λόγον, ὥσπερ ἐλέχθη· δοκεῖ γὰρ ἡ ἀλλοίωσις οὐχ ὑπὸ τῶν ὁμοίων, ἀλλ' ὑπὸ τῶν ἐναντίων εἶναι. καίτοι καὶ τοῦτο δεῖται πίστεως, εἰ ἀλλοίωσις ἡ αἴσθησις εἴ τε τὸ ἐναντίον τοῦ ἐναντίου κριτικόν. τὸ δὲ μετὰ λύπης ἅπασαν εἶναι [ψεῦδος] οὔτ' ἐκ τῆς χρήσεως ὁμολογεῖται, τὰ μὲν ⟨γὰρ⟩ μεθ' ἡδονῆς τὰ δὲ πλεῖστα ἄνευ λύπης ἐστίν, οὔτ' ἔστι τῶν εὐλόγων. ἡ μὲν γὰρ αἴσθησις κατὰ φύσιν, οὐδὲν

trated by ⟨our experience when an impression⟩ long persists[89] and when the exciting objects are present in excess. For dazzling colours and excessively loud sounds cause pain and we cannot long endure[90] the same objects. The larger animals have more perfect powers of sense, and sense perception varies in general with the size ⟨of the organs of sense⟩. For animals that have large clear lustrous eyes see large objects and such as are distant; [91] while of animals with small eyes the opposite is true.

And likewise of hearing. For large animals hear 30 loud sounds and sounds far away, and the more minute sounds escape them; while small animals hear sounds that are minute and close at hand.[92] And similarly of smell: for rarefied air has a stronger odour, since it is odorous when heated and rendered less dense. A large animal when breathing, accordingly, inhales the dense along with the subtile, while the small animal inhales merely the subtile; [93] large animals as a consequence have the more perfect sensory power. For an odour near by is more intense than one remote, he holds, because it is denser, and in scattering becomes faint. Roughly, then, his view is, that large animals perceive no 'subtile odour', [94] and small animals no odour that is dense.

Now there is a certain reasonableness, as I have 31 said,[95] in explaining sense perception by the interplay of opposites; for alteration is held to be caused, not by similars, but by opposites. And yet even here one might entertain a doubt whether sense perception actually is an alteration, and whether an opposite is cognizant of its opposite. But as for the thesis that sense perception is universally conjoined with pain, this finds no warrant in experience, inasmuch as some objects are actually perceived with pleasure, and most of them at least without pain. Nor is it reasonable.[96] For sense perception is in accord with nature, and no

δὲ τῶν φύσει βίᾳ καὶ μετὰ λύπης, ἀλλὰ μᾶλλον μεθ᾽ ἡδονῆς, ὅπερ καὶ φαίνεται συμβαῖνον. τὰ γὰρ πλείω καὶ πλεονάκις ἡδόμεθα καὶ αὐτὸ δὲ τὸ αἰσθάνεσθαι χωρὶς τῆς
32 περὶ ἕκαστον ἐπιθυμίας διώκομεν.   ἔτι δ᾽ ἐπεὶ καὶ ἡδονὴ καὶ λύπη γίνεται διὰ τῆς αἰσθήσεως, ἅπαν δὲ φύσει πρὸς τὸ βέλτιόν ἐστι, καθάπερ ἡ ἐπιστήμη, μᾶλλον ἂν εἴη μεθ᾽ ἡδονῆς ἢ μετὰ λύπης. ἁπλῶς δ᾽ εἴπερ μηδὲ τὸ διανοεῖσθαι μετὰ λύπης, οὐδὲ τὸ αἰσθάνεσθαι· τὸν αὐτὸν γὰρ ἔχει λόγον ἑκάτερον πρὸς τὴν αὐτὴν χρείαν. ἀλλὰ μὴν οὐδὲ αἱ τῶν αἰσθητῶν ὑπερβολαὶ καὶ τὸ τοῦ χρόνου πλῆθος οὐδὲν σημεῖον ὡς μετὰ λύπης ἐστίν, ἀλλὰ μᾶλλον ὡς ἐν συμμετρίᾳ τινὶ καὶ κράσει πρὸς τὸ αἰσθητὸν ἡ αἴσθησις. διόπερ ἴσως τὸ μὲν ἐλλεῖπον ἀναίσθητον, τὸ δ᾽ ὑπερβάλλον λύπην
33 τε ποιεῖ καὶ φθείρει.   συμβαίνει τοίνυν τὸ κατὰ φύσιν ἐκ τοῦ παρὰ φύσιν σκοπεῖν· ἡ γὰρ ὑπερβολὴ παρὰ φύσιν. ἐπεὶ τό γε ἀπ᾽ ἐνίων καὶ ἐνίοτε λυπεῖσθαι, καθάπερ καὶ ἥδεσθαι, φανερὸν καὶ ὁμολογούμενον· ὥστ᾽ οὐδὲν μᾶλλον διά γε τοῦτο μετὰ λύπης ἢ μεθ᾽ ἡδονῆς ἐστιν, ἀλλ᾽ ἴσως μετ᾽ οὐδετέρου κατά γε τὸ ἀληθές· οὐδὲ γὰρ ἂν δύναιτο κρίνειν, ὥσπερ οὐδὲ ἡ διάνοια συνεχῶς οὖσα μετὰ λύπης ἢ ἡδονῆς. ἀλλὰ τοῦτο μὲν ἀπὸ μικρᾶς ἀρχῆς ἐφ᾽ ὅλην
34 μετήνεγκε τὴν αἴσθησιν.   ὅταν δὲ λέγῃ τὰ μείζω μᾶλλον αἰσθάνεσθαι καὶ ἁπλῶς κατὰ τὸ μέγεθος τῶν αἰσθη-

such process does violence and brings pain, but the rather it has pleasure as its accompaniment,—a law whose operation is quite manifest. For as a rule we take pleasure in things, and perception itself is something sought by us, apart from any desire we may have for the particular ⟨object perceived⟩.

Moreover since pleasure and pain alike arise from 32 sense perception, and yet all that accords with nature tends to produce good rather that evil [97]—as is the case also with the knowledge process,—⟨perception⟩ would be linked more intimately with pleasure than with pain. In a word, if understanding is not painful, clearly sense perception is not; for they both stand in the same relation to the same ⟨kind of⟩ need.[98]

Nor does the effect of excessively intense stimuli and of stimulation long continued prove that perception is ⟨invariably⟩ conjoined with pain, but rather that sense perception implies a certain correspondence and a composition suited to the object. And this perhaps is why a deficient stimulation passes unperceived, and an excessive one causes pain and is destructive.

Now our author, we see, arrives at his interpretation of 33 what is normal and according to nature, from what is exceptional and contrary to nature; for excess [99] is contrary to nature. For it is patent and not to be denied that we receive pain now and then from various sources, even as we do pleasure. Upon this showing, consequently, ⟨perception⟩ is no more invariably connected with pain than with pleasure, but in strict truth is inseparably connected with neither. For, like thought, ⟨perception⟩ could discern nothing, were it unceasingly attended by pleasure or by pain. Nevertheless our author, starting from so slight a warrant, applies his principle to perception universally.

When Anaxagoras says that larger animals have 34 better powers of sense, and that sense perception varies in general [100] with the size of the organs of sense, one

τηρίων εἶναι τὴν αἴσθησιν, τὸ μὲν αὐτῶν ἔχει τινὰ ἀπορίαν, οἷον πότερον τὰ μικρὰ μᾶλλον ἢ τὰ μεγάλα τῶν ζῴων αἰσθητικά· δόξειε γὰρ ἂν ἀκριβεστέρας αἰσθήσεως εἶναι τὰ μικρὰ μὴ λανθάνειν, καὶ ἅμα τὸ τὰ ἐλάττω δυνάμενον καὶ τὰ μείζω κρίνειν οὐκ ἄλογον. ἅμα δὲ καὶ δοκεῖ περὶ ἐνίας αἰσθήσεις βέλτιον ἔχειν τὰ μικρὰ τῶν μεγάλων, ὥστε ταύτῃ
35 μὲν χείρων ἡ τῶν μειζόνων αἴσθησις.   εἰ δ' αὖ φαίνεται καὶ πολλὰ λανθάνειν τὰ μικρά [τῶν μειζόνων οἷον οἱ ψόφοι, χρώματα], βελτίων ἡ τῶν μειζόνων· ἅμα δὲ καὶ εὔλογον, ὥσπερ καὶ τὴν ὅλην τοῦ σώματος κρᾶσιν, ὁμοίως ἔχειν καὶ τὰ περὶ τὰς αἰσθήσεις. τοῦτο μὲν οὖν, ὥσπερ ἐλέχθη, διαπορήσειεν ἄν τις, εἰ ἄρα καὶ δεῖ λέγειν οὕτως· οὐ γὰρ ἐν τοῖς ὁμοίοις γένεσιν ἀφώρισται κατὰ τὸ μέγεθος, ἀλλὰ κυριώτατα ἴσως ἡ τοῦ σώματος διάθεσίς τε καὶ κρᾶσις. τὸ δὲ πρὸς τὰ μεγέθη τὴν συμμετρίαν ἀποδιδόναι τῶν αἰσθητῶν ἔοικεν ὁμοίως λέγειν Ἐμπεδοκλεῖ· τῷ γὰρ ἐναρμόττειν τοῖς πόροις ποιεῖ τὴν αἴσθησιν. πλὴν ἐπὶ τῆς ὀσφρήσεως ἴδιον συμβαίνει δυσχερές· ὄζειν μὲν γάρ φησι τὸν λεπτὸν ἀέρα μᾶλλον, ὀσφραίνεσθαι δὲ ἀκριβέστερον ὅσα τὸν πυκνὸν ἢ τὸν μανὸν ἕλκει.

36 περὶ δὲ τῆς ἐμφάσεως κοινή τίς ἐστιν ἡ δόξα· σχεδὸν γὰρ οἱ πολλοὶ τὸ ὁρᾶν οὕτως ὑπολαμβάνουσι διὰ τὴν γινομένην ἐν τοῖς ὀφθαλμοῖς ἔμφασιν. τοῦτο δὲ οὐκέτι συνεῖδον ὡς οὔτε τὰ μεγέθη σύμμετρα τὰ ὁρώμενα τοῖς ἐμφαινομένοις οὔτε ἐμφαίνεσθαι πολλὰ ἅμα καὶ τἀναντία

Theophrastus on the Senses

of these propositions raises the question whether small animals or large animals have better powers of sense. For it would seem to be essential to keener sense perception that minute objects should not escape it. And we might reasonably suppose, too, that an animal with power to discern smaller objects could also discern the larger. Indeed it is held that, so far as certain of the senses are concerned, small animals are superior to large ones; and, in so far, consequently the perceptive power of the larger animals would be inferior. But on the other hand, if it appear that many objects 35 actually do escape ⟨the senses of⟩ small animals, then the ⟨sense perception⟩ of larger animals is superior. At the same time it were reasonable to suppose that what is true of the entire composition of the body will hold also of matters connected with sense perception. We may well doubt, then, as was said, the propriety of any such assertion.[101] For in analogous cases things are not determined by size; but the most important factors seem to be the body's general state and its composition. In making the correspondence between ⟨the senses and⟩ their objects depend on size, Anaxagoras seems to be speaking after the manner of Empedocles, who explains sense perception by the supposition that ⟨emanations⟩ fit into the passages ⟨of sense⟩. In the case of smell, however, there is a special difficulty: for he asserts that rarefied air is the more odorous; and yet that the animals which inhale the dense air have a keener sense of smell than those inhaling the subtile.

Anaxagoras' doctrine of the visual image is one some- 36 what commonly held; for nearly everyone assumes that seeing is occasioned by the reflection in the eyes. They took no account of the fact, however, that the size of objects seen is incommensurate with the size of their reflection; and that it is impossible to have many contrasting objects reflected at the same time; and,

δυνατόν, ἔτι δὲ κίνησις καὶ διάστημα καὶ μέγεθος ὁρατὰ μέν, ἔμφασιν δὲ οὐ ποιοῦσιν. ἐνίοις δὲ τῶν ζῴων οὐδὲν ἐμφαίνεται, καθάπερ τοῖς σκληροφθάλμοις καὶ τοῖς ἐνύδροις. ἔτι δὲ καὶ τῶν ἀψύχων διά γε τοῦτο πολλὰ ἂν ὁρῷεν· καὶ γὰρ ἐν ὕδατι καὶ χαλκῷ καὶ ἑτέροις πολλοῖς ἐστιν ἀνάκλασις.

37 φησὶ δὲ καὶ αὐτὸς ἐμφαίνεσθαι μὲν εἰς ἄλληλα ⟨τὰ⟩ χρώματα, μᾶλλον δὲ τὸ ἰσχυρὸν εἰς τὸ ἀσθενές· ὥστε ἑκάτερον μὲν ἐχρῆν ὁρᾶν, μᾶλλον δὲ ⟨τὸ⟩ μέλαν καὶ ὅλως ⟨τὸ⟩ ἀσθενέστερον. διὸ καὶ τὴν ὄψιν ὁμόχρων ποιεῖ τῇ νυκτὶ καὶ τὸ φῶς αἴτιον τῆς ἐμφάσεως. καίτοι πρῶτον μὲν τὸ φῶς ὁρῶμεν αὐτὸ δι' οὐδεμιᾶς ἐμφάσεως, ἔπειτα οὐδὲν ἧττον τὰ μέλανα τῶν λευκῶν οὐκ ἔχει φῶς. ἔτι δὲ κἀν τοῖς ἄλλοις ἀεὶ τὴν ἔμφασιν ὁρῶμεν εἰς τὸ λαμπρότερον καὶ καθαρώτερον γινομένην, ὥσπερ καὶ αὐτὸς λέγει τοὺς ὑμένας τῶν ὀμμάτων λεπτοὺς εἶναι καὶ λαμπρούς. τιθέασι δὲ καὶ τὴν ὄψιν αὐτὴν οἱ πολλοὶ πυρός, ⟨ὡς⟩ τούτου τὰς χρόας μετεχούσας μᾶλλον. Ἀναξαγόρας μὲν οὖν, ὥσπερ ἐλέχθη, κοινήν τινα ταύτην καὶ παλαιὰν δόξαν ἀναφέρει. πλὴν ἴδιον ἐπὶ πάσαις λέγει ταῖς αἰσθήσεσι καὶ μάλιστα ἐπὶ τῇ ὄψει, διότι τὸ μέγα αἰσθανόμενόν ἐστιν, οὐ δηλοῖ δὲ τὰς σωματικωτέρας αἰσθήσεις.

38 Κλείδημος δὲ μόνος ἰδίως εἴρηκε περὶ τῆς ὄψεως· αἰσθάνεσθαι γάρ φησι τοῖς ὀφθαλμοῖς μόνον ὅτι διαφανεῖς· ταῖς ⟨δ'⟩ ἀκοαῖς ὅτι ἐμπίπτων ὁ ἀὴρ κινεῖ· ταῖς δὲ ῥισὶν

Theophrastus on the Senses

farther, that motion, distance, and size are visual objects and yet produce no image.[102] And with some animals nothing whatever is reflected,—for example, with those that have horny eyes, or that live in the water. Moreover according to this theory many *lifeless* things would possess the power of sight; for there is a reflection certainly in water, in bronze, and in many other things.

His own statement is that colours are reflected in one another,[103] but particularly the strong in the weak; consequently each of these—but especially black and the weaker colours generally—should possess the power of sight.[104] For the reason just given, he holds that the organ of vision is of the same colour as the night,[105] and that light is the cause of the visual reflection. But in the first place, we see light itself, without any image of it whatsoever; and in the second place, black objects and white objects alike lack light.[106] And furthermore in other cases we are all the while seeing reflection arise in what is more brilliant and pure,—a fact entirely in keeping with his own statement that the membranes of the eyes are fine and lustrous. Now most ⟨scientists⟩ assume that the organ of vision itself is of fire, since colours partake of this element especially. And Anaxagoras himself, as I have said, upholds this rather common and hoary doctrine;[107] save that in the case of each and every sense he offers something original, and particularly of sight when he sets forth the part which size here plays in perception. But of the senses that have a more material character he offers no such clear account. 37

Clidemus alone[108] spoke with originality in regard to vision; for the perceptive power of our eyes, he says, is due solely to their being transparent. We perceive with our ears because the air bursts in upon them and causes there a motion. With our nostrils we perceive in the 38

ἐφελκομένους τὸν ἀέρα· τοῦτον γὰρ ἀναμείγνυσθαι· τῇ δὲ γλώσσῃ τοὺς χυμοὺς καὶ τὸ θερμὸν καὶ τὸ ψυχρὸν διὰ τὸ σομφὴν εἶναι· τῷ δὲ ἄλλῳ σώματι παρὰ μὲν ταῦτ' οὐθέν, αὐτῶν δὲ τούτων καὶ τὸ θερμὸν καὶ τὰ ὑγρὰ καὶ τὰ ἐναντία· μόνον δὲ τὰς ἀκοὰς αὐτὰς μὲν οὐδὲν κρίνειν, εἰς δὲ τὸν νοῦν διαπέμπειν, οὐχ ὥσπερ Ἀναξαγόρας ἀρχὴν ποιεῖ πάντων τὸν νοῦν.

39 Διογένης δ' ὥσπερ τὸ ζῆν καὶ τὸ φρονεῖν τῷ ἀέρι καὶ τὰς αἰσθήσεις ἀνάπτει· διὸ καὶ δόξειεν ἂν τῷ ὁμοίῳ ποιεῖν (οὐδὲ γὰρ τὸ ποιεῖν εἶναι καὶ πάσχειν, εἰ μὴ πάντα ἦν ἐξ ἑνός)· τὴν μὲν ὄσφρησιν τῷ περὶ τὸν ἐγκέφαλον ἀέρι· τοῦτον γὰρ ἄθρουν εἶναι καὶ σύμμετρον τῇ ὀσμῇ· τὸν γὰρ ἐγκέφαλον αὐτὸν μανὸν καὶ ⟨τὰ⟩ φλεβία, λεπτότατον δ' ἐν οἷς ἡ διάθεσις ἀσύμμετρος, καὶ οὐ μείγνυσθαι ταῖς ὀσμαῖς· ὡς εἴ τις εἴη τῇ κράσει σύμμετρος, δῆλον ὡς αἰσθανόμενον 40 ἄν. τὴν δ' ἀκοήν, ὅταν ὁ ἐν τοῖς ὠσὶν ἀὴρ κινηθεὶς ὑπὸ τοῦ ἔξω διαδῷ πρὸς τὸν ἐγκέφαλον. τὴν δὲ ὄψιν [ὁρᾶν] ἐμφαινομένων εἰς τὴν κόρην, ταύτην δὲ μειγνυμένην τῷ ἐντὸς ἀέρι ποιεῖν αἴσθησιν· σημεῖον δέ· ἐὰν γὰρ φλεγμασία γένηται τῶν φλεβῶν, οὐ μείγνυσθαι τῷ ἐντὸς οὐδ' ὁρᾶν ὁμοίως τῆς ἐμφάσεως οὔσης. τὴν δὲ γεῦσιν τῇ γλώττῃ διὰ τὸ μανὸν καὶ ἁπαλόν. περὶ δὲ ἁφῆς οὐδὲν ἀφώρισεν οὔτε πῶς οὔτε τίνων ἐστίν. ἀλλὰ μετὰ ταῦτα

Theophrastus on the Senses

act of inhaling the air, for there the air enters into some kind of combination. Savours and heat and cold are perceived by means of the tongue because it is spongy. With the rest of the body we perceive nothing other than the ⟨qualities⟩ named; and even of these ⟨qualities, there come to us from the body outside the special sense organs, only⟩ warmth and moisture [109] and their opposites. The ears, he maintains by way of exception, are of themselves incapable of passing judgment, but must ever report to the reason ⟨what they receive⟩. Yet he does not, like Anaxagoras, regard reason as the source of all.

Diogenes connects the senses with the air, even as he 39 connects with it both life and thought. He would accordingly seem to ascribe ⟨perception⟩ to likeness; for, he holds, there would be neither activity nor passivity unless all things were from a single ⟨source⟩.[110] Smelling is effected by the air about the brain; since the air is massed there [111] and is commensurate with odour; while the brain of itself, with its ducts,[112] is already of light consistency. But ⟨the cephalic air⟩ [113] in some whose condition departs from this proper measure is too attenuated [114] and does not unite with the odours. Thus it is evident that perception occurs in anyone whose composition has this correspondence.

Hearing arises when the air within the ears is set in 40 motion by the external ⟨air⟩ and transmits ⟨this motion⟩ to the brain. Sight arises when objects are reflected in the pupil, but it [115] occasions perception only when mingled with the internal air. This is capable of proof: for if the ducts become inflamed, there is no union with the internal ⟨air⟩, and sight is impossible although the image is still there as before. Taste arises in the tongue because of its open and soft texture. As for touch, he offers no explanation either of its mode of action or of the objects with which it is concerned.

The Greek Physiological Psychology

πειρᾶται λέγειν, διὰ τί συμβαίνει τὰς αἰσθήσεις ἀκριβεστέρας
41 εἶναι καὶ τῶν ποίων. ὄσφρησιν μὲν οὖν ὀξυτάτην οἷς
ἐλάχιστος ἀὴρ ἐν τῇ κεφαλῇ· τάχιστα γὰρ μείγνυσθαι· καὶ
πρὸς τούτοις ἐὰν ἕλκῃ διὰ μακροτέρου καὶ στενοτέρου· θᾶττον
γὰρ οὕτω κρίνεσθαι· διόπερ ἔνια τῶν ζῴων ὀσφραντικώτερα
τῶν ἀνθρώπων εἶναι· οὐ μὴν ἀλλὰ συμμέτρου γε οὔσης
τῆς ὀσμῆς τῷ ἀέρι πρὸς τὴν κρᾶσιν μάλιστα ἂν αἰσθάνεσθαι
τὸν ἄνθρωπον. ἀκούειν δ' ὀξύτατα, ὧν αἵ τε φλέβες
λεπταὶ καὶ τὸ περὶ † τῇ αἰσθήσει καὶ τῇ ἀκοῇ τέτρηται βραχὺ
καὶ λεπτὸν καὶ ἰθὺ καὶ πρὸς τούτοις τὸ οὖς ὀρθὸν ἔχει
καὶ μέγα· κινούμενον γὰρ τὸν ἐν τοῖς ὠσὶν ἀέρα κινεῖν
τὸν ἐντός. ἐὰν δὲ εὐρυτέρα ᾖ, κινουμένου τοῦ ἀέρος ἦχον
εἶναι καὶ τὸν ψόφον ἄναρθρον διὰ τὸ μὴ προσπίπτειν πρὸς
42 ἠρεμοῦν. ὁρᾶν δ' ὀξύτατα ὅσα τε τὸν ἀέρα καὶ τὰς
φλέβας ἔχει λεπτάς, ὥσπερ ἐπὶ τῶν ἄλλων, καὶ ὅσα τὸν
ὀφθαλμὸν λαμπρότατον. μάλιστα δ' ἐμφαίνεσθαι τὸ ἐναντίον
χρῶμα· διὸ τοὺς μελανοφθάλμους μεθ' ἡμέραν καὶ τὰ λαμπρὰ
μᾶλλον ὁρᾶν, τοὺς δ' ἐναντίους νύκτωρ. ὅτι δὲ ὁ ἐντὸς
ἀὴρ αἰσθάνεται μικρὸν ὢν μόριον τοῦ θεοῦ, σημεῖον εἶναι,
διότι πολλάκις πρὸς ἄλλα τὸν νοῦν ἔχοντες οὔθ' ὁρῶμεν οὔτ'
43 ἀκούομεν. ἡδονὴν δὲ καὶ λύπην γίνεσθαι τόνδε τὸν τρό-
πον· ὅταν μὲν πολὺς ὁ ἀὴρ μίσγηται τῷ αἵματι καὶ κουφίζῃ
κατὰ φύσιν ὢν καὶ κατὰ πᾶν τὸ σῶμα διεξιών, ἡδονήν· ὅταν

Theophrastus on the Senses

He then attempts to state upon what depends the greater acuteness of the senses, and in what kinds ⟨of creatures⟩ this is found.

Smell, to begin with, is keenest in those who have least air in the head,—for then this air most readily unites ⟨with the odours⟩,—and in those, furthermore, who inhale through an unusually long,[116] narrow ⟨passage⟩, for ⟨odour⟩ is thus more readily detected. Some animals in consequence are keener of smell than are men. Yet man's perceptive power is extremely acute whenever the odour corresponds to the ⟨cephalic⟩ air in point of composition.

Those have sharpest hearing whose ducts[117] are delicate and in whom the passage to the seat of sensation[118] and of hearing is short, delicate, and straight, and in whom the external ear, furthermore, is erect and large; for the air in ⟨the more external parts of⟩ the ears, when set in motion, moves the air within. But if ⟨the organs of hearing⟩ be too wide and open, there is a ringing in the ears when the air is set in motion, and the sound ⟨which we wish to hear⟩ becomes inarticulate because it does not come upon ⟨the internal air⟩ at rest.

Vision is keenest in such animals as have their ⟨internal⟩ air and their ducts refined—as is true of the other ⟨senses⟩,—and have an exceedingly lustrous eye. But since the eye reflects better a colour that stands in contrast with it, black-eyed[119] persons have a vision superior by day and for brilliant objects, while those with eyes of opposite hue see better by night. That the internal air, however, is the real agent of perception —being a tiny fragment of divinity—is proved by this, that when our minds are engrossed in other things we often neither see nor hear.[120]

Pleasure and pain, he holds, arise in the following way. Whenever the air mingles in large quantities with the blood and sublimates it,—since the air is now in its normal state and pervades the entire body,—there is

41

42

43

δὲ παρὰ φύσιν καὶ μὴ μίσγηται συνιζάνοντος τοῦ αἵματος καὶ ἀσθενεστέρου καὶ πυκνοτέρου γινομένου, λύπην. ὁμοίως καὶ θάρσος καὶ ὑγίειαν καὶ τἀναντία. κριτικώτατον δὲ ἡδονῆς τὴν γλῶτταν· ἁπαλώτατον γὰρ εἶναι καὶ μανὸν καὶ τὰς φλέβας ἁπάσας ἀνήκειν εἰς αὐτήν· διὸ σημεῖά τε πλεῖστα τοῖς κάμνουσιν ἐπ' αὐτῆς εἶναι· καὶ τῶν ἄλλων ζῴων τὰ χρώματα μηνύειν· ὁπόσα γὰρ ἂν ᾖ καὶ ὁποῖα, τοσαῦτα ἐμφαίνεσθαι. τὴν μὲν οὖν αἴσθησιν οὕτω καὶ διὰ 44 τοῦτο γίνεσθαι. φρονεῖν δ', ὥσπερ ἐλέχθη, τῷ ἀέρι καθαρῷ καὶ ξηρῷ· κωλύειν γὰρ τὴν ἰκμάδα τὸν νοῦν· διὸ καὶ ἐν τοῖς ὕπνοις καὶ ἐν ταῖς μέθαις καὶ ἐν ταῖς πλησμοναῖς ἧττον φρονεῖν· ὅτι δὲ ἡ ὑγρότης ἀφαιρεῖται τὸν νοῦν, σημεῖον, διότι τὰ ἄλλα ζῷα χείρω τὴν διάνοιαν· ἀναπνεῖν τε γὰρ τὸν ἀπὸ τῆς γῆς ἀέρα καὶ τροφὴν ὑγροτέραν προσφέρεσθαι. τοὺς δὲ ὄρνιθας ἀναπνεῖν μὲν καθαρόν, φύσιν δὲ ὁμοίαν ἔχειν τοῖς ἰχθύσι· καὶ γὰρ τὴν σάρκα στιφράν, καὶ τὸ πνεῦμα οὐ διιέναι διὰ παντός, ἀλλὰ ἱστάναι περὶ τὴν κοιλίαν· διὸ τὴν μὲν τροφὴν ταχὺ πέττειν, αὐτὸ δ' ἄφρον εἶναι· συμβάλλεσθαι δέ τι πρὸς τῇ τροφῇ καὶ τὸ στόμα καὶ τὴν γλῶτταν· οὐ γὰρ δύνασθαι συνεῖναι ἀλλήλων. τὰ δὲ φυτὰ διὰ τὸ μὴ εἶναι κοῖλα μηδὲ ἀναδέ- 45 χεσθαι τὸν ἀέρα παντελῶς ἀφῃρῆσθαι τὸ φρονεῖν. ταὐτὸν δ' αἴτιον εἶναι καὶ ὅτι τὰ παιδία ἄφρονα· πολὺ γὰρ ἔχειν τὸ ὑγρόν, ὥστε μὴ δύνασθαι διὰ παντὸς διιέναι τοῦ σώματος, ἀλλὰ ἐκκρίνεσθαι περὶ τὰ στήθη· διὸ νωθῆ τε εἶναι καὶ ἄφρονα· ὀργίλα δὲ καὶ ὅλως ὀξύρροπα καὶ εὐμετάπτωτα διὰ τὸ ἐκ μικρῶν κρίνεσθαι τὸν ἀέρα πολύν· ὅπερ καὶ τῆς

Theophrastus on the Senses

pleasure. But when ⟨the condition is⟩ abnormal and the air no longer unites with the blood, then the blood settles and becomes too sluggish and thick, and there is pain. In like manner ⟨he explains⟩ daring and health and their opposites. The tongue, he holds, is pre-eminently the judge of pleasure,[121] for it is exceedingly soft and of open texture and all the ducts lead into it. Very many symptoms with the sick are consequently found here in the tongue.[122] And in other animals ⟨the tongue⟩ reveals the colours ⟨of their skin⟩, for the variety and character ⟨of these colours⟩ are ⟨there⟩ reflected.[123] Such is the manner and occasion, then, of perception's rise.

Thinking, as was said,[124] is due to pure dry air; for moisture[125] clogs the intellect. Thought is at a low ebb consequently in sleep and in one's cups and in repletion. That moisture robs one of reason is proved by this, that the other living creatures are inferior of understanding, for they breathe air that comes from the earth and they take moister nourishment. It is true that birds breathe air that is pure, while yet their nature remains like that of fish; for the flesh ⟨of birds⟩ is firm and compact, and their breath is not allowed to penetrate the entire ⟨body⟩ but is checked in the region of the belly. As a result, it speedily digests the food, while ⟨the animal⟩[126] itself remains witless. But the character of their mouth and tongue aids and abets the food ⟨in making them witless⟩, for birds cannot understand one another.[127] Plants are entirely bereft of thought because they are not hollow and consequently do not receive the air.

The same principle explains also why young children lack understanding; for they are excessively moist, and in consequence ⟨the air⟩ cannot make its way throughout the body but is set apart in the breast, leaving them sluggish and witless. They are passionate and impetuous in general and flighty because the air in large quantities is excreted from their tiny bodies.

λήθης αἴτιον εἶναι· διὰ γὰρ τὸ μὴ ἰέναι διὰ παντὸς τοῦ σώματος οὐ δύνασθαι συνεῖναι· σημεῖον δέ· καὶ γὰρ τοῖς ἀναμιμνησκομένοις τὴν ἀπορίαν εἶναι περὶ τὸ στῆθος, ὅταν δὲ εὕρωσιν, διασκίδνασθαι καὶ ἀνακουφίζεσθαι τῆς λύπης.

46 Διογένης μὲν οὖν πάντα βουλόμενος ἀνάπτειν τῷ ἀέρι πολλῶν ἀπολείπεται πρὸς πίστιν. οὔτε γὰρ τὴν αἴσθησιν οὔτε τὴν φρόνησιν ἴδιον ποιεῖ τῶν ἐμψύχων. ἴσως γὰρ καὶ ἀέρα τοιοῦτον καὶ κρᾶσιν καὶ συμμετρίαν ἐνδέχεται πανταχοῦ καὶ πᾶσιν ὑπάρχειν, εἰ δὲ μή, τοῦτο αὐτὸ λεκτέον. ἔτι δὲ καὶ ἐν αὐταῖς ταῖς διαφόροις αἰσθήσεσιν, ὥστε ἐνδέχεσθαι τὰ τῆς ὄψεως τὴν ἀκοὴν κρίνειν καὶ ἅπερ ἡμεῖς τῇ ὀσφρήσει, ταῦτα ἄλλο τι ζῷον ἑτέρᾳ διὰ τὸ τὴν αὐτὴν ἔχειν κρᾶσιν· ὥστε καὶ τῇ περὶ τὸν θώρακα ἀναπνοῇ κρίνειν τότε τὰς ὀσμάς· ἐνδέχεται γὰρ ἐνίοτε σύμμετρον εἶναι ταύταις.

47 εὐήθη δὲ καὶ τὰ περὶ τὴν ὄψιν, ὡς τῷ ἀέρι τῷ ἐντὸς ὁρῶμεν· ἀλλὰ ἐλέγχει μέν πως τοὺς τὴν ἔμφασιν ποιοῦντας, οὐ μὴν αὐτὸς λέγει τὴν αἰτίαν. ἔπειτα τὸ μὲν αἰσθάνεσθαι καὶ ἥδεσθαι καὶ φρονεῖν τῇ τε ἀναπνοῇ καὶ τῇ μίξει τοῦ αἵματος ἀποδίδωσι. πολλὰ δὲ τῶν ζῴων τὰ μὲν ἄναιμα, τὰ δὲ ὅλως οὐκ ἀναπνεῖ· καὶ εἰ δεῖ διὰ παντὸς τοῦ σώματος διιέναι τὴν ἀναπνοήν, ἀλλὰ ⟨μὴ⟩ μορίων τινῶν (μικροῦ γὰρ ἕνεκα τοῦτ' ἔστιν), οὐθὲν ἂν κωλύοι διά γε τοῦτο καὶ τὰ πάντα καὶ μεμνῆσθαι καὶ φρονεῖν. * * * ἔτι δὲ εἰ καὶ τοῦτο συνέβαινεν, οὐκ ἂν ἦν ἐμποδών. οὐ γὰρ ἐν ἅπασι τοῖς

Theophrastus on the Senses

This is the cause of forgetfulness also; for since the air does not penetrate the entire body, one cannot understand.[128] Which is proven by this: that when we try to remember, there is a feeling of oppression in the breast; but when ⟨the missing thought⟩ is found, ⟨the air⟩ is 'dispelled' and the weight of pain is lifted.

In his effort to connect everything with the air, Diogenes fails at many points to produce conviction. For he makes neither sense perception nor thought a peculiar mark of things animate. For presumably such air and in such combination and correspondence can exist everywhere and in everything; if not, he ought to make this point explicit. Moreover ⟨this condition might occur⟩ in the different senses themselves, and consequently it would be possible for hearing to detect the objects of sight, and what we arrive at by smell some other creature should reach by some other ⟨sense⟩ because ⟨this other sense⟩ had a composition the same ⟨as that of our sense of smell⟩. And so, according to this theory, it would also be possible for us to detect odours by the breath taken into the chest, for ⟨this air⟩ might sometimes be proportionate to the odours.

His theory of vision, moreover,—that we see by means of the internal air,—is childish indeed. Yet in a measure he refutes those who regard the reflection ⟨as the cause of sight⟩, although he does not assign the ⟨true⟩ cause himself. Furthermore he attributes perception, pleasure, and thought to respiration and to the mingling ⟨of air⟩ with the blood. But many animals are either bloodless or do not breathe at all. And were it necessary for the breath to penetrate the entire body and not merely certain special parts,—for this is introduced merely for the sake of a small part ⟨of the theory⟩—there would be nothing in this to prevent all ⟨parts of the body⟩[129] from remembering and thinking. . . . But even if this were the case,[130] it would offer no difficulty. For reason does not have its seat in all our members—in

The Greek Physiological Psychology

μέρεσιν ὁ νοῦς, οἷον ἐν τοῖς σκέλεσι καὶ τοῖς ποσίν, ἀλλὰ ἐν ὡρισμένοις, δι' ὧν καὶ οἱ ἐν ἡλικίᾳ καὶ μέμνηνται καὶ

48 φρονοῦσιν.   εὔηθες δὲ καὶ τὸ τοὺς ἀνθρώπους διαφέρειν τῷ καθαρώτερον ἀναπνεῖν, ἀλλ' οὐ τὴν φύσιν, καθάπερ καὶ τὰ ἔμψυχα τῶν ἀψύχων. ἐχρῆν γὰρ εὐθὺς μεταλλάξαντα τόπον διαφέρειν τῷ φρονεῖν καὶ τῶν ἀνθρώπων δὲ τοὺς ἐν τοῖς ὑψηλοῖς ἐμφρονεστέρους εἶναι, τῶν πάντων δὲ μάλιστα τοὺς ὄρνιθας· οὐ γὰρ τοσοῦτον ἡ τῆς σαρκὸς διαφέρει φύσις, ὅσον ἡ τοῦ ἀέρος καθαριότης. ἔτι δὲ τὰ φυτὰ μὴ φρονεῖν διὰ τὸ μὴ ἔχειν κενόν· οἷς δ' ἐνυπάρχει, ταῦτα πάντα φρονεῖν. Διογένης μὲν οὖν, ὥσπερ εἴπομεν, ἅπαντα προθυμούμενος ἀνάγειν εἰς τὴν ἀρχὴν πολλὰ διαμαρτάνει τῶν εὐλόγων.

49   Δημόκριτος δὲ περὶ μὲν αἰσθήσεως οὐ διορίζει, πότερα τοῖς ἐναντίοις ἢ τοῖς ὁμοίοις ἐστίν. εἰ μὲν γὰρ ⟨τῷ⟩ ἀλλοιοῦσθαι ποιεῖ τὸ αἰσθάνεσθαι, δόξειεν ἂν τοῖς διαφόροις· οὐ γὰρ ἀλλοιοῦται τὸ ὅμοιον ὑπὸ τοῦ ὁμοίου· πάλιν δ' ⟨εἰ⟩ τὸ μὲν αἰσθάνεσθαι καὶ ἁπλῶς ἀλλοιοῦσθαι ⟨τῷ⟩ πάσχειν, ἀδύνατον δέ, φησί, τὰ μὴ ταὐτὰ πάσχειν, ἀλλὰ κἂν ἕτερα ὄντα ποιῇ οὐχ ⟨ᾗ⟩ ἕτερα ἀλλ' ᾗ ταὐτόν τι ὑπάρχει, τοῖς ὁμοίοις. διὸ περὶ μὲν τούτων ἀμφοτέρως ἔστιν ὑπολαβεῖν. περὶ ἑκάστης δ' ἤδη τούτων ἐν μέρει

50 πειρᾶται λέγειν.   ὁρᾶν μὲν οὖν ποιεῖ τῇ ἐμφάσει· ταύτην

Theophrastus on the Senses

our legs and feet, for instance—but in determinate parts, even those by whose means, at the proper age, we exercise memory and the power of thought.

Childlike, too, is his idea that men differ from animals—not in their essential nature, as animate things differ from inanimate,—but because they breathe purer air. For then one ought to show a difference of intelligence directly upon change of place, and highlanders should be more intellectual than other men, and birds should surpass them all. For the character of the ⟨birds'⟩ flesh[131] differs ⟨from that of men and the higher animals⟩ by no means so greatly as does the purity of the air ⟨they breathe⟩. Moreover, ⟨it is childish to hold⟩ that plants lack the power of thought because they are not hollow,[132] and that all those things that actually are hollow possess this power. Thus Diogenes, in his zeal to derive everything from his principle ⟨the air⟩, as we have indicated, strays repeatedly from the path of likelihood. 48

Democritus in his account of sense perception does not make it entirely clear whether it is due to contrast or to similarity. For in so far as he ascribes the action of the senses to an alteration, it would seem to depend on contrast; for the like is never altered by the like. On the other hand, sense perception would seem to depend on similarity in so far as he ascribes the perceptive process and, in a word, alteration to the fact that something is acted upon. For things that are not the same cannot be acted upon, he says; but even when things that are different do act, ⟨their action is⟩ not due to their difference but to the presence in them of something identical. Upon such matters as these he may consequently be understood either way. He now undertakes to discuss the ⟨senses⟩ each in turn. 49

Vision he explains by the reflection ⟨in the eye⟩, of which he gives a unique account. For the reflection 50

δὲ ἰδίως λέγει· τὴν γὰρ ἔμφασιν οὐκ εὐθὺς ἐν τῇ κόρῃ γίνεσθαι, ἀλλὰ τὸν ἀέρα τὸν μεταξὺ τῆς ὄψεως καὶ τοῦ ὁρωμένου τυποῦσθαι συστελλόμενον ὑπὸ τοῦ ὁρωμένου καὶ τοῦ ὁρῶντος· ἅπαντος γὰρ ἀεὶ γίνεσθαί τινα ἀπορροήν· ἔπειτα τοῦτον στερεὸν ὄντα καὶ ἀλλόχρων ἐμφαίνεσθαι τοῖς ὄμμασιν ὑγροῖς· καὶ τὸ μὲν πυκνὸν οὐ δέχεσθαι, τὸ δὲ ὑγρὸν διιέναι. διὸ καὶ τοὺς ὑγροὺς τῶν σκληρῶν ὀφθαλμῶν ἀμείνους εἶναι πρὸς τὸ ὁρᾶν, εἰ ὁ μὲν ἔξω χιτὼν ὡς λεπτότατος καὶ πυκνότατος εἴη, τὰ δ' ἐντὸς ὡς μάλιστα σομφὰ καὶ κενὰ πυκνῆς καὶ ἰσχυρᾶς σαρκός, ἔτι δὲ ἰκμάδος παχείας τε καὶ λιπαρᾶς, καὶ αἱ φλέβες ⟨αἱ⟩ κατὰ τοὺς ὀφθαλμοὺς εὐθεῖαι καὶ ἄνικμοι, ὡς ὁμοσχημονεῖν τοῖς ἀποτυπουμένοις· τὰ γὰρ ὁμόφυλα μάλιστα ἕκαστον γνωρίζειν.

51 Πρῶτον μὲν οὖν ἄτοπος ἡ ἀποτύπωσις ἡ ἐν τῷ ἀέρι. δεῖ γὰρ ἔχειν πυκνότητα καὶ μὴ θρύπτεσθαι τὸ τυπούμενον, ὥσπερ καὶ αὐτὸς λέγει παραβάλλων τοιαύτην εἶναι τὴν ἐντύπωσιν οἷον εἰ ἐκμάξειας εἰς κηρόν. ἔπειτα μᾶλλον ἐν ὕδατι τυποῦσθαι δυνατὸν ὅσῳ πυκνότερον· ἧττον δὲ ὁρᾶται, καίτοι προσῆκε μᾶλλον. ὅλως δὲ ἀπορροὴν ποιοῦντα τῆς μορφῆς ὥσπερ ἐν τοῖς περὶ τῶν εἰδῶν τί δεῖ τὴν ἀποτύπωσιν ποιεῖν; αὐτὰ γὰρ ἐμφαίνεται τὰ εἴδωλα.

52 εἰ δὲ δὴ τοῦτο συμβαίνει καὶ ὁ ἀὴρ ἀπομάττεται καθάπερ κηρὸς ὠθούμενος καὶ πυκνούμενος, πῶς καὶ ποία τις ἡ ἔμφασις γίνεται; δῆλον γὰρ ὡς ἀντιπρόσωπος ⟨ὁ⟩ τύπος ἔσται τῷ ὁρωμένῳ καθάπερ ἐν τοῖς ἄλλοις. τοιούτου δ'

does not arise immediately in the pupil. On the contrary, the air between the eye and the object of sight is compressed by the object and the visual organ, and thus becomes imprinted; since there is always an effluence of some kind arising from everything. Thereupon this imprinted air, because it is solid and is of a hue contrasting ⟨with the pupil⟩, is reflected in the eyes, which are moist. A dense substance does not receive ⟨this reflection⟩, but what is moist gives it admission. Moist eyes accordingly have a better power of vision than have hard eyes; provided their outer tunic be exceedingly fine and close-knit, and the inner ⟨tissues⟩ be to the last degree spongy and free from dense and stubborn flesh, and free too,[133] from thick oily moisture; and provided, also, the ducts connected with the eyes be straight and dry that they may "perfectly conform" to the entering imprints. For each knows best its kindred.

Now in the first place this imprint upon the air is 51 an absurdity. For the substance receiving such an imprint must have a certain consistence and not be 'fragile'; even as Democritus himself, in illustrating the character of the "impression", says that "it is as if one were to take a mould in wax". In the second place, an object could make a better imprint upon water ⟨than upon air⟩, since water is denser. While the theory would require us to see more distinctly ⟨an object in water⟩, we actually see it less so. In general, why should Democritus assume this *imprint*, when in his discussion of forms[134] he has supposed an *emanation* that conveys the object's form? For these images ⟨due to emanation⟩ would be reflected.

But if such an imprint actually occurs and the air is 52 moulded like wax that is squeezed and pressed, how does the reflection ⟨in the eye⟩ come into existence, and what is its character? For the imprint here as in other cases will evidently face the object seen. But since this is

ὄντος ἀδύνατον ἐξ ἐναντίας ἔμφασιν γίνεσθαι μὴ στραφέντος τοῦ τύπου. τοῦτο δ᾽ ὑπὸ τίνος ἔσται καὶ πῶς δεικτέον· οὐχ οἷόν τε γὰρ ἄλλως γίνεσθαι τό ὁρᾶν. ἔπειτα ὅταν ὁρᾶται πλείονα κατὰ τὸν αὐτὸν τόπον, πῶς ἐν τῷ αὐτῷ ἀέρι πλείους ἔσονται τύποι; καὶ πάλιν πῶς ἀλλήλους ὁρᾶν ἐνδέχεται; τοὺς γὰρ τύπους ἀνάγκη συμβάλλειν ἑαυτοῖς, ἑκάτερον ἀντιπρόσωπον ὄντα ἀφ᾽ ὧν ἐστιν. ὥστε τοῦτο

53 ζήτησιν ἔχει. καὶ πρὸς τούτῳ διὰ τί ποτε ἕκαστος αὐτὸς αὑτὸν οὐχ ὁρᾷ; καθάπερ γὰρ τοῖς τῶν πέλας ὄμμασιν οἱ τύποι καὶ τοῖς ἑαυτῶν ἐμφαίνοιντ᾽ ἄν, ἄλλως τε καὶ εἰ εὐθὺς ἀντιπρόσωποι κεῖνται καὶ ταὐτὸ συμβαίνει πάθος ὥσπερ ἐπὶ τῆς ἠχοῦς. ἀνακλᾶσθαι γάρ φησι καὶ πρὸς αὐτὸν τὸν φθεγξάμενον τὴν φωνήν. ὅλως δὲ ἄτοπος ἡ τοῦ ἀέρος τύπωσις. ἀνάγκη γὰρ ἐξ ὧν λέγει πάντα ἐναποτυποῦσθαι τὰ σώματα καὶ πολλὰ ἐναλλάττειν, ὃ καὶ πρὸς τὴν ὄψιν ἐμπόδιον ἂν εἴη καὶ ἄλλως οὐκ εὔλογον. ἔτι δὲ εἴπερ ἡ τύπωσις διαμένει, καὶ μὴ φανερῶν [ὄντων] μηδὲ πλησίον ὄντων τῶν σωμάτων ἐχρῆν ὁρᾶν εἰ καὶ μὴ νύκτωρ, ἀλλὰ μεθ᾽ ἡμέραν. καίτοι τούς γε τύπους οὐχ ἧττον εἰκὸς διαμένειν νυκτός, ὅσῳ ἐμψυχότερος ὁ ἀήρ.

54 ἀλλ᾽ ἴσως τὴν ἔμφασιν ὁ ἥλιος ποιεῖ [καὶ] τὸ φῶς ὥσπερ ⟨ἀκτῖνα⟩ ἐπιφέρων ἐπὶ τὴν ὄψιν, καθάπερ ἔοικε βούλεσθαι λέγειν. ἐπεὶ τό γε τὸν ἥλιον ἀπωθοῦντα ἀφ᾽ ἑαυτοῦ καὶ ἀποπληττόμενον πυκνοῦν τὸν ἀέρα, καθάπερ φησίν, ἄτοπον· διακρίνειν γὰρ πέφυκε μᾶλλον. ἄτοπον δὲ

Theophrastus on the Senses

so, it is impossible for a reflection facing us to arise unless this imprint is turned around. What would cause this reversal, and what the manner of its operation, ought, however, to be shown; for in no other way could vision come to pass. Moreover when several objects are seen in one and the same place, how can so many imprints be made upon the self-same air? And again, how could we possibly see each other? For the imprints would inevitably clash, since each of them would be facing ⟨the person⟩ from whom it sprung. All of which gives us pause.

Furthermore, why does not each person see himself? 53 For the imprints ⟨from ourselves⟩ would be reflected in our own eyes quite as they are in the eyes of our companions, especially if these imprints directly face us and if the effect here is the same as with an echo, —since Democritus says that ⟨in the case of the echo⟩ the vocal sound is reflected back to him who utters it. Indeed the whole idea of imprints made on the air is extravagant. For we should be forced to believe, from what he says, that all bodies are producing imprints ⟨in the air⟩, and that great numbers of them are sending ⟨their impressions⟩ across one another's path,—a state of things at once embarrassing to sight and improbable on other grounds. If the impression moreover endures, we ought to see bodies that are out of sight [135] and remote,—if not by night, at all events by day. And yet it would be but fair to assume that these imprints would persist at night, since then the air is so much cooler.[136]

Possibly, however, the reflection in the eye is caused 54 by the sun, in sending light in upon the visual sense in the form of rays,—as Democritus seems to mean. For the idea that the sun "drives the air from itself and, in thus repelling, condenses it", as he says,—this is indefensible; since the sun by its very nature disperses the air. He is unfortunate, too, in regarding visual per-

καὶ τὸ μὴ μόνον τοῖς ὄμμασιν, ἀλλὰ καὶ τῷ ἄλλῳ σώματι μεταδιδόναι τῆς αἰσθήσεως. φησὶ γὰρ διὰ τοῦτο κενότητα καὶ ὑγρότητα ἔχειν δεῖν τὸν ὀφθαλμόν, ἵν' ἐπὶ πλέον δέχηται καὶ τῷ ἄλλῳ σώματι παραδιδῷ. ἄλογον δὲ καὶ τὸ μάλιστα μὲν ὁρᾶν φάναι τὰ ὁμόφυλα, τὴν δὲ ἔμφασιν ποιεῖν τοῖς ἀλλόχρωσιν ὡς οὐκ ἐμφαινομένων τῶν ὁμοίων. τὰ δὲ μεγέθη καὶ τὰ διαστήματα πῶς ἐμφαίνεται, καίπερ
55 ἐπιχειρήσας λέγειν οὐκ ἀποδίδωσιν. περὶ μὲν οὖν ὄψεως ἰδίως ἔνια βουλόμενος λέγειν πλείω παραδίδωσι ζήτησιν. τὴν δ' ἀκοὴν παραπλησίως ποιεῖ τοῖς ἄλλοις. εἰς γὰρ τὸ κενὸν ἐμπίπτοντα τὸν ἀέρα κίνησιν ἐμποιεῖν, πλὴν ὅτι κατὰ πᾶν μὲν ὁμοίως τὸ σῶμα εἰσιέναι, μάλιστα δὲ καὶ πλεῖστον διὰ τῶν ὤτων, ὅτι διὰ πλείστου τε κενοῦ διέρχεται καὶ ἥκιστα διαμίμνει. διὸ καὶ κατὰ μὲν τὸ ἄλλο σῶμα οὐκ αἰσθάνεσθαι, ταύτῃ δὲ μόνον. ὅταν δὲ ἐντὸς γένηται, σκίδνασθαι διὰ τὸ τάχος· τὴν γὰρ φωνὴν εἶναι πυκνουμένου τοῦ ἀέρος καὶ μετὰ βίας εἰσιόντος. ὥσπερ οὖν ἐκτὸς ποιεῖ τῇ ἀφῇ τὴν αἴσθησιν, οὕτω καὶ
56 ἐντός. ὀξύτατον δ' ἀκούειν, εἰ ὁ μὲν ἔξω χιτὼν εἴη πυκνός, τὰ δὲ φλεβία κενὰ καὶ ὡς μάλιστα ἄνικμα καὶ εὔτρητα κατά τε τὸ ἄλλο σῶμα καὶ τὴν κεφαλὴν καὶ τὰς ἀκοάς, ἔτι δὲ τὰ ὀστᾶ πυκνὰ καὶ ὁ ἐγκέφαλος εὔκρατος καὶ τὸ περὶ αὐτὸν ὡς ξηρότατον· ἀθρόον γὰρ ἂν οὕτως εἰσιέναι τὴν φωνὴν ἅτε διὰ πολλοῦ κενοῦ καὶ ἀνίκμου καὶ εὐτρήτου

Theophrastus on the Senses

ception as a function not only of the eyes but of the rest of the body as well; for he says that the eye must contain emptiness and moisture, in order that it may the more readily receive ⟨impressions⟩ and transmit ⟨them⟩ to the rest of the body. Farther, it is unreasonable to declare that what is 'kindred' to the organ of sight is preëminently the object of vision, and yet to explain the reflection ⟨in the eye⟩ by colour-contrast, on the ground that colours of the eyes' own hue are not reflected in them. And though he tries to explain how magnitudes and distances are reflected, he does not succeed. Thus Democritus in his endeavour to say something unique with regard to vision has bequeathed us the problem even farther from solution.

His explanation of hearing is very much like others'. 55 For the air, he holds, bursts into the ⟨aural⟩ cavity and sets up a commotion. And while it gains entrance to the body in this same manner at every point, yet it enters more fully and freely through the ears because there it traverses the largest empty space, where least it "tarries". In consequence no part of the body perceives ⟨sounds⟩ save this ⟨sensory region⟩.[137] But once the commotion has been started within, it is "sent broadcast" by reason of its velocity; for sound,[138] he holds, arises as the air is being condensed [139] and is making forcible entry ⟨into the body⟩. So he explains sensation within the body, just as he explains perception external to it, by contact.

Hearing is keenest, he maintains, when the outer 56 tunic [140] is tough and the ducts are empty and unusually free from moisture and are well-bored in the rest of the body as well as in the head and ears; when, too, the bones are dense and the brain is well-tempered and that which surrounds [141] it is exceedingly dry. For the sound thus enters compact, since it traverses a cavity large and dry and with good orifices, and swiftly

The Greek Physiological Psychology

εἰσιοῦσαν, καὶ ταχὺ σκίδνασθαι καὶ ὁμαλῶς κατὰ τὸ σῶμα
57 καὶ οὐ διεκπίπτειν ἔξω. τὸ μὲν οὖν ἀσαφῶς ἀφορίζειν ὁμοίως ἔχει τοῖς ἄλλοις. ἄτοπον δὲ καὶ ἴδιον ⟨τὸ⟩ κατὰ πᾶν τὸ σῶμα τὸν ψόφον εἰσιέναι, καὶ ὅταν εἰσέλθῃ διὰ τῆς ἀκοῆς διαχεῖσθαι κατὰ πᾶν, ὥσπερ οὐ ταῖς ἀκοαῖς, ἀλλ' ὅλῳ τῷ σώματι τὴν αἴσθησιν οὖσαν. οὐ γὰρ κἂν συμπάσχῃ τι τῇ ἀκοῇ, διὰ τοῦτο καὶ αἰσθάνεται. πάσαις γὰρ τοῦτό γε ὁμοίως ποιεῖ, καὶ οὐ μόνον ταῖς αἰσθήσεσιν ἀλλὰ καὶ τῇ ψυχῇ. καὶ περὶ μὲν ὄψεως καὶ ἀκοῆς οὕτως ἀποδίδωσι, τὰς δὲ ἄλλας αἰσθήσεις σχεδὸν ὁμοίως ποιεῖ τοῖς πλείστοις.
58 περὶ δὲ τοῦ φρονεῖν ἐπὶ τοσοῦτον εἴρηκεν ὅτι γίνεται συμμέτρως ἐχούσης τῆς ψυχῆς κατὰ τὴν κρῆσιν· ἐὰν δὲ περίθερμός τις ἢ περίψυχρος γένηται, μεταλλάττειν φησί· δι' ὅ τι καὶ τοὺς παλαιοὺς καλῶς τοῦθ' ὑπολαβεῖν ὅτι ἐστὶν ἀλλοφρονεῖν. ὥστε φανερόν, ὅτι τῇ κράσει τοῦ σώματος ποιεῖ τὸ φρονεῖν, ὅπερ ἴσως αὐτῷ καὶ κατὰ λόγον ἐστὶ σῶμα ποιοῦντι τὴν ψυχήν. αἱ μὲν οὖν περὶ αἰσθήσεως καὶ τοῦ φρονεῖν δόξαι σχεδὸν αὗται καὶ τοσαῦται τυγχάνουσιν οὖσαι παρὰ τῶν πρότερον.

the sound is "sent broadcast" impartially through the body and does not again escape.

Such hazy definition is found in other writers as well. Yet it is absurd, while original, to say that sound permeates the entire body, and that when it has entered by the organ of hearing it is spread to every nook and cranny, as though perception here were due not to the ears but to the body entire. For if ⟨the rest of the body⟩ is somehow affected conjointly with the organ of hearing, it by no means follows that the perception depends upon the ⟨body as a whole⟩. For the ⟨entire body⟩ [142] acts thus in the case of every sense; and not of the senses only, but of the soul as well.

Thus he accounts for sight and hearing. As for our other senses, his treatment hardly differs from that of the mass of writers.

Concerning thought, Democritus says merely that "it arises when the soul's composition is duly proportioned". But if one becomes excessively hot or cold, he says, thinking is transformed; and it was for some such reason, the ancients well believed, that the mind became 'deranged'. Thus it is clear that he explains thought by the composition of the body,—a view perhaps not unreasonable in one who regards the soul itself as corporeal.

In sum and substance, then, these are the conclusions with regard to perception and thinking, which have come down to us from the earlier investigators.

The Greek Physiological Psychology

59 Περὶ δὲ τῶν αἰσθητῶν, τίς ἡ φύσις καὶ ποῖον ἕκαστόν ἐστιν, οἱ μὲν ἄλλοι παραλείπουσιν. τῶν μὲν γὰρ ὑπὸ τὴν ἀφὴν περὶ βαρέος καὶ κούφου καὶ θερμοῦ καὶ ψυχροῦ λέγουσιν, οἷον ὅτι τὸ μὲν μανὸν καὶ λεπτὸν θερμόν, τὸ δὲ πυκνὸν καὶ παχὺ ψυχρόν, ὥσπερ Ἀναξαγόρας διαιρεῖ τὸν ἀέρα καὶ τὸν αἰθέρα. σχεδὸν δὲ καὶ τὸ βαρὺ καὶ τὸ κοῦφον τοῖς αὐτοῖς καὶ ἔτι ταῖς ἄνω καὶ κάτω φοραῖς, καὶ πρὸς τούτοις περί τε φωνῆς ὅτι κίνησις τοῦ ἀέρος, καὶ περὶ ὀσμῆς ὅτι ἀπορροή τις. Ἐμπεδοκλῆς δὲ καὶ περὶ τῶν χρωμάτων, καὶ ὅτι τὸ μὲν λευκὸν τοῦ πυρὸς τὸ δὲ μέλαν τοῦ ὕδατος. οἱ δὲ ἄλλοι τοσοῦτον μόνον, ὅτι τό τε λευκὸν καὶ τὸ μέλαν ἀρχαί, τὰ δ' ἄλλα μειγνυμένων γίνεται τούτων. καὶ γὰρ Ἀναξαγόρας ἁπλῶς εἴρηκε περὶ αὐτῶν.

60 Δημόκριτος δὲ καὶ Πλάτων ἐπὶ πλεῖστόν εἰσιν ἡμμένοι, καθ' ἕκαστον γὰρ ἀφορίζουσι· πλὴν ὁ μὲν οὐκ ἀποστερῶν τῶν αἰσθητῶν τὴν φύσιν, Δημόκριτος δὲ πάντα πάθη τῆς αἰσθήσεως ποιῶν. ποτέρως μὲν οὖν ἔχει τἀληθὲς οὐκ ἂν εἴη λόγος. ἐφ' ὅσον δὲ ἑκάτερος ἧπται

Theophrastus on the Senses

[PART II. THE OBJECTS OF SENSE]

WHAT may be the intrinsic character and quality of 59 each of the senses' *objects*, the writers other ⟨than Democritus and Plato⟩ fail to state. Of the objects perceived by touch, they discuss the heavy and the light, the warm and the cold, saying that the rare and fine is hot; the dense and thick, cold,—which is the distinction Anaxagoras makes between air and aether.[143] And in general ⟨they explain⟩ weight and lightness by the same ⟨causes⟩—that is to say, by 'tendencies' respectively upward and downward; and they further agree that sound is a movement of the air, and that odour is an emanation. Empedocles discusses the colours also, and holds that white is composed of fire, and black of water. The other investigators confine themselves to the statement that white and black are the fundamental colours and that the rest are derived from these by mixture. For even Anaxagoras treats of the ⟨colours⟩ in only a loose and general way.[144]

Democritus and Plato, however, are the investigators 60 who go into the question most fully, for they define the object of each sense; although ⟨Plato⟩ never robs these objects of their external reality, whereas Democritus reduces them one and all to effects in our sensuous faculty. Where the truth itself lies, is not the question we are now discussing.[145] Let our aim be rather to report the range of each author's treatment and the

The Greek Physiological Psychology

καὶ πῶς ἀφώρικε πειραθῶμεν ἀποδοῦναι, πρότερον εἰπόντες τὴν ὅλην ἔφοδον ἑκατέρου. Δημόκριτος μὲν οὖν οὐχ ὁμοίως λέγει περὶ πάντων, ἀλλὰ τὰ μὲν τοῖς μεγέθεσι τὰ δὲ τοῖς σχήμασιν ἔνια δὲ τάξει καὶ θέσει διορίζει. Πλάτων δὲ σχεδὸν ἅπαντα πρὸς τὰ πάθη καὶ τὴν αἴσθησιν ἀποδίδωσιν. ὥστε δόξειεν ἂν ἑκάτερος ἐναντίως τῇ ὑποθέσει 61 λέγειν. ὁ μὲν γὰρ πάθη ποιῶν τῆς αἰσθήσεως καθ᾽ αὑτὰ διορίζει τὴν φύσιν· ὁ δὲ καθ᾽ αὑτὰ ποιῶν ταῖς οὐσίαις πρὸς τὰ πάθη τῆς αἰσθήσεως ἀποδίδωσι.

Βαρὺ μὲν οὖν καὶ κοῦφον τῷ μεγέθει διαιρεῖ Δημόκριτος· εἰ γὰρ διακριθείη καθ᾽ ἓν ἕκαστον, εἰ καὶ κατὰ σχῆμα διαφέροι, σταθμὸν ἂν ἐπὶ μεγέθει τὴν φύσιν ἔχειν. οὐ μὴν ἀλλ᾽ ἔν γε τοῖς μεικτοῖς κουφότερον μὲν εἶναι τὸ πλέον ἔχον κενόν, βαρύτερον δὲ τὸ ἔλαττον. ἐν ἐνίοις μὲν οὕτως εἴρηκεν. 62 ἐν ἄλλοις δὲ κοῦφον εἶναί φησιν ἁπλῶς τὸ λεπτόν. παραλησίως δὲ καὶ περὶ σκληροῦ καὶ μαλακοῦ. σκληρὸν μὲν γὰρ εἶναι τὸ πυκνόν, μαλακὸν δὲ τὸ μανόν, καὶ τὸ μᾶλλον δὲ καὶ ἧττον καὶ τὰ λοιπὰ κατὰ λόγον. διαφέρειν δέ τι τὴν θέσιν καὶ τὴν ἐναπόληψιν τῶν κενῶν τοῦ σκληροῦ καὶ μαλακοῦ καὶ βαρέος καὶ κούφου. διὸ σκληρότερον μὲν εἶναι σίδηρον, βαρύτερον δὲ μόλυβδον· τὸν μὲν γὰρ σίδηρον ἀνωμάλως συγκεῖσθαι καὶ τὸ κενὸν ἔχειν πολλαχῇ καὶ κατὰ μεγάλα, πεπυκνῶσθαι δὲ κατὰ ἔνια, ἁπλῶς δὲ πλέον ἔχειν

Theophrastus on the Senses

precise definitions he gives, stating by way of preface his general method.

Democritus has no uniform account of all ⟨the sensory objects⟩: some he distinguishes by the size ⟨of their atoms⟩, others by the shape, and a few by the ⟨atomic⟩ order and position. Plato, on the other hand, refers nearly all of them to effects in us, and to our perceptive faculty. Consequently each of these authors would seem to speak directly counter to his own postulate. For the one of them, who would have sensory objects to be but effects in our perceptive faculty, actually describes a reality resident in the objects themselves;[146] while the other, who attributes the objects' character to their own intrinsic being, ends by ascribing it to the passive change of our perceptive faculty.

Heaviness and lightness, to begin with, Democritus distinguishes in terms of size. For if we were to divide each substance into its ⟨atomic⟩ units, then even though these were to differ in shape, he contends, their reality would have as its standard ⟨of weight⟩ their size.[147] In the case of compounds, on the contrary, a substance that contains more of void is lighter; one that contains less is heavier. This at least is what he says in certain passages. In others, he holds that it is simply its fineness that makes a substance light.

And he speaks in almost the same terms of the hard and of the soft. For him anything is hard that is compact; it is soft if loose; while the different degrees, and so on, ⟨of such qualities are also explained⟩ in accord with this idea. Yet the position and grouping of the void spaces that make substances hard or soft differ in some respects from those that make them heavy or light. Consequently though iron is harder than lead, lead is heavier. For iron is of uneven composition, and its void spaces are many and of large extent, although here and there iron is condensed; but speaking generally it con-

κενόν. τὸν δὲ μόλυβδον ἔλαττον ἔχοντα κενὸν ὁμαλῶς συγκεῖσθαι ⟨καὶ⟩ κατὰ πᾶν ὁμοίως· διὸ βαρύτερον μέν, 63 μαλακώτερον δ' εἶναι τοῦ σιδήρου. περὶ μὲν ⟨οὖν⟩ βαρέος καὶ κούφου καὶ σκληροῦ καὶ μαλακοῦ ἐν τούτοις ἀφορίζει. τῶν δὲ ἄλλων αἰσθητῶν οὐδενὸς εἶναι φύσιν, ἀλλὰ πάντα πάθη τῆς αἰσθήσεως ἀλλοιουμένης, ἐξ ἧς γίνεσθαι τὴν φαντασίαν. οὐδὲ γὰρ τοῦ ψυχροῦ καὶ τοῦ θερμοῦ φύσιν ὑπάρχειν, ἀλλὰ τὸ σχῆμα μεταπῖπτον ἐργάζεσθαι καὶ τὴν ἡμετέραν ἀλλοίωσιν· ὅ τι γὰρ ἂν ἄθρουν ᾖ, τοῦτ' ἐνισχύειν ἑκάστῳ, τὸ δ' εἰς μακρὰ διανενημένον ἀναίσθητον εἶναι. σημεῖον δ' ὡς οὐκ εἰσὶ φύσει τὸ μὴ ταὐτὰ πᾶσι φαίνεσθαι τοῖς ζῴοις ἀλλ' ὃ ἡμῖν γλυκύ, τοῦτ' ἄλλοις πικρὸν καὶ ἑτέροις ὀξὺ καὶ ἄλλοις δριμὺ τοῖς 64 δὲ στρυφνόν, καὶ τὰ ἄλλα δ' ὡσαύτως. ἔτι δ' αὐτοὺς μεταβάλλειν τῇ κρήσει κατὰ τὰ πάθη καὶ τὰς ἡλικίας· ᾗ καὶ φανερὸν ὡς ἡ διάθεσις αἰτία τῆς φαντασίας. ἁπλῶς μὲν οὖν περὶ τῶν αἰσθητῶν οὕτω δεῖν ὑπολαμβάνειν. οὐ μὴν ἀλλ' ὥσπερ καὶ τὰ ἄλλα καὶ ταῦτα ἀνατίθησι τοῖς σχήμασι· πλὴν οὐχ ἁπάντων ἀποδίδωσι τὰς μορφάς, ἀλλὰ μᾶλλον τῶν χυλῶν καὶ τῶν χρωμάτων, καὶ τούτων ἀκριβέστερον διορίζει τὰ περὶ τοὺς χυλοὺς ἀναφέρων τὴν 65 φαντασίαν πρὸς ἄνθρωπον. τὸν μὲν οὖν ὀξὺν εἶναι τῷ σχήματι γωνοειδῆ τε καὶ πολυκαμπῆ καὶ μικρὸν καὶ λεπτόν. διὰ γὰρ τὴν δριμύτητα ταχὺ καὶ πάντῃ διαδύεσθαι, τραχὺν δ' ὄντα καὶ γωνοειδῆ συνάγειν καὶ

tains more void spaces ⟨than does lead⟩. But lead, though it has less of the void, is of even and uniform composition throughout; and so, while heavier than iron, lead is softer. Such is his account of the heavy, 63 the light, the hard, and the soft.

As for the other sensory objects, he holds that none has an objective reality, but that one and all are effects in our sensuous faculty as it undergoes alteration,—and that from this faculty arises the inner presentation. For not even of heat or cold is there for him an objective reality; but configuration,[148] in "undergoing a change", effects a qualitative alteration in us also; since what is massed together in anything prevails in it,[149] and what is widely diffused is imperceptible.

Proof that ⟨these sensory qualities⟩ are not objectively real is found in the fact that they do not appear the same to all creatures: what is sweet to us is bitter to others, and to still others it is sour or pungent or astringent; and similarly of the other ⟨sensory qualities⟩.[150]

Moreover Democritus holds that "men vary in com- 64 position" according to their condition and age; whence it is evident that a man's physical state accounts for his inner presentation. So we must in general, according to him, hold this view regarding sensory objects. Nevertheless here too, as elsewhere, he falls back upon ⟨atomic⟩ figures;[151] yet he does not recount the shapes ⟨of the atoms⟩ of all ⟨the sensory objects⟩, but centres his attention upon those of the tastes and of colours; and even of these, he describes with greater precision the ⟨figures⟩ connected with taste, although he refers the presentation itself to ⟨the sentience of⟩ man.

What is 'sour', he holds, is at once 'angular' in its 65 ⟨atomic⟩ figure and is 'twisted', minute, and thin. By its keenness it swiftly slips in and penetrates everywhere, and by its roughness and 'angularity' it draws the parts together and binds them. It also heats the

συσπᾶν· διὸ καὶ θερμαίνειν τὸ σῶμα κενότητας ἐμποιοῦντα· μάλιστα γὰρ θερμαίνεσθαι τὸ πλεῖστον ἔχον κενόν. τὸν δὲ γ λ υ κ ὺ ν ἐκ περιφερῶν συγκεῖσθαι σχημάτων κοὐκ ἄγαν μικρῶν· διὸ καὶ διαχεῖν ὅλως τὸ σῶμα καὶ οὐ βιαίως καὶ οὐ ταχὺ πάντα περαίνειν· τοὺς ⟨δ'⟩ ἄλλους ταράττειν, ὅτι διαδύνων π λ α ν ᾷ τὰ ἄλλα καὶ ὑγραίνει· ὑγραινόμενα δὲ καὶ ἐκ τῆς τάξεως κινούμενα συρρεῖν εἰς τὴν κοιλίαν· ταύτην γὰρ εὐπορώτατον εἶναι διὰ τὸ ταύτῃ πλεῖστον εἶναι
66 κενόν. τὸν δὲ σ τ ρ υ φ ν ὸ ν ἐκ μεγάλων σχημάτων καὶ πολυγωνίων καὶ περιφερὲς ἥκιστ' ἐχόντων· ταῦτα γὰρ ὅταν εἰς τὰ σώματα ἔλθῃ, ἐπιτυφλοῦν ἐμπλάττοντα τὰ φλεβία καὶ κωλύειν συρρεῖν· διὸ καὶ τὰς κοιλίας ἱστάναι. τὸν δὲ π ι κ ρ ὸ ν ἐκ μικρῶν καὶ λείων καὶ περιφερῶν τὴν περιφέρειαν εἰληχότα καὶ καμπὰς ἔχουσαν· διὸ καὶ γλισχρὸν καὶ κολλῶδη. ἁ λ μ υ ρ ὸ ν δὲ τὸν ἐκ μεγάλων καὶ οὐ περιφερῶν, ἀλλ' ἐπ' ἐνίων μὲν σ κ α λ η ν ῶ ν, ⟨ἐπὶ δὲ πλείστων οὐ σκαληνῶν⟩ διὸ οὐδὲ π ο λ υ κ α μ π ῶ ν (βούλεται δὲ σ κ α λ η ν ὰ λέγειν, ἅπερ παράλλαξιν ἔχει πρὸς ἄλληλα καὶ συμπλοκήν)· μεγάλων μέν, ὅτι ἡ ἁλμυρὶς ἐπιπολάζει· μικρὰ γὰρ ὄντα καὶ τυπτόμενα τοῖς περιέχουσι μείγνυσθαι ἂν τῷ παντί· οὐ περιφερῶν δ' ὅτι τὸ μὲν ἁλμυρὸν τραχὺ τὸ δὲ περιφερὲς λεῖον· οὐ σ κ α λ η ν ῶ ν δὲ διὰ τὸ μὴ π ε ρ ι π λ ά τ τ ε σ θ α ι,
67 διὸ ψ α φ α ρ ὸ ν ε ἶ ν α ι. τὸν δὲ δ ρ ι μ ὺ ν μικρὸν καὶ

Theophrastus on the Senses

body, in consequence, since it produces emptiness within;[152] for whatever has most of empty space ⟨amongst its atoms⟩ is most heated.

'Sweet' consists of ⟨atomic⟩ figures that are rounded and not too small; wherefore it quite softens the body by its gentle action, and unhastening makes its way throughout. Yet it disturbs the other ⟨savours⟩,[153] for it slips in among the other ⟨atomic figures⟩ and "leads them from their accustomed ways" and moistens them. And the ⟨atomic figures⟩ thus moistened and disturbed in their arrangement flow into the belly, which is most accessible, since empty space is there in greatest measure.

The 'astringent' taste, according to Democritus, is 66 derived from ⟨atomic⟩ figures that are large and of many angles and are least rounded. For when these enter our bodies, they clog and occlude the ducts and prevent ⟨their contents⟩ from intermingling, and consequently stay the action of the bowels.

'Bitter' is composed of small, smooth, round ⟨atomic figures⟩ whose surfaces moreover are furnished with hooks; as a consequence bitter is sticky and viscous.

The taste derived from large ⟨atoms⟩ that are unrounded,—some of them are 'crooked', yet for the most part they are regular [154]—this taste is 'saline'; ⟨its atoms⟩ therefore are not provided with 'many hooks'; (by 'crooked' ⟨atoms⟩ he means such as overlap and become entangled in one another). ⟨The saline quality is derived⟩ from large ⟨atoms⟩ because salt comes to the surface of bodies;[155] while if ⟨its atoms⟩ were small and were battered against the surrounding ⟨particles⟩, they would mingle with the whole; from unrounded ⟨atoms⟩, because what is saline is rough while the rounded is smooth; from ⟨atoms⟩ that are not 'crooked', because these do not "stick to one another",[156] and in consequence they "crumble apart".

The 'pungent' savour according to him is small, 67

περιφερῆ καὶ γωνιοειδῆ, σκαληνὸν δὲ οὐκ ἔχειν. τὸν μὲν γὰρ δριμὺν πολυγώνιόν τε ὄντα τῇ τραχύτητι θερμαίνειν καὶ διαχεῖν διὰ τὸ μικρὸν εἶναι καὶ περιφερῆ καὶ γωνιοειδῆ· καὶ γὰρ τὸ γωνιοειδὲς εἶναι τοιοῦτον. ὡσαύτως δὲ καὶ τὰς ἄλλας ἑκάστου δυνάμεις ἀποδίδωσιν ἀνάγων εἰς τὰ σχήματα. ἁπάντων δὲ τῶν σχημάτων οὐδὲν ἀκέραιον εἶναι καὶ ἀμιγὲς τοῖς ἄλλοις, ἀλλ' ἐν ἑκάστῳ πολλὰ εἶναι καὶ τὸν αὐτὸν ἔχειν λείου καὶ τραχέος καὶ περιφεροῦς καὶ ὀξέος καὶ τῶν λοιπῶν. οὗ δ' ἂν ἐνῇ πλεῖστον, τοῦτο μάλιστα ἐνισχύειν πρός τε τὴν αἴσθησιν καὶ τὴν δύναμιν, ἔτι δὲ εἰς ὁποίαν ἕξιν ἂν εἰσέλθῃ· διαφέρειν γὰρ οὐκ ὀλίγον καὶ τοῦτο διὰ τὸ αὐτὸ τἀναντία, καὶ τἀναντία τὸ αὐτὸ πάθος ποιεῖν
68 ἐνίοτε. καὶ περὶ μὲν τῶν χυλῶν οὕτως ἀφώρικεν.

ἄτοπον δ' ἂν φανείη πρῶτον μὲν τὸ μὴ πάντων ὁμοίως ἀποδοῦναι τὰς αἰτίας, ἀλλὰ βαρὺ μὲν καὶ κοῦφον καὶ μαλακὸν καὶ σκληρὸν καὶ μεγέθει καὶ σμικρότητι καὶ τῷ μανῷ καὶ πυκνῷ, θερμὸν δὲ καὶ ψυχρὸν καὶ τὰ ἄλλα τοῖς σχήμασιν. ἔπειτα βαρέος μὲν καὶ κούφου καὶ σκληροῦ καὶ μαλακοῦ καθ' αὑτὰ ποιεῖν φύσεις (μέγεθος μὲν γὰρ καὶ σμικρότης καὶ τὸ πυκνὸν καὶ τὸ μανὸν οὐ πρὸς ἕτερόν ἐστι), θερμὸν δὲ καὶ ψυχρὸν καὶ τὰ ἄλλα πρὸς τὴν αἴσθησιν, καὶ ταῦτα πολλάκις λέγοντα διότι τοῦ θερμοῦ τὸ σχῆμα σφαι-
69 ροειδές. ὅλως δὲ μέγιστον ἐναντίωμα καὶ κοινὸν ἐπὶ πάντων, ἅμα μὲν πάθη ποιεῖν τῆς αἰσθήσεως, ἅμα δὲ τοῖς σχήμασι διορίζειν· καὶ τὸ αὐτὸ φαίνεσθαι τοῖς μὲν πικρὸν

round, and angular,[157] but not irregular. Having many angles, this taste heats and melts by reason of its roughness, because it is small, round, and angular; for the angular too has this character.[158]

In a like manner he accounts for all the other effects of each ⟨savour⟩ by referring them to figures. But no one of all these figures is present, he holds, pure and without admixture of the others; on the contrary, there is a multitude of them in each savour, and the selfsame taste includes figures that are smooth, rough, round, sharp, and so on. The preponderant figure, however, exerts the most influence upon the faculty of sense and determines the ⟨savour's⟩ effect; and, moreover, the condition in which it finds ⟨us influences the result⟩. For it makes a great difference ⟨what our condition is⟩, inasmuch as the same substance at times causes opposite feeling, and opposite substances cause the same feeling.[159] Such is Democritus's account of tastes. 68

In the first place, it might seem odd not to assign causes to all ⟨sensory qualities⟩ according to a uniform principle, but to explain heaviness and lightness, softness and hardness, by the fact that ⟨the atoms⟩ are large or small, and rare or dense,[160] while heat and cold and the rest are explained by the figures ⟨of the atoms⟩.[161] In the second place, ⟨it seems strange⟩ to ascribe a resident and objective reality to the qualities heavy, light, hard, and soft (for the properties large and small, dense and rare are not relative to something other than ⟨the substance itself⟩), and then to make heat, cold, and the rest entirely relative to sense, and this though he repeatedly says that the figure of heat is spherical.

But the one glaring inconsistency running through the whole account is, that he no sooner declares ⟨savours⟩ to be subjective effects in sense than he distinguishes them by their figures; and he points out that the same substance appears bitter to some persons and 69

τοῖς δὲ γλυκὺ τοῖς δ' ἄλλως· οὔτε γὰρ οἷόν ⟨τε⟩ τὸ σχῆμα πάθος εἶναι οὔτε ταὐτὸν τοῖς μὲν σφαιροειδὲς τοῖς δ' ἄλλως (ἀνάγκη δ' [εἴπερ] ἴσως, εἴπερ τοῖς μὲν γλυκὺ τοῖς δὲ πικρόν) οὐδὲ κατὰ τὰς ἡμετέρας ἕξεις μεταβάλλειν τὰς μορφάς. ἁπλῶς δὲ τὸ μὲν σχῆμα καθ' αὑτό ἐστι, τὸ δὲ γλυκὺ καὶ ὅλως τὸ αἰσθητὸν πρὸς ἄλλο καὶ ἐν ἄλλοις, ὥς φησιν. ἄτοπον δὲ καὶ τὸ πᾶσιν ἀξιοῦν ταὐτὸ φαίνεσθαι τῶν αὐτῶν αἰσθανομένοις καὶ τούτων τὴν ἀλήθειαν ἐλέγχειν, καὶ ταῦτα εἰρηκότα πρότερον τὸ τοῖς ἀνομοίως διακειμένοις ἀνόμοια φαίνεσθαι καὶ πάλιν τὸ μηθὲν μᾶλλον ἕτερον ἑτέρου
70 τυγχάνειν τῆς ἀληθείας.   εἰκὸς γὰρ τὸ βέλτιον τοῦ χείρονος καὶ τὸ ὑγιαῖνον τοῦ κάμνοντος· κατὰ φύσιν γὰρ μᾶλλον. ἔτι δὲ εἴπερ μὴ ἔστι φύσις τῶν αἰσθητῶν διὰ τὸ μὴ ταὐτὰ πᾶσι φαίνεσθαι, δῆλον ὡς οὐδὲ τῶι ζῴων οὐδὲ τῶν ἄλλων σωμάτων· οὐδὲ γὰρ περὶ τούτων ὁμοδοξοῦσι. καίτοι εἰ μὴ καὶ διὰ τῶν αὐτῶν γίνεται πᾶσι τὸ γλυκὺ καὶ τὸ πικρόν, ἀλλ' ἥ γε φύσις τοῦ πικροῦ καὶ τοῦ γλυκέος ἡ αὐτὴ φαίνεται πᾶσιν. ὅπερ καὶ αὐτὸς ἂν δόξειεν ἐπιμαρτυρεῖν. πῶς γὰρ ἂν τὸ ἡμῖν πικρὸν ἄλλοις ἦν γλυκὺ καὶ στρυφνόν, εἰ μή τις ἦν ὡρισμένη φύσις αὐτῶν;
71 ἔτι δὲ ποιεῖ σαφέστερον ἐν οἷς φησι γίνεσθαι μὲν ἕκαστον καὶ εἶναι κατ' ἀλήθειαν, ἰδίως δ' ἐπὶ πικροῦ μοῖραν ἔχειν συνέσεως. ὥστε διά τε τούτων ἐναντίον ἂν φανείη τὸ

Theophrastus on the Senses

sweet to others and has still a third quality for some other group. For the figure cannot possibly be a subjective effect, nor can one and the same figure be spherical for certain persons and of another shape for others (although such an assumption were perhaps inevitable if what is sweet for some is bitter for others), nor can the shapes ⟨of atoms⟩ change according to differences of state in us. And, in general, the ⟨atomic⟩ figure has an absolute existence, while sweetness and the sensuous object generally, as he says, is relative and existent in something beyond itself.

It is strange, furthermore, to insist that to all those who perceive the same things there comes the same subjective appearance,[162] and to examine the true character of these things, when he has already said that to persons in different conditions there come different subjective appearances, and again that no one attains the truth of things better than does another. For it is 70 probable that ⟨in the attainment of truth⟩ the better surpasses the worse, and the well the sick; since ⟨the better and healthier⟩ are more in accord with the reality of things.[163]

But if there be no objective reality in sensory objects because they do not appear the same to all, there is manifestly none in animals or other bodies; for men disagree about these things, too. And yet even if the cause of sweet and bitter is not the same for us all, at least the bitterness [164] and sweetness appear the same for all. Democritus himself seems a witness to this; for how could that which is bitter for us be sweet or astringent for others, unless these very qualities had a definite nature? This he makes even more explicit in 71 those passages where he says that the being of anything and the process by which it originated are real;[165] and particularly when he says of bitter, that "⟨here we⟩ have a portion of understanding."[166] Upon such a showing, consequently, there would seem to be a general

The Greek Physiological Psychology

μὴ ποιεῖν φύσιν τινὰ τῶν αἰσθητῶν καὶ πρὸς τούτοις ὅπερ ἐλέχθη καὶ πρότερον, ὅταν σχῆμα μὲν ἀποδιδῷ τῆς ⟨πικρᾶς⟩ οὐσίας ὥσπερ καὶ τῶν ἄλλων, μὴ εἶναι δὲ λέγῃ φύσιν· ἢ γὰρ οὐδενὸς ὅλως ἢ καὶ τούτων ἔσται, τῆς αὐτῆς γε ὑπαρχούσης αἰτίας. ἔτι δὲ τὸ θερμόν τε καὶ ψυχρόν, ἅπερ ἀρχὰς τιθέασιν, εἰκὸς ἔχειν τινὰ φύσιν, εἰ δὲ ταῦτα καὶ τὰ ἄλλα. νῦν δὲ σκληροῦ μὲν καὶ μαλακοῦ καὶ βαρέος καὶ κούφου ποιεῖ τιν' οὐσίαν, ἅπερ οὐχ ἧττον ἔδοξε λέγεσθαι πρὸς ἡμᾶς, θερμοῦ δὲ καὶ ψυχροῦ καὶ τῶν ἄλλων οὐδενός. καίτοι τό γε βαρὺ καὶ κοῦφον ὅταν διορίζῃ τοῖς μεγέθεσιν, ἀνάγκη τὰ ἁπλᾶ πάντα τὴν αὐτὴν ἔχειν ὁρμὴν τῆς φορᾶς, ὥστε μιᾶς τινος ἂν ὕλης εἴη καὶ τῆς αὐτῆς φύσεως.

72 ἀλλὰ περὶ μὲν τούτων ἔοικε συνηκολουθηκέναι τοῖς ποιοῦσιν ὅλως τὸ φρονεῖν κατὰ τὴν ἀλλοίωσιν, ἥπερ ἐστὶν ἀρχαιοτάτη δόξα. πάντες γὰρ οἱ παλαιοὶ καὶ [οἱ] ποιηταὶ καὶ σοφοὶ κατὰ τὴν διάθεσιν ἀποδιδόασι τὸ φρονεῖν. τῶν δὲ χυλῶν ἑκάστῳ τὸ σχῆμα ἀποδίδωσι πρὸς τὴν δύναμιν ἀφομοιῶν τὴν ἐν τοῖς πάθεσιν· ὅπερ οὐ μόνον ἐξ ἐκείνων, ἀλλὰ καὶ ἐκ τῶν αἰσθητηρίων ἔδει συμβαίνειν ἄλλως τε καὶ εἰ πάθη τούτων ἐστίν. οὐ γὰρ πᾶν τὸ σφαιροειδὲς οὐδὲ τὰ ἄλλα σχήματα τὴν αὐτὴν ἔχει δύναμιν, ὥστε καὶ ⟨κατὰ τὸ⟩ [κάτω] ὑποκείμενον ἔδει διορίζειν, πότερον ἐξ

contradiction in his refusal to ascribe any objective reality to sensory objects. But there is, besides, the special contradiction indicated above, when he assigns a figure to the bitter,[167] as he does to the other ⟨savours⟩, and yet says that ⟨the bitter⟩ has no objective reality.[168] For either no ⟨sensory object⟩ has external reality, or else these tastes have such reality, since a common cause underlies them.[169]

Moreover both heat and cold, which are supposed to be the primal source of things, probably have some objective reality; but if these, then the others also. He does, however, ascribe a certain substantive being to the qualities hard and soft, and heavy and light;—although in spite of this they seem to be counted ⟨among the qualities⟩ relative to us;—but he does not ascribe such substantive being to heat, and cold, and the rest. And yet, as he distinguishes the heavy and the light by the size [170] ⟨of their atoms⟩, he ought to hold that all simple ⟨bodies⟩ have an impulse to move in the same direction; [171] and consequently they would be of one and the same 'matter' and would have a common nature. Yet upon such questions he seems to have followed those who make thought entirely a matter of change, a doctrine from hoary antiquity; since all the ancients, whether poets or sages, represented thought as dependent upon ⟨bodily⟩ disposition.

But in assigning an ⟨atomic⟩ figure to each of the savours, Democritus has made this figure correspond to the effect [172] which the savour produces in our feelings. The ⟨figure therefore should be deduced⟩, not from the ⟨external savours⟩ merely, but from our sense organs as well; above all, if these savours themselves are but subjective effects in these sense-organs. A spherical figure does not have the same 'power' in every case, nor does any other figure; ⟨a savour⟩ must consequently be characterized with reference to the substrate affected,[173] by stating whether it is composed of what is like or

ὁμοίων ἢ ἐξ ἀνομοίων ἐστί, καὶ πῶς ἡ τῶν αἰσθήσεων ἀλλοίωσις γίνεται, καὶ πρὸς τούτοις ὁμοίως ἐπὶ πάντων ἀποδοῦναι τῶν διὰ τῆς ἁφῆς καὶ μὴ μόνον τὰ περὶ γεῦσιν. ἀλλὰ καὶ ταῦτα μὲν ἤτοι διαφοράν τινα ἔχει πρὸς τοὺς χυλούς, ἣν ἔδει διελεῖν, ἢ καὶ παρεῖται δυνατὸν ὂν ὁμοίως

73 εἰπεῖν. τῶν δὲ χρωμάτων ἁπλᾶ μὲν λέγει τέτταρα. λευκὸν μὲν οὖν εἶναι τὸ λεῖον. ὃ γὰρ ἂν μὴ τραχὺ μηδ' ἐπισκιάζον ᾖ μηδὲ δυσδίοδον, τὸ τοιοῦτο πᾶν λαμπρὸν εἶναι. δεῖ δὲ καὶ εὐθύτρυπα καὶ διαυγῆ τὰ λαμπρὰ εἶναι. τὰ μὲν οὖν σκληρὰ τῶν λευκῶν ἐκ τοιούτων σχημάτων συγκεῖσθαι οἷον ἡ ἐντὸς πλὰξ τῶν κογχυλίων· οὕτω γὰρ ἂν ἄσκια καὶ εὐαγῆ καὶ εὐθύπορα εἶναι. τὰ ⟨δὲ⟩ ψαθυρὰ καὶ εὔθρυπτα ἐκ περιφερῶν μέν, λοξῶν δὲ τῇ θέσει πρὸς ἄλληλα καὶ κατὰ δύο συζεύξει, τὴν δ' ὅλην τάξιν ἔχειν ὅτι μάλιστα ὁμοίαν. τοιούτων δ' ὄντων ψαθυρὰ μὲν εἶναι, διότι κατὰ μικρὸν ἡ σύναψις· εὔθρυπτα δέ, ὅτι ὁμοίως κεῖνται· ἄσκια δέ, διότι λεῖα καὶ πλατέα· λευκότερα δ' ἀλλήλων τῷ τὰ σχήματα τὰ εἰρημένα καὶ ἀκριβέστερα καὶ ἀμιγέστερα εἶναι καὶ τὴν τάξιν καὶ τὴν θέσιν ἔχειν μᾶλλον

74 τὴν εἰρημένην. τὸ μὲν οὖν λευκὸν ἐκ τοιούτων εἶναι σχημάτων.

τὸ δὲ μέλαν ἐκ τῶν ἐναντίων, ἐκ τραχέων καὶ σκαληνῶν καὶ ἀνομοίων· οὕτω γὰρ ἂν σκιάζειν καὶ οὐκ εὐθεῖς εἶναι

Theophrastus on the Senses

unlike ⟨the substance of the sense organ⟩, and how the change in the sensuous faculty comes to pass. And furthermore there should be offered an explanation applicable alike to all the sensory qualities that arise by touch, and not merely to those involved in taste.[174] And yet these qualities ⟨arising by touch⟩ either show some difference when compared with savours—a difference which he should make clear—or else he has neglected to tell us what is the common explanation that here is possible.

The simple colours, he says, are four. What is smooth is white; since what neither is rough nor casts shadows nor is hard to penetrate,—all such substances are brilliant. But brilliant substances must also have open passages and be translucent. Now white substances that are hard have the structure just described,—for instance, the inner surface of cockle shells; for the substance here would be shadowless, 'gleaming', and with straight passages. But the white substances that are loose and friable are composed of round particles, yet with these placed oblique to one another and oblique in their conjunction by pairs,[175] while the arrangement as a whole is uniform in the extreme. With such a structure these substances are loose because ⟨their particles are⟩ in contact only over a small ⟨portion of their surface⟩; friable, because their composition is so uniform; shadowless, because they are smooth and flat. But those substances are whiter, compared with one another, in which the figures are more exactly as described above and are freer from admixture with other figures and whose order and position more nearly conform to the given description. From such figures, then, is white derived.

Black is composed of figures the very opposite ⟨to those of white⟩,—figures rough, irregular, and differing from one another. For these cast shadows, and the passages amongst them are not straight nor easy to

73

74

τοὺς πόρους οὐδ' εὐδιόδους. ἔτι δὲ τὰς ἀπορροίας νωθεῖς καὶ ταραχώδεις· διαφέρειν γάρ τι καὶ τὴν ἀπορροὴν τῷ ποιὰν εἶναι πρὸς τὴν φαντασίαν, ἣν γίνεσθαι διὰ τὴν ἐναπόληψιν τοῦ ἀέρος ἀλλοίαν.

75 ἐρυθρὸν δ' ἐξ οἷωνπερ καὶ τὸ θερμόν, πλὴν ἐκ μειζόνων. ἐὰν γὰρ αἱ συγκρίσεις ὦσι μείζους ὁμοίων ὄντων τῶν σχημάτων, μᾶλλον ἐρυθρὸν εἶναι. σημεῖον δ' ὅτι ἐκ τοιούτων τὸ ἐρυθρόν· ἡμᾶς τε γὰρ θερμαινομένους ἐρυθραίνεσθαι καὶ τὰ ἄλλα τὰ πυρούμενα, μέχρις ἂν οὗ ἔχῃ τὸ τοῦ πυροειδοῦς. ἐρυθρότερα δὲ τὰ ἐκ μεγάλων ὄντα σχημάτων οἷον τὴν φλόγα καὶ τὸν ἄνθρακα τῶν χλωρῶν ξύλων ἢ τῶν αὔων. καὶ τὸν σίδηρον δὲ καὶ τὰ ἄλλα τὰ πυρούμενα· λαμπρότατα μὲν γὰρ εἶναι τὰ πλεῖστον ἔχοντα καὶ λεπτότατον πῦρ, ἐρυθρότερα δὲ τὰ παχύτερον καὶ ἔλαττον. διὸ καὶ ἧττον εἶναι θερμὰ τὰ ἐρυθρότερα· θερμὸν [μὲν] γὰρ τὸ λεπτόν. τὸ δὲ χλωρὸν ἐκ τοῦ στερεοῦ καὶ τοῦ κενοῦ συνεστάναι μεικτὸν ἐξ ἀμφοῖν, τῇ θέσει δὲ καὶ τάξει ⟨διαλλάττειν⟩ αὐτῶν

76 τὴν χρόαν. τὰ μὲν οὖν ἁπλᾶ χρώματα τούτοις κεχρῆσθαι τοῖς σχήμασιν· ἕκαστον δὲ καθαρώτερον, ὅσῳ ἂν ἐξ ἀμιγεστέρων ᾖ. τὰ δὲ ἄλλα κατὰ τὴν τούτων μῖξιν. οἷον τὸ μὲν χρυσοειδὲς καὶ τὸ τοῦ χαλκοῦ καὶ πᾶν τὸ τοιοῦτον ἐκ τοῦ λευκοῦ καὶ τοῦ ἐρυθροῦ· τὸ μὲν γὰρ λαμπρὸν ἔχειν ἐκ τοῦ λευκοῦ, τὸ δὲ ὑπέρυθρον ἀπὸ τοῦ ἐρυθροῦ· πίπτειν γὰρ εἰς τὰ κενὰ τοῦ λευκοῦ τῇ μίξει τὸ ἐρυθρόν. ἐὰν δὲ προστεθῇ τούτοις τὸ χλωρόν, γίνεσθαι τὸ κάλλιστον χρῶμα, δεῖν δὲ μικρὰς τοῦ χλωροῦ τὰς συγκρίσεις εἶναι· μεγάλας γὰρ οὐχ οἷόν τε συγκειμένων οὕτω τοῦ λευκοῦ καὶ τοῦ ἐρυθροῦ. διαφόρους δὲ ἔσεσθαι τὰς χρόας τῷ πλέον καὶ

Theophrastus on the Senses

thread. Their effluences, too, are sluggish and confused; for the character of the effluence also makes a difference in the inner presentation, as this emanation is changed by its retention of air.[176]

Red is composed of figures such as enter into heat, save that those of red are larger. For if the aggregations [177] be larger although the figures are the same, they produce the quality of redness rather ⟨than of heat⟩.[178] Evidence that redness is derived from such ⟨figures⟩ [179] is found in the fact that we redden as we become heated, as do other things placed in the fire until they have a fiery colour. Those substances are redder that are composed of large figures—for example, the flame and coals of green wood ⟨are redder⟩ than those of dry.[180] And iron, too, and other things placed in fire ⟨become redder⟩. Those are most luminous, however, that contain the most fire and the subtilest, while those are redder that have coarser ⟨fire⟩ and less of it. Redder things, accordingly, are not so hot; for what is subtile is hot.[181]

Green is composed of both the solid and the void,—the hue varying with the position and order of these constituents.

Such are the figures which the simple colours possess; and each of these colours is the purer the less the admixture of other figures. The other colours are derived from these by mixture.

Golden and copper-colour and all such tones, for instance, come from white and red, their brilliance being derived from the white, their ruddiness from the red component; for in combination the red sinks into the empty spaces of the white. Now if green be added to white and red, there results the most beautiful colour; but the green component must be small, for any large admixture would not comport with the union of white with red. The tint will vary according to the amount ⟨of green⟩ that is introduced.

75

76

The Greek Physiological Psychology

77 ἔλαττον λαμβάνειν. τὸ δὲ πορφυροῦν ἐκ λευκοῦ καὶ μέλανος καὶ ἐρυθροῦ, πλείστην μὲν μοῖραν ἔχοντος τοῦ ἐρυθροῦ, μικρὰν δὲ τοῦ μέλανος, μέσην δὲ τοῦ λευκοῦ· διὸ καὶ ἡδὺ φαίνεσθαι πρὸς τὴν αἴσθησιν. ὅτι μὲν οὖν τὸ μέλαν καὶ τὸ ἐρυθρὸν αὐτῷ ἐνυπάρχει, φανερὸν εἶναι τῇ ὄψει, διότι δὲ τὸ λευκόν, τὸ λαμπρὸν καὶ διαυγὲς σημαίνειν· ταῦτα γὰρ ποιεῖν τὸ λευκόν. τὴν δ' ἴσατιν ἐκ μέλανος σφόδρα καὶ χλωροῦ, πλείονα δὲ μοῖραν ἔχειν τοῦ μέλανος· τὸ δὲ πράσινον ἐκ πορφυροῦ καὶ τῆς ἰσάτιδος, ἢ ἐκ χλωροῦ καὶ πορφυροειδοῦς.... τὸ γὰρ θεῖον εἶναι τοιοῦτον καὶ μετέχειν τοῦ λαμπροῦ. τὸ δὲ κυανοῦν ἐξ ἰσάτιδος καὶ πυρώδους, σχημάτων δὲ περιφερῶν καὶ βελονοειδῶν, ὅπως

78 τὸ στίλβον τῷ μέλανι ἐνῇ. τὸ δὲ καρύινον ἐκ χλωροῦ καὶ κυανοειδοῦς· ἐὰν δὲ πλέον τοῦ χλωροῦ μειχθῇ, φλογοειδὲς γίνεσθαι· τῷ γὰρ ἀσκίῳ τὸ μελανόχρων ἐξείργεσθαι. σχεδὸν δὲ καὶ τὸ ἐρυθρὸν τῷ λευκῷ μειχθὲν χλωρὸν ποιεῖν εὐαγὲς καὶ οὐ μέλαν· διὸ καὶ τὰ φυόμενα χλωρὰ τὸ πρῶτον εἶναι πρὸ τοῦ θερμανθῆναι καὶ διαχεῖσθαι. καὶ πλήθει μὲν τοσούτων ἐπιμέμνηται χρωμάτων, ἄπειρα δὲ εἶναι καὶ τὰ χρώματα καὶ τοὺς χυλοὺς κατὰ τὰς μίξεις, ἐάν τις τὰ μὲν ἀφαιρῇ τὰ δὲ προστιθῇ καὶ τῶν μὲν ἔλαττον μίσγῃ τῶν δὲ πλέον. οὐθὲν γὰρ ὅμοιον ἔσεσθαι θάτερον θατέρῳ.

79 Πρῶτον μὲν οὖν τὸ πλείους ἀποδοῦναι τὰς ἀρχὰς ἔχει τινὰ ἀπορίαν· οἱ γὰρ ἄλλοι τὸ λευκὸν καὶ τὸ μέλαν, ὡς τούτων ἁπλῶν ὄντων μόνων· ἔπειτα τὸ μὴ πᾶσι τοῖς λευκοῖς μίαν ποιῆσαι τὴν μορφήν, ἀλλ' ἑτέραν τοῖς σκληροῖς καὶ

Theophrastus on the Senses

Crimson comes from white, black,[182] and red,—the largest 'portion' being red, that of black small, and of white midway; for thus it makes an appearance delightful to the sense. That black and red are present in it is patent to the eye: its brilliance and lustre testify to the presence of white; for white produces such effects.

Woad hue is composed of deep black and golden green, but with the major 'portion' black. Leek green is of crimson and woad, or of golden green and purplish. . . . For sulphur colour is of this character, with a dash of brilliance.[183] Indigo is a mixture of woad and fiery red,[184] with round figures and figures needle-shaped to give a gleam to the colour's darkness.[185]

Brown is derived from golden green and deep blue; but if more of the golden green be mixed, flame-colour is the result; for the blackness is expelled because ⟨the golden green⟩[186] is shadowless. And red, too, when mixed with white, gives almost a 'pure' golden green,[187] and not a black;[188] which accounts for the fact that plants at first are of such a green before there is a heating and dispersion.[189]

This completes the tale of colours he recounts; although he holds that the colours, like the savours, are endless in number according to their combinations,—according as we remove some and add others and 'combine' them in varying proportion. For no one of these colours would be the same as another.

But first of all, his increase of the number of primaries presents a difficulty; for the other investigators propose white and black as the only simple colours. And in the second place, there is a difficulty when he fails to assign one and the same shape to all kinds of white, but attributes a different shape to

77

78

79

The Greek Physiological Psychology

τοῖς ψαθυροῖς. οὐ γὰρ εἰκὸς ἄλλην αἰτίαν εἶναι τοῖς διαφόροις κατὰ τὴν ἀφήν· οὐδ' ἂν ἔτι τὸ σχῆμα αἴτιον εἴη τῆς διαφορᾶς, ἀλλὰ μᾶλλον ἡ θέσις· ἐνδέχεται γὰρ καὶ τὰ περιφερῆ καὶ ἁπλῶς πάντα ἐπισκιάζειν ἑαυτοῖς. σημεῖον δέ· καὶ γὰρ αὐτὸς ταύτην φέρει τὴν πίστιν, ὅσα τῶν λείων μέλανα φαίνεται. διὰ γὰρ τὴν σύμφυσιν καὶ τὴν τάξιν ὡς τὴν αὐτὴν ἔχοντα τῷ μέλανι φαίνεσθαι τοιαῦτα. καὶ πάλιν ὅσα λευκὰ τῶν τραχέων. ἐκ μεγάλων γὰρ εἶναι ταῦτα καὶ τὰς συνδέσεις οὐ περιφερεῖς, ἀλλὰ προκρόσσας, καὶ τῶν σχημάτων τὰς μορφὰς ἀγνυμένας, ὥσπερ ἡ ἀνάβασις καὶ τὰ πρὸ τῶν τειχῶν ἔχει χώματα· τοιοῦτον γὰρ ὂν ἄσκιον εἶναι καὶ οὐ
80 κωλύεσθαι τὸ λαμπρόν.   πρὸς δὲ τούτοις πῶς λέγει καὶ ζῴων τὸ λευκὸν ἐνίων γίνεσθαι μέλαν, εἰ τεθείησαν οὕτως, ὥστ' ἐπισκιάζειν; ὅλως δὲ τοῦ διαφανοῦς καὶ τοῦ λαμπροῦ μᾶλλον ἔοικε τὴν φύσιν ἢ τοῦ λευκοῦ λέγειν. τὸ γὰρ εὐδίοπτον εἶναι καὶ μὴ ἐπαλλάττειν τοὺς πόρους τοῦ διαφανοῦς ἐστι, πόσα δὲ λευκὰ τοῦ διαφανοῦς; ἔτι δὲ τὸ μὲν εὐθεῖς εἶναι τῶν λευκῶν τοὺς πόρους, τῶν δὲ μελάνων ἐπαλλάττειν, ὡς εἰσιούσης τῆς φύσεως ὑπολαβεῖν ἔστιν. ὁρᾶν δέ φησι διὰ τὴν ἀπορροὴν καὶ τὴν ἔμφασιν τὴν εἰς τὴν ὄψιν· εἰ δὲ τοῦτ' ἐστι, τί διοίσει τοὺς πόρους κεῖσθαι κατ' ἀλλήλους ἢ ἐπαλλάττειν; οὐδὲ τὴν ἀπορροὴν ἀπὸ τοῦ κενοῦ πως γίνεσθαι ῥᾴδιον ὑπολαβεῖν· ὥστε λεκτέον τούτου

Theophrastus on the Senses

the 'hard' whites from that which he ascribes to the whites of 'loose texture.' For it is improbable that ⟨the whiteness⟩ would have a different cause in substances differing merely in their tactile character. And, too, the cause of the difference ⟨between white and black⟩ would not lie in the figure ⟨of the constituent particles⟩, but in their position.[190] For round figures, and indeed every kind of figure whatever, can cast shadows upon one another. And this is evident, for Democritus himself gives this reason for the smooth things that look black; for they appear thus, he holds, because they have the internal combination and arrangement characteristic of black. And again, ⟨in giving his reason⟩ for the white things that are rough; these are of large particles, he holds, and their junctions are not rounded off but are 'battlemented',[191] and the shapes of the figures are broken,[192] like the earthworks in the approach to a city's wall. For such an arrangement, he says, throws no shadow, and brilliance is not hindered.

Moreover, how can he say that the whiteness of certain creatures becomes black if they be so placed that shadows are cast?[193] He seems really to be talking about the nature of transparency and brilliance, rather than of whiteness. For to be easily seen through and to have passages that do not run zig-zag are features of transparency; but how many transparent substances are white? And further, to assume straight passages in substances that are white, and passages zig-zag in those that are black, implies that the very structure of the object enters ⟨our sense organ⟩.[194] Vision, he says, is due to an emanation and to the reflection in the organ of sight. But if this be so, what difference does it make whether the passages ⟨in the object⟩ lie end to end or zig-zag? Nor is it easy to believe that an emanation can by any possibility arise from the void.[195] The cause of this, therefore, should be stated. For he seems to derive

τὴν αἰτίαν. ἔοικε γὰρ ἀπὸ τοῦ φωτὸς ἢ ἀπὸ ἄλλου τινὸς ποιεῖν τὸ λευκόν· διὸ καὶ τὴν παχύτητα τοῦ ἀέρος αἰτιᾶται
81 πρὸς τὸ φαίνεσθαι μέλαν. ἔτι δὲ πῶς τὸ μέλαν ἀποδίδωσιν, οὐ ῥᾴδιον καταμαθεῖν· ἡ σκιὰ γὰρ μέλαν τι καὶ ἐπιπρόσθησίς ἐστι τοῦ λευκοῦ· διὸ πρῶτον τὸ λευκὸν τὴν φύσιν. ἅμα δὲ οὐ μόνον τὸ ἐπισκιάζειν, ἀλλὰ καὶ τὴν παχύτητα τοῦ ἀέρος καὶ τῆς εἰσιούσης ἀπορροῆς αἰτιᾶται καὶ τὴν ταραχὴν τοῦ ὀφθαλμοῦ. πότερον δὲ ταῦτα συμβαίνει διὰ τὸ μὴ εὐδίοπτον ἢ καὶ ἄλλῳ γίνοιτ' ἂν καὶ ποίῳ [ἢ μέλαν], οὐ διασαφεῖ.

82 ἄτοπον δὲ καὶ τὸ τοῦ χλωροῦ μὴ ἀποδοῦναι μορφήν, ἀλλὰ μόνον ἐκ τοῦ στερεοῦ καὶ τοῦ κενοῦ ποιεῖν. κοινὰ γὰρ ταῦτά γε πάντων καὶ ἐξ ὁποιωνοῦν ἔσται σχημάτων. χρῆν δ' ὥσπερ κἂν τοῖς ἄλλοις ἴδιόν τι ποιῆσαι, καὶ εἰ μὲν ἐναντίον τῷ ἐρυθρῷ, καθάπερ τὸ μέλαν τῷ λευκῷ, τὴν ἐναντίαν ἔχειν μορφήν· εἰ δὲ μὴ ἐναντίον, αὐτὸ τοῦτ' ἄν τις θαυμάσειεν, ὅτι τὰς ἀρχὰς οὐκ ἐναντίας ποιεῖ· δοκεῖ γὰρ ἅπασιν οὕτως. μάλιστα δὲ χρῆν τοῦτο διακριβοῦν, ποῖα τῶν χρωμάτων ἁπλᾶ καὶ διὰ τί τὰ μὲν σύνθετα τὰ δὲ ἀσύνθετα· πλείστη γὰρ ἀπορία περὶ τῶν ἀρχῶν. ἀλλὰ τοῦτο μὲν ἴσως χαλεπόν. ἐπεὶ καὶ τῶν χυμῶν εἴ τις δύναιτο τοὺς ἁπλοῦς ἀποδοῦναι, μᾶλλον ἂν ὅδε λέγοι. περὶ δὲ ὀσμῆς προσαφορίζειν παρῆκεν πλὴν τοσοῦτον, ὅτι τὸ λεπτὸν ἀπορρέον ἀπὸ τῶν βαρέων ποιεῖ τὴν ὀδμήν. ποῖον δέ τι τὴν φύσιν ὂν ὑπὸ τίνος πάσχει, οὐκέτι προσέ-

whiteness from light or something else; and accordingly offers the grossness of the air as also a reason why things seem dark.

His explanation of black, farther, is not easy to comprehend; for a shadow is (in his theory) something black, and at the same time it is an obscuration [196] of what is white; white is therefore essentially prior ⟨to black⟩.[197] Yet with this, he attributes ⟨black⟩ not only to shading but to the grossness of the air and of the entering emanation, as well as to disturbance of the eye. But whether these arise from mere opacity, or from some other source, and if so, what the character ⟨of this farther source may be⟩, he does not reveal.

It is singular, also, to assign no shape to green but to constitute it merely of the solid and the void.[198] For these are present in all things, of whatsoever figures they are composed. He should have given some distinctive ⟨figure⟩ to green, as he has to the other colours. And if he holds ⟨green⟩ to be the opposite of red,[199] as black is of white, it ought to have an opposite shape; but if in his view it is not the opposite, this itself would surprise us that he does not regard his first principles[200] as opposites, for that is the universally accepted doctrine. Most of all, though, he should have determined with accuracy which colours are simple, and why some colours are compound and others not; for there is the gravest difficulty with regard to the first principles.[201] Yet this would doubtless prove a difficult task. For if one could say, of tastes for example, which of them are simple, there would be more in what one [202] said ⟨than is found in Democritus upon them⟩. As for smell, he says nothing definite except that something subtile emanating from heavy substances is the cause of odour. But what its character is, and by what this process is effected—which is perhaps the most important point of all,—on this we have never a word.

θηκεν, ὅπερ ἴσως ἦν κυριώτατον. Δημόκριτος μὲν οὖν οὕτως ἔνια παραλείπει.

83 Πλάτων δὲ θερμὸν μὲν εἶναί φησι τὸ διακρῖνον δι᾽ ὀξύτητα τῶν γωνιῶν· ψυχρὸν δὲ ὅταν δι᾽ ὑγρότητα ἐκκρίνοντα τὰ ἐλάττω καὶ μὴ δυνάμενα εἰσιέναι τὰ μείζω κύκλῳ περιωθῇ· τῇ γὰρ μάχῃ τρόμον καὶ τῷ πάθει ῥῖγος εἶναι ὄνομα. σκληρὸν <δέ>, ᾧ ἂν ἡ σὰρξ ὑπείκῃ, μαλακὸν δέ, ὃ ἂν τῇ σαρκί, καὶ πρὸς ἄλληλα ὁμοίως. ὑπείκειν δὲ τὸ μικρὰν ἔχον βάσιν. βαρὺ δὲ καὶ κοῦφον τῷ μὲν ἄνω καὶ κάτω διορίζειν οὐ δεῖν, οὐ γὰρ εἶναι τοιούτων φύσιν· ἀλλὰ κοῦφον μὲν εἶναι τὸ εἰς τὸν παρὰ φύσιν τόπον ῥᾳδίως ἑλκόμενον, βαρὺ δὲ τὸ χαλεπῶς. τραχὺ δὲ καὶ λεῖον ὡς
84 ἱκανῶς ὄντα φανερὰ παραλείπει καὶ οὐ λέγει. ἡδὺ δὲ καὶ λυπηρόν, τὸ μὲν εἰς φύσιν ἀθρόον πάθος, τὸ δὲ παρὰ φύσιν καὶ βίᾳ [λυπηρόν], τὰ δὲ μέσα καὶ ἀναίσθητα ἀνὰ λόγον. διὸ καὶ κατὰ τὸ ὁρᾶν οὐκ εἶναι λύπην οὐδ᾽ ἡδονὴν τῇ διακρίσει καὶ συγκρίσει. περὶ δὲ χυμῶν ἐν μὲν τοῖς περὶ ὕδατος τέτταρα λέγει ὕδατος εἴδη· ἐν χυλοῖς μὲν οἶνον ὀπὸν ἔλαιον μέλι, ἐν δὲ τοῖς πάθεσι τὸν γεώδη χυμόν· καὶ διὰ ταῦτα συνάγοντα τοὺς χυλοὺς καὶ συγκρίνοντα, τὰ μὲν τραχύτερα στρυφνὰ εἶναι, τὰ δὲ ἧττον αὐστηρά. τὸ δὲ

Theophrastus on the Senses

There are some things of this kind, then, that Democritus has neglected.

Plato holds [203] that a substance is *hot* which by the sharpness of its angles divides ⟨the body⟩.[204] But whenever, by reason of their fluidity, the larger particles expel the smaller, and—since they are unable to enter amongst them—yet encompass and compress them, this is *cold*. 'Shivering' is our name for the conflict ⟨between these particles⟩; while the affection is known as 'chill'.[205] *Hard* is whatever the flesh yields to; *soft*, whatever yields to the flesh; and ⟨the hardness and softness of objects⟩ relative to one another are explained in like fashion. Those particles yield that have a small base.[206] *Heavy* and *light* should not be defined, he maintains, by resort to the relations 'up' and 'down'; for these have no objective reality. But anything is light when it is with ease drawn to a place opposed to its own nature; it is heavy when this is done with difficulty.[207] Of *rough* and *smooth* he has nothing to say, passing them by as of a character clear enough.[208]

With regard to pleasure and pain,[209] he explains pleasure as a sudden and violent experience of return to the natural state; pain, as a sudden experience of forcible disturbance of the natural state; while the intermediate and imperceptible changes are explained in conformity with this. In the case of sight, accordingly, there is no pain or pleasure from the dissolution and recombining.

As for the savours,[210] Plato when treating of water[211] mentions four of its kinds;[212] amongst the saps are wine, verjuice, oil, and honey. But in treating of the feelings produced in us,[213] ⟨he adds⟩ an earthy savour.[214] And as these [215] coagulate and compact the organic juices,[216] the rougher are *astringent*; the less rough,

83

84

The Greek Physiological Psychology

ῥυπτικὸν τῶν πόρων καὶ ἀποκαθαρτικὸν ἁλμυρόν· τὸ δὲ σφόδρα ῥυπτικόν, ὥστε καὶ ἐκτήκειν, πικρόν. τὰ δὲ θερμαινόμενα καὶ ἄνω φερόμενα καὶ διακρίνοντα δριμέα· τὰ δὲ κυκῶντα ὀξέα· τὰ δὲ σὺν τῇ ὑγρότητι τῇ ἐν τῇ γλώττῃ καὶ
85 διαχυτικὰ καὶ συστατικὰ εἰς τὴν φύσιν γλυκέα.   τὰς δὲ ὀσμὰς εἴδη μὲν οὐκ ἔχειν, ἀλλὰ τῷ λυπηρῷ καὶ ἡδεῖ διαφέρειν. εἶναι δὲ τὴν ὀσμὴν ὕδατος μὲν λεπτότερον, ἀέρος δὲ παχύτερον. σημεῖον δὲ ὅτι ὅταν ἐπιφράξαντες ἀνασπῶσιν, ἄνευ ὀσμῆς τὸ πνεῦμα εἰσέρχεται· διὸ καθάπερ καπνὸν καὶ ὁμίχλην εἶναι τῶν σωμάτων ἀόρατον. εἶναι δὲ καπνὸν μὲν μεταβολὴν ἐξ ὕδατος εἰς ἀέρα, ὁμίχλην δὲ τὴν ἐξ ἀέρος εἰς ὕδωρ. φωνὴν δὲ εἶναι πληγὴν ὑπὸ ἀέρος ἐγκεφάλου καὶ αἵματος δι' ὤτων μέχρι ψυχῆς· ὀξεῖαν δὲ καὶ βαρεῖαν τὴν ταχεῖαν καὶ βραδεῖαν· συμφωνεῖν δ' ὅταν ἡ ἀρχὴ
86 τῆς βραδείας ὁμοία ᾖ τῇ τελευτῇ τῆς ταχείας.   τὸ δὲ χρῶμα φλόγα εἶναι ἀπὸ τῶν σωμάτων σύμμετρα μόρια ἔχουσαν τῇ ὄψει· λευκὸν μὲν τὸ διακριτικόν, μέλαν δὲ τὸ συγκριτικὸν ἀνὰ λόγον [δὲ] τοῖς περὶ τὴν σάρκα θερμοῖς καὶ ψυχροῖς καὶ τοῖς περὶ τὴν γλῶσσαν στρυφνοῖς καὶ δριμέσι· λαμπρὸν δὲ τὸ πυρῶδες λευκόν, . . . τὰ δὲ ἄλλα ἐκ τούτων· ἐν οἷς δὲ λόγοις, οὐδ' εἴ τις εἰδείη χρῆναι λέγειν φησίν, ὧν οὐκ ἔχομεν εἰκότα λόγον ἢ ἀναγκαῖον· οὐδ' εἰ πειρωμένῳ μὴ γίγνοιτο, οὐθὲν ἄτοπον, ἀλλὰ τὸν θεὸν δύνασθαι τοῦτο δρᾶν. ἃ μὲν οὖν εἴρηκε καὶ πῶς ἀφώρικε, σχεδὸν ταῦτά ἐστιν.

Theophrastus on the Senses

harsh. Those that rinse and purge the passages ⟨of taste⟩ are *saline*; such as are excessively detergent, even to the pitch of dissolution, are *bitter*.[217] Substances that are filled with heat[218] and are borne upward ⟨in the head⟩ and disintegrate ⟨the very tissues⟩ are *pungent*; those that cause a confusion are *sharp*; while those are *sweet* that, in company with the tongue's own moisture, relax or contract[219] ⟨the tissues⟩ back to their natural state.

Odours, according to Plato,[220] admit of no ⟨true⟩ classification, but are distinguished by their painful or pleasant ⟨effect⟩. Odour[221] is subtiler than water, though less refined than air; the proof is this, that if we inhale through an obstruction, the breath enters without odour. Thus odour is a kind of invisible vapour or mist from bodies; vapour being a transition from water to air, mist the transition from air to water.

Sound,[222] he holds,[223] is a shock produced by the air—a shock through the ears to the brain and blood and penetrating to the soul.[224] Tones are high and low, respectively, when swift and slow; they are in concord when the beginning of the slow tone is like[225] the end of the swift.

Colour, for Plato,[226] is a flame from bodies, a flame whose parts correspond to the organ of vision. What disintegrates ⟨the organ⟩ is *white*; what redintegrates it is *black*,—a contrast analogous to hot and cold in the case of the flesh, and to astringent and pungent in the case of the tongue.[227] Fiery white is *brilliant*.[228] . . . The rest of the colours are compounded of these. But as for the precise proportions, he says that one ought not to state them, even if one knew, since we have neither a necessary nor a probable account to give of them; or should one, upon experiment, find the event far otherwise, there need be no surprise; for God alone can bring such things to pass. This gives fairly well his thought and his mode of explanation.

87 Ἄτοπον δὲ καὶ τοῦτο· πρῶτον μὲν τὸ μὴ πάντα ὁμοίως ἀποδοῦναι μηδὲ ὅσα τοῦ αὐτοῦ γένους. ὁρίσας γὰρ τὸ θερμὸν σχήματι τὸ ψυχρὸν οὐχ ὡσαύτως ἀπέδωκεν. ἔπειτ' εἰ μαλακὸν τὸ ὑπεῖκον, φανερὸν ὅτι τὸ ὕδωρ καὶ ὁ ἀὴρ καὶ τὸ πῦρ ἐστι μαλακά· φησὶ γὰρ ὑπείκειν τὸ μικρὰν ἔχον βάσιν, ὥστε τὸ πῦρ ἂν εἴη μαλακώτατον. δοκεῖ δὲ τούτων οὐθὲν οὐδ' ὅλως τὸ μὴ ἀντιμεθιστάμενον εἶναι μαλακόν, ἀλλὰ τὸ εἰς τὸ βάθος ὑπεῖκον ἄνευ μεταστάσεως.

88 ἔτι δὲ τὸ βαρὺ καὶ κοῦφον οὐχ ἁπλῶς, ἀλλ' ἐπὶ τῶν γεωδῶν ἀφώρικε· τούτων γὰρ δοκεῖ τὸ μὲν βαρὺ χαλεπῶς, τὸ δὲ κοῦφον ῥᾷον ἄγεσθαι πρὸς ἀλλότριον τόπον. τὸ δὲ πῦρ καὶ ὁ ἀὴρ ταῖς εἰς τοὺς οἰκείους τόπους φοραῖς κοῦφα καὶ ἔστι καὶ δοκεῖ. διόπερ οὐκ ἔσται τὸ μὲν πλεῖον τῶν ὁμογενῶν ἔχον βαρύ, τὸ δὲ ἔλαττον κοῦφον· τὸ μὲν γὰρ πῦρ ὅσῳ ἂν ᾖ πλεῖον, κουφότερον, ἀλλ' ἄνω μὲν τιθεμένου τοῦ πυρὸς ἐφαρμόσουσιν οἱ λόγοι καὶ οὗτος κἀκεῖνος, ἐνταῦθα δ' οὐδέτερος. ὡσαύτως δὲ καὶ ἐπὶ τῆς γῆς· ἄνωθεν γὰρ δεῦρο θᾶττον οἰσθήσεται τὸ πλέον. ὥστε οὐχ ἁπλῶς ἡ γῆ καὶ τὸ πῦρ ἐστι τὸ μὲν βαρὺ τὸ δὲ κοῦφον, ἀλλ' ἑκάτερον πρὸς τὸν τόπον· οὐδ' ὁμοίως ἐνταῦθα κἀκεῖ τὸ γεῶδες, ἀλλ' ἀνάπαλιν· ἐνταῦθα μὲν τὸ ἔλαττον, ἐκεῖ δὲ τὸ πλέον ἔχον τῶν ὁμογενῶν κουφότερον.

89 ταῦτα δὲ πάντα συμβαίνει διὰ τὸ μὴ ἁπλῶς περὶ κούφου καὶ βαρέος, ἀλλὰ περὶ τοῦ γεώδους ἀφορίζειν. τῶν δὲ

Theophrastus on the Senses

Yet the following might well surprise one. First of all, he gives no uniform account of all ⟨our sensory objects⟩, not even of those that belong to the same class. For he describes heat in terms of figure,[229] but he has not given a like account of cold. Then, if whatever is yielding is soft, evidently water and air and fire are soft. And since he says that any substance is yielding whose elements have a small base, fire would be the softest of all. But none of these statements is widely accepted, nor in general is it held that a thing is soft that moves freely around and behind ⟨the entering body⟩; but only what yields in 'depth', without ⟨free⟩ change of place.[230] 87

Furthermore he does not define heaviness and lightness universally, but ⟨only⟩ in the case of things of earth;[231] for it is held that, of these, a heavy object is one that is borne to an alien place with difficulty; a light one, with ease. But fire and air are held to be, and actually are, light by very tending toward their proper places. Hence it is not true that the body with more of kindred substance is heavy; and the one with less, light.[232] For the more of fire we take, the lighter it is. Of Plato's two statements,[233] then, both hold true if fire be placed on high; but neither holds of fire here on earth. And similarly in the case of earth; for from on high the greater mass would be borne hither more swiftly.[234] Earth and fire therefore ⟨for Plato⟩ are not universally heavy or light, but each is either, according to mere position. Nor would earth ⟨have the same character⟩ here and there,[235] but quite the reverse; here the mass with less of kindred matter, there the mass with more, would be the lighter. All of which arises from Plato's defining heaviness and lightness, not as they are universally, but for the special case of things of earth. 88

89

The Greek Physiological Psychology

χυλῶν τὰς μὲν φύσεις οὐ λέγει τίς ἕκαστος, εἰ ἄρα τέσσαρες αἱ πᾶσαι διαφοραί, τὰ δὲ πάθη τὰ συμβαίνοντα ἀπ' αὐτῶν δηλοῖ. συνάγειν γὰρ τοὺς πόρους τὸ στρυφνὸν ἢ στυπτικὸν καὶ καθαίρειν τὸ ἁλμυρόν, ὅπερ πάθος ἐστὶν ἡμέτερον· ὁμοίως δὲ καὶ τὰ ἄλλα. ζητοῦμεν δὲ τὴν οὐσίαν μᾶλλον καὶ διὰ τί ταῦτα δρῶσιν, ἐπεὶ τά γε πάθη θεωροῦμεν.

90 ἀπορήσειε δ' ἄν τις καὶ περὶ τῶν ὀσμητῶν εἰ ἔστιν εἴδη· καὶ γὰρ τοῖς πάθεσι καὶ ταῖς ἡδοναῖς διαφέρουσιν, ὥσπερ οἱ χυλοί. καὶ ἅμα δόξειεν ἂν ὁμοίως ἔχειν ἐπὶ πάντων. περὶ δὲ τῆς ὀσμῆς ὅτι μὲν ἀπορροή τίς ἐστι καὶ ἀνάπνευσις τοῦ ἀέρος, σχεδὸν ὁμολογεῖται. τὸ δὲ ἀφομοιοῦν καπνῷ καὶ ὀμίχλῃ ταὐτά τε λέγειν οὐκ ἀληθές. οὐδὲ γὰρ αὐτὸς φαίνεται ποιεῖν· τὸν μὲν γὰρ ἐξ ὕδατος εἰς ἀέρα, τὴν δ' ὀμίχλην ἐξ ἀέρος εἰς ὕδωρ λέγει μεταβάλλειν. καίτοι δοκεῖ γ' ἀνάπαλιν ἔχειν ἐπὶ τῆς ὀμίχλης, διὸ καὶ παύεται

91 τὰ ὕδατα γινομένης ὀμίχλης. ἐνδεεστέρως ⟨δὲ⟩ καὶ ὁ τῆς φωνῆς εἴρηται λόγος· οὔτε γὰρ κοινὸς ἅπασι τοῖς ζῴοις ἐστὶν οὔτε τὴν αἰτίαν λέγει τῆς αἰσθήσεως βουλόμενος. ἔτι δὲ οὐ τὸν ψόφον καὶ τὴν φωνήν, ἀλλὰ τὴν ἡμετέραν αἴσθησιν ἔοικεν ἀφορίζειν. περὶ δὲ χρωμάτων σχεδὸν ὁμοίως Ἐμπεδοκλεῖ λέγει· τὸ γὰρ σύμμετρα ἔχειν μόρια τῇ ὄψει τῷ τοῖς πόροις ἐναρμόττειν ἐστίν.* ἄτοπον δὲ τὸ μόνην ταύτην ἀποδιδόναι τῶν αἰσθήσεων·

Theophrastus on the Senses

Of the sapid substances, he fails to state what severally are their natures, even were we to suppose that their distinct varieties are precisely four;[236] he merely sets forth the affections they occasion. For he says that the astringent or 'puckering' taste contracts the passages,[237] and that the saline taste cleanses them,—which is but an affection in ourselves. And the rest of the savours are treated after a like manner. But what we seek—since the affections themselves are clear as day—is rather the reality behind them and why they produce their results.

Regarding the objects of smell, too, one could well doubt whether there might not be differences of kind. For they differ in their affections, as well as in the pleasures they give us, quite as do the savours. Indeed ⟨the two groups⟩ would seem to be governed alike in all respects. As for smell itself, it is generally agreed that there is some emanation and that there is an inhalation of air. But it is incorrect to liken odour to vapour and mist, and to say that vapour and mist are identical. Nor does he himself seem actually so to regard them; for vapour is in transition from water to air, he says, while mist is in transition from air to water. And yet in regard to mist the very opposite is generally held to be the fact; for when mist arises water disappears.

Rather unsatisfactory, too, is the definition he gives of sound:[238] for this definition is not applicable to all creatures impartially; and although he tries, he does not state the cause of the sensation. Moreover he seems to be defining, not sound itself, whether inarticulate or vocal, but the sensory process in us.

As for the colours, he agrees in general with Empedocles, since his idea that particles are proportioned to the organ of sight [239] ⟨amounts to the thought⟩ that certain elements fit into the passages ⟨of sense⟩.[240] It is absurd, however, to represent ⟨in such a manner⟩[241] only this single one of our senses; as it is, also, to

The Greek Physiological Psychology

ἔτι δὲ τὸ ἁπλῶς τὸ χρῶμα φλόγα λέγειν· τὸ μὲν γὰρ λευκὸν ἔχει τινὰ ὁμοιότητα, τὸ δὲ μέλαν ἐναντίον ἂν φανείη. τὴν δὲ τῶν ἄλλων μῖξιν † τὸ ἀφαιρεῖν ὅλως οὐκ ἐνδέχεται ἀποδοῦναι ταῖς αἰτίαις, δεῖται δέ τινος λόγου καὶ πίστεως.

say without exception that colour is a flame. For while in some respects the colour white resembles flame, black would seem to be flame's opposite. And in depriving ⟨of all rational necessity⟩²⁴² the mixture which produces the other ⟨colours⟩, he has on the whole made it impossible to assign them to their causes, and has left ⟨his case⟩ in need of argument and warrant.

III

NOTES UPON THE TRANSLATION AND TEXT OF THEOPHRASTUS'S DE SENSIBUS

III

NOTES UPON THE TRANSLATION AND TEXT OF THEOPHRASTUS'S *DE SENSIBUS*

(Upon the title of the *De Sensibus*, see p. 15.)

1. The meaning of the word αἴσθησις would be more accurately represented here by "sensation and sense perception"; but this is too cumbrous for frequent repetition. Nor have I found it possible to render αἴσθησις by any constant English expression. According to need, it has been variously translated as "sense" or "sensation" or "sense perception".

2. Or, "Anaxagoras and Heraclitus and their followers."

3. Theophrastus here mentions only those whose attitude toward the question whether perception is due to likeness or to difference is clearest to him. Clidemus, for example, is not here included, perhaps because he was concerned only with the particular process in each sense and had nothing to say as to the *general* character of perception. Other writers whose view Theophrastus later reports, do not fall readily into the one or the other group. Thus Diogenes of Apollonia is placed doubtfully or by inference with the 'likeness' party (§ 39); Alcmaeon is declared not to belong to the 'likeness' party (§ 25), while yet there is no sufficient reason to place him definitely and

The Greek Physiological Psychology

positively in the opposing camp. Democritus, Theophrastus says (§ 49), can be placed in either group, according as we give emphasis to one or another aspect of his theory.

Of Heraclitus we have nothing in Theophrastus's present treatise save this brief reference; and Philippson would here substitute Δημόκριτον for Ἡράκλειτον. But since Theophrastus explicitly says later that Democritus belongs to either party, this emendation does not seem especially happy. Yet in spite of Theophrastus's own hesitation in regard to Democritus and to Diogenes, Beare (p. 209) says: "For Diogenes, as for Empedocles and Democritus, it was axiomatic that *like* is perceived by *like*."

As for Plato, so far as the direct evidence goes, Theophrastus is partly right and partly wrong in placing him among those whose principle is that of 'likeness'. Aristotle (*De Anima* 404^b), giving as his authority the *Timaeus* and Plato's own lectures on Philosophy, likewise places Plato in the 'likeness' party. But, judging by Plato's writings which we have, it is true that statements in *Timaeus* 30, 39 E, 45 B-C, 63, esp. 63 E (cf. also *Lysis* 214 ff., and *Republic* 837 A) show his general sympathy with the principle of likeness, and his readiness specifically to apply it to the process of vision (*Timaeus* 45 B-C); yet his wider principle in explaining perception is that sensation and sense perception are due to transmitted *motions*, and not transmitted *substances*. Whether there shall be a perception aroused in the soul depends not on the likeness between the particular object and some constituent of the body but upon the mobility of the parts of the body and upon the mere *arrival* of the movement at the seat of consciousness. The mechanical shock and its transmission as a quantity is the important thing; not its kinship or similarity with the soul. In his general theory of *perception*, then, Plato seems not to have been a party to the ancient dispute, in which Aristotle and Theophrastus were interested; he

Notes on the Translation and Text

adopts neither the principle of likeness nor that of difference; nor, as does Aristotle, does he adopt both.

4. The statement that all save Empedocles gave stepmotherly treatment to the senses taken severally, cannot refer to all of Theophrastus's predecessors; for, as we shall see, Theophrastus's own account indicates something quite different to be true of such men as Alcmaeon, Diogenes, and Democritus. Nor will his statement well apply merely to the men whose names appear in this introductory classification; for the several senses are taken up by Anaxagoras. Nor is the statement true if Theophrastus means merely that, with the exception of Empedocles, none makes apparent in each sense the operation of the general principle of likeness or of difference. Besides Empedocles, who observes in each sense the principle of similarity, Anaxagoras connects each with that of opposition.

The puzzle may possibly be less puzzling if we assume that something has disappeared from the text, and that Theophrastus is referring simply to those members of the *likeness* party whom he has named,—Parmenides, Empedocles, and Plato: for of Parmenides his statement seems entirely true; and of Plato, it agrees with Theophrastus's later assertion (§§ 5 f.) that Plato confines his attention almost wholly to sight and hearing, so far as the sensory process itself is concerned, while taking a wider view when he treats of the external 'objects' of perception. The present statement then would harmonize with the later statement, although the later itself is not wholly justified. See note 12.

5. Or, "correspondence". This necessary 'symmetria' may mean either of two things: a due proportion of heat and cold, each to the other; or a certain correspondence with the object that is to be perceived, i.e., that heat itself, even though it be the element more favourable to knowledge, can know only its 'like'. The context would perhaps seem to favour the first of these alternatives; but

the frequent use of συμμετρία by Theophrastus to indicate an appropriate relation between inner power and outer object supports the second.

6. Students differ greatly in their interpretation of this passage. Diels' translation of the opening clause is: "Denn wie sich der Sinn jedesmal verhält in bezug auf die Mischung seiner vielfach irrenden Organe, so tritt er dem Menschen nahe." (*Vorsokr.* I, 163.) Burnet renders πολυπλάγκτων, "flexible" in his 1st edit. (p. 188), "erring" in the 2nd (p. 202). The closing words of the quotation —τὸ γὰρ πλέον ἐστὶ νόημα are translated by Diels, "Denn das Mehrere ist der Gedanke"; by Burnet (p. 202), "For their thought is that of which there is more in them." Zeller (*Ph. d. Gr.* I, 579 f., note) takes πλέον as rightly interpreted by Theophrastus to mean τὸ ὑπερβάλλον, '*das mehrere,*' in which, as we have just seen, Diels follows him.

Professor Taylor translates the verses as follows: "For just as thought at any time finds the mixture in their erring organs, so does it come to men. For it is the same thing which thinks in all men and every man, viz., the substance of the organs, for their thought is that of which there is more in them." And he adds: "My reason for taking πολυπλάγκτων to mean 'erring' rather than 'flexible' is that the metaphor of 'wandering' is Orphic, the thought being that the soul is a fallen deity who keeps missing the way back to her heavenly home, and it has long been recognized that the mise-en-scène and vocabulary of Parmenides' poem are largely Orphic. Also since Parmenides thought sense-perception illusory, the sense 'erring' is more to the point."

After some hesitation, however, I have thought it perhaps well to keep, by the term "far-wandering", the more vivid metaphor of the original.

7. Perhaps it should be said that Parmenides fails to make any clear *distinction* between sensation and thought. For unless Theophrastus had some other evidence than is

Notes on the Translation and Text

to be found in the verses just quoted, Parmenides certainly does not *assert* their identity. In fact he elsewhere assumes their difference. See, e.g., Fr. 1, ll. 33 ff. (*Vorsokr.* I, 150 f.); and cf. *Ph. d. Gr.* I, 580 n.

8. Diels (*Dox.* 499 n.) understands this passage to mean, rather, that remembering and forgetting arise from the mixture of *sense and understanding*. But if sense and understanding are treated by Parmenides as identical,—which Theophrastus has just asserted,—how could he well explain anything by a 'mixture' of *them*? That the mixture is of heat and cold, is held—and justly, one must think,—by Philippson (p. 89). Similarly Karsten (*Philos. Graec. Vet. Op.* I, 267) supplements τούτων in this passage by (τῶν στοιχείων). (See *Dox.* 499 n. 24.)

9. Or, possibly, "the state of thought".

10. Namely, *cold*. So Philippson and Diels. The passage has been taken, quite unwarrantably, to mean a perception by opposition (so Fairbanks: *First Philosophers of Greece*, 107). But Theophrastus expressly says (§1) that Parmenides' principle is that of similarity; and moreover, the thought that perception can also occur by reason of opposition is irreconcilable with the substance of the present context, where it is asserted that the cold and silent corpse can perceive only cold and silence (i.e., 'similars').

11. The account which Theophrastus gives of Plato's doctrine of sense perception seems to be drawn exclusively from the *Timaeus*. Succeeding notes will call attention to the more particular passages which he may have had in mind.

12. It should be borne in mind that Theophrastus divides his present work into two distinct parts: the first (§§ 1–58)—dealing with the perceptive processes, physiological and psychological,—which he calls in the opening line of § 1, περὶ αἰσθήσεως; and the second (§§ 59–91)—dealing with the external objects and stimuli of perception—which he calls, in the opening line of § 59, περὶ τῶν

αἰσθητῶν. In § 6 and again in § 60, Theophrastus clearly recognizes that Plato dealt with the objects and stimuli of each and all the senses. We may consequently understand him to be speaking here of only that portion of Plato's doctrine which dealt with the inner, the psychological and physiological, aspect of perception. Yet with even this silent limitation of Theophrastus's statement, we can hardly justify it; nor its counterpart in § 6,—the statement that Plato tells us nothing of smell, taste, and touch. See *Timaeus*, especially 61 D–62 C, and 65 C–67 A.

13. The use of ὄψις, 'vision', for '⟨the organ of⟩ vision' is so frequent that the brackets in this expression—as well as in the corresponding phrase, '⟨the organ of⟩ hearing', for ἀκοή,—will hereafter be omitted.

14. The organ of vision, for Plato (cf. note following), includes in its action an efflux from the eye, as Theophrastus goes on to say. Professor Taylor would prefer here the translation, "having parts (or particles) which fit into the visual stream".

15. The words of Plato which Theophrastus may have had before him, are here set beside those of the present account.

Timaeus 45 B.	THEOPHRASTUS § 5.
τοῦ πυρὸς ὅσον τὸ μὲν κάειν οὐκ ἔσχε, τὸ δὲ παρέχειν φῶς ἥμερον, οἰκεῖον ἑκάστης ἡμέρας, σῶμα ἐμηχανήσαντο γίγνεσθαι. τὸ γὰρ ἐντὸς ἡμῶν ἀδελφὸν ὂν τούτου πῦρ εἰλικρινὲς ἐποίησαν διὰ τῶν ὀμμάτων ῥεῖν, λεῖον καὶ πυκνὸν ὅλον μέν, μάλιστα δὲ τὸ μέσον συμπιλήσαντες τῶν ὀμμάτων, ὥστε τὸ μὲν ἄλλο ὅσον παχύτερον στέγειν πᾶν, τὸ τοιοῦτον δὲ μόνον αὐτὸ καθαρὸν διηθεῖν.	καὶ τὴν μὲν ὄψιν ποιεῖ πυρός

Notes on the Translation and Text

67 C.

... ἃ σύμπαντα μὲν χρόας ἐκαλέσαμεν, φλόγα τῶν σωμάτων ἑκάστων ἀπορρέουσαν, ὄψει σύμμετρα μόρια ἔχουσαν πρὸς αἴσθησιν.

Cf. 67 D and 45 C, D.

(διὸ καὶ τὸ χρῶμα φλόγα τιν' ἀπὸ τῶν σωμάτων σύμμετρα μόρια τῇ ὄψει ἔχουσαν), ὡς ἀπορροῆς τε γινομένης

καὶ δέον συναρμόττειν ἀλλήλοις ἐξιοῦσαν μέχρι τινὸς συμφύεσθαι τῇ ἀπορροῇ καὶ οὕτως ὁρᾶν ἡμᾶς.

From the wording it seems improbable that Theophrastus had the passage in *Theaet.* 156 D–E in mind. And if Theophrastus had borne in mind *Republic* 507 C–E, we should not have had his astonishing neglect of *light*, which is so important in Plato's theory of vision.

16. Theophrastus may here refer to the Pythagorean doctrine of an outgoing act of vision, which in mirroring is turned back upon itself (Aët. IV, 14, 3; *Dox.* 405). And the evidence seems fairly strong that Empedocles held the idea that something issued from the eye as well as entered it (Aristotle 437^b 23 ff.; *Vorsokr.* I, 253; cf. Aët. IV, 13, 4, *Dox.* 403). Beare (p. 49 and cf. p. 12) thinks that probably Alcmaeon and the Pythagoreans are here meant; and in Burnet (p. 224), this probability regarding Alcmaeon becomes, on Beare's authority, an actuality. Professor Taylor suggests as the translation here: "those who say that the visual stream impinges on the object" (reading φέρεσθαί ⟨τι⟩).

17. This would clearly refer to Democritus and to the main part, at least, of Empedocles' theory of vision. But if we are wholly to trust Aristotle's interpretation, Empedocles too, like Plato, would stand 'midway', since vision with him also had an outgoing and an incoming process. (See the preceding note; and for Plato, esp. *Timaeus* 45). In what we know of the theories of vision held by Anaxagoras, Clidemus, and Diogenes of Apol-

The Greek Physiological Psychology

Ionia (and even of Alcmaeon, so far as explicit statement goes) there is nothing to make it clear that these men believed in aught but an action from the object to the eye, with no action in the reverse direction.

18. The word φωνή means strictly 'vocal sound', as Beare (p. 106) consistently translates it. But here it seems clearly to be used for sound in general, since no theorist would well assume that the ear fastidiously neglected all sounds save those of the voice. Cf. the use of φωνή and ψόφος discussed in notes 138, 222, and 238.

19. Theophrastus has here kept faithfully many of Plato's own words, while yet dealing somewhat freely with the original.

Timaeus 67 B.	THEOPHRASTUS § 6.
ὅλως μὲν οὖν φωνὴν θῶμεν τὴν δι' ὤτων ὑπ' ἀέρος ἐγκεφάλου τε καὶ αἵματος μέχρι ψυχῆς πληγὴν διαδιδομένην, τὴν δὲ ὑπ' αὐτῆς κίνησιν, ἀπὸ τῆς κεφαλῆς μὲν ἀρχομένην, τελευτῶσαν δὲ περὶ τὴν τοῦ ἥπατος ἕδραν, ἀκοήν.	ἀκοὴν δὲ διὰ τῆς φωνῆς ὁρίζεται· φωνὴν γὰρ εἶναι πληγὴν ὑπ' ἀέρος ἐγκεφάλου καὶ αἵματος δι' ὤτων μέχρι ψυχῆς, τὴν δ' ὑπὸ ταύτης κίνησιν ἀπὸ κεφαλῆς μέχρι ἥπατος ἀκοήν. Cf. the repetition, almost exact, of a part of this in § 85.

In the *Placita* (*Dox.* 406) the air which is important for hearing is spoken of explicitly as *in the head,*—τὸν ἐν τῇ κεφαλῇ ἀέρα.

"You know of course that there has been considerable dispute about the exact way in which Plato meant the definition here referred to to be construed (*Timaeus* 67 B). A note on the point might be in place. There is a good discussion in Cook Wilson's brochure *On the Interpretation of Plato's Timaeus*, p. 99. Of course there is no ambiguity in the version given by Theophrastus, and perhaps his

Notes on the Translation and Text

authority ought to decide the question what the right construction in Plato is." (A. E. T.)

20. For the limitation which must be imposed upon this statement, see note 12; and for its untruth even when so limited, see the *Timaeus*, especially 61 D–62 C, and 65 C–67 A.

21. One feels obliged to translate ὅλως οὐδὲν thus, as does Beare (p. 141), even though such a statement is patently untrue. If we were to understand ὅλως to mean 'in general,' or 'in the nature of a general theory,' the statement is still untrue, although the offence of Theophrastus or of some scribe is then a shade milder.

22. See §§ 83 ff.

23. The term translated here and elsewhere as 'object' often includes what we should call the 'stimulus.' The effluence entering the 'pores' of the sense-organ would hardly be regarded by us as the real object of perception; it is rather the means by which the object is perceived. But while several of these early investigators clearly in thought distinguished the thing perceived and the effluence from that thing, they yet included them both under a common term which can hardly be translated otherwise than as 'object'.

24. "διευτονεῖν is rather more than 'pass through.' It is to keep their τόνος as they go through, or, as Diels puts it, to keep their original impetus, to 'keep on their course with their original velocity,' 'to pass through steadily'". (A. E. T.)

25. The omission of any reference to water at this point in the text of the MSS. has troubled critics. Diels at first (*Dox.* 500) adopted Karsten's ⟨καὶ ὕδωρ⟩ after πῦρ; later (in the text of the *Vorsokr.*) he withdrew this emendation and wrote ⟨ὕδωρ καὶ⟩ after περὶ αὐτό. Since it is so doubtful whether Theophrastus or even Empedocles here mentioned water at all; and, if so, in what precise connection, one might well be inclined to reject both of these conjectures: and so I have done. Fairbanks, using the

The Greek Physiological Psychology

first of them, translates: "What is in the eye is fire and water, and what surrounds it is earth and air." But the words of the text would lend themselves better to the idea that Theophrastus is describing the composition of the eye-ball in both cases, and that the earth and air are not external to the eye, but are constituents of the eye's *tunics* —the sclerotic coat, the cornea, etc. So Beare (14 f.); and cf. Burnet (p. 284 f.). Professor Taylor writes "that by the ἀήρ round the fire in the eye Empedocles means water-vapour, not atmospheric air." This would be an additional reason for leaving the text as the MSS. give it, and not inserting καὶ ὕδωρ or ὕδωρ καὶ, with Diels.

26. A fuller statement, in Empedocles' own words, is to be found in Aristotle *De Sensu* 437^b, where Aristotle also attempts to interpret the passage.

27. This and the doctrine of 'pores', is not, so far as I know, to be traced in Greek thought to an earlier source than Empedocles. Applied to all the senses, it seems to have been his contribution to the general theory of perception.

28. Diels in the *Vorsokr.* inserts after ὁμοίως the words ⟨ἀλλὰ τὰς μὲν ἐκ τῶν ὁμοίων⟩. But there seems no warrant for assuming that Empedocles ever held that some eyes were composed only of 'similars'. Beare's rendering (which is like Wimmer's)—"All eyes are not constituted alike of the contrary elements" (Beare, p. 20)—seems to me more nearly in accord with what we know of Empedocles' doctrine; and I have accordingly preferred not to add Diels' words to the text, but have ventured, at Professor Taylor's suggestion, to enclose τὰς δ' in brackets, these words seeming an obstacle to the probable meaning.

29. That is (as I understand it) not outside the eye, but less confined to its centre, while still within the eye-ball.

30. There is difficulty at this point, due to over-compression in the style, or possibly to confusion in the thought itself. Difference in power of vision seems to be

Notes on the Translation and Text

attributed (1) to a difference of *position* of the fire in the eye; some eyes are with fire at their centre, while with others it is less central, although in all eyes the fire is enclosed in 'earth and air'; and (2), when contrasting day-vision with night-vision, to a difference of *quantity* of fire in the eyes, although one is not clear in what respect the amount of fire possessed by animals with night-vision is greater;—greater than is found in animals with day-vision, or greater than the amount of water in their own eyes. Beare (p. 20) takes the latter view. But the fact that the best vision, according to Empedocles, is when fire and water are present in equal measure, makes it probable that the meaning here is 'less fire than is present in eyes with night-vision'; i.e., for day-vision there is an advantage in having the eye's fire somewhat diminished, if yet it does not fall below the point where it is equal to the water—this being the optimal proportion.

Alternatives 1 and 2 given above in this note might after all be reduced to identity, if we were to consider that the *position* of the fire might be a 'function' of its *amount*: that if there is more of fire it is less confined to the centre of the eye; but in more nearly filling the eye, it naturally will lie nearer its surface. Professor Taylor writes: "Your explanation of what is meant by the 'more' or 'less' of fire I believe to be the natural and obvious one. I understand the process thus. In the animals whose eyes contain less than a certain amount of fire, extra fire from the sun makes its way in by day, but at night this extra supply is not available. So they see better by day than they do by night (not necessarily better than other animals do by day). Those which have less than a certain proportion of water, on the other hand, can receive a fresh supply of dark mist or vapour from outside at night; hence they discern things better by night than by day, because it is by the water in the eye that we see the dark hues of things."

31. I.e., 'water'.

32. "Empedocles means, I suppose, that *all* animals

are more or less dazed by brilliant light, even those that have an excess of fire in the eye. The point, I think is that from his general theory that 'like is known by like' you would suppose that in the sunlight, when colours are brightest, the more fire an animal had in its eye the better it could see the 'bright' things around it. But this is not so, for the sunlight gets into the eye and chokes up the pores so that the water in the eye by which the darker colours are seen is unable to do its work and the animal is just blinded and dazzled by light, and the more easily the greater amount of fire, as compared with water, it already had in its eye." (A. E. T.)

33. ἕως ἂν ... ἀποκριθῇ τὸ ὕδωρ: "'until the water is isolated' (or 'cut off') or 'intercepted'—i.e., until its 'passages' are occupied by the fire. It does not cease to be there but is rendered inactive by the stopping up of the πόροι through which it would otherwise issue forth and be operative." (A. E. T.) This in objection to my thought that ἀποκριθῇ here might mean "separated and expelled".

34. One might expect him here to say 'water' instead of 'air'; but Theophrastus's report seems entirely clear upon this point (cf. § 14). Diels feels that ἀήρ is here used in its epic sense; and Beare (p. 20 n.) likewise understands ἀήρ here to mean 'moist air'; and cf. Burnet, p. 284 n.

35. Or, "⟨the ears⟩." The reading of the MSS. here is ἔξωθεν,—by sounds *external* to the head, or ears.

36. It is doubtful whether Empedocles had in mind the concha or something more within. Cf. Beare, pp. 95 f. I have inclined to the belief that he is here speaking of the concha (for which the expression σάρκινον ὄζον would seem to be appropriate) acting as the *bell* of a trumpet, rather than as a trumpet entire (*Phil. d. Gr.* I, 860), or as a bell in the usual sense (Aët. IV, 16, 1), or as a 'gong' (Beare, 95). The form of the description in § 21, however makes one less certain that the concha is meant; it may well be that Empedocles had in mind some bell-like or

Notes on the Translation and Text

trumpet-like portion of the ear less external,—perhaps the ampullae, which with some portion of their conjoined 'canals' might suggest a twisted trumpet with its 'bell.' The objection raised by Diels that the trumpet-shape of the outer-ear would do for sounds *issuing from* the head, but not for sounds *entering*, does not seem to me weighty; for Empedocles may have had in mind some general resonant function of the concha, irrespective of the direction in which the sound was travelling. A 'gong' or 'bell,' however, would be open to the objection that it gives forth but one predominant pitch when struck, (although Beare, 96 n., would have κώδων to resound 'sympathetically') whereas the MSS. text implies that Empedocles was thinking of a form that repeats *various* sounds that come to it; and this the 'bell' of a trumpet actually does. Those who interpret κώδων as 'gong' or as 'bell' in its simpler sense therefore feel drawn to change ἴσων to ἔσω (so Schneider, followed by Philippson, by Beare, and by Burnet). The rendering I have hesitatingly given seems to provide reasonably for the two distinct operations in Theophrastus's account, namely, that of the 'bell' and that of the sound in the solid parts. This more internal sound seems to be the final and essential operation, to which the action of the 'bell' is but preliminary.

"I think you are right about κώδων as meaning the 'bell of a trumpet'; you might refer to Sophocles, *Ajax* 17, for this sense, χαλκοστόμου κώδωνος ὡς Τυρσηνικῆς. But I feel sure that κώδωνα τῶν ἴ σ ω ν ἤχων must be corrupt. I do not see how ἴσος by itself could mean *gleichgestimmt* (Diels), or 'of equal period with,' which I take to be the meaning rather obscurely conveyed by your rendering. This would, I think, require some such word as ἰσ‹οταχ›ῶν. (Unless it is, after all, a mistake for ἔσω, written first εἴσω and then ἴσω.)" (A. E. T.)

37. Diels' translation is: "Denn aus ihnen (*den Elementen*) ist alles passlich zusammengefügt und durch sie denken, freuen und ärgern sie sich."

The Greek Physiological Psychology

38. Cf. Diels, *Vorsokr.* 261 (Fr. 105) and *Dox.* 582, 15 (Plut. *Stromat.* 10).

39. "ἀραιὸν here may refer to the individual parcel of earth, fire, or what not, so that the sense would be 'loose and rare', or 'apart and rare'? (Of course either μανὸν or ἀραιὸν by itself means 'thin', 'rare' as opposed to πυκνόν, but it is at least possible that Theophrastus means to mention *two* defects, (1) too great a distance between the different 'elements' in the organ, (2) undue 'thinness' in the layer of one of these elements itself. E.g. in the eye the fire may (1) not be near enough to the water surrounding it, or (2) may not itself be as compact as it should be. Of course (2) involves the existence of empty space, but Aristotle has pointed out that the whole theory of πόροι is affected by confusion on this very point (*de Generatione* 326^b 6.)" (A. E. T.)

40. The contrast is (1) between intelligence and stupidity, and (2) between inertness and impulsive energy,—the one contrast being in the intellectual and sensory region; the other, in that of action. We have here, so far as I know, our earliest record of a theory of temperament.

41. Cf. Burnet, pp. 284 ff., where §§ 7-11 will be found translated; his rendering gives in some places a different meaning from that here offered.

42. The later portion of this paragraph, with its assertion of the identity, for Empedocles, of sense perception, mixture, and growth, would indicate that Theophrastus is here thinking of the difference not merely between the organic and the inorganic, but of (*a*) creatures endowed with *sentience*, (*b*) creatures marked by *growth*, but not sentient, and (*c*) lifeless things which undergo *mixture* and increase, but neither grow nor are sentient.

43. Or, possibly, "have an advantage over".

44. The 'asymmetria' of the mixture, here spoken of, might mean that the two elements, fire and water, are not present in the eye in equal measure. But it is far more probable that it means a proportion of these elements that

Notes on the Translation and Text

is ill-adapted to the special situation—as, e.g., a surplus of internal light in the eye by day, since now the internal fire becomes still more excessive by supplement from the light without. See § 8.

45. There would be no excuse in fact or in logic for saying that creatures would perceive 'everything'. I have understood πάντων in the indefinite sense of 'all manner of things'.

46. Philippson emends the text here by changing αἴσθησις to ἀναισθησία. This seems reasonable if Empedocles meant that *both* likeness and contact were indispensable for the sensory process; for then there would be no propriety in saying, as Theophrastus does, that mere contact would be sufficient to cause perception. But if we keep the text of the MSS., Theophrastus seems to be saying that Empedocles explains sense perception in two ways—by likeness and by contact; and that in the latter case to have the particles of the stimulus merely *touch* the sensory passages, without exactly 'fitting' them, should be enough.

47. The word συμμετρία, here translated "commensurateness", I have felt unable to render throughout by any single word. The English word "symmetry", which others have used for it, does not seem to me happy. In contrast with τὸ ὅμοιον, which stands for likeness of *quality*, it represents here a *spatial* correspondence; and so I have expressed it when translating ἀσυμμετρίαν just below. Elsewhere in the present translation "proportion" has occasionally been used.

48. In some respects this statement might seem overdrawn. For at least in the case of vision, Empedocles seems to assume that the effluence *is* qualitatively like the passages into which it 'fits',—the effluence from dark objects fitting into the passages of water; from light objects, into the passages of fire. (See § 7.) Yet one might well doubt whether Empedocles meant that all 'dark' objects gave off effluences composed literally of *water*.

The Greek Physiological Psychology

49. I.e., with his general theory; since in the case of pain Empedocles' principle of similarity is abandoned.

50. *Vorsokr.* I, 234. The context of these two verses in the larger fragment shows that Empedocles is describing Hatred, as opposed to Love, and is here saying nothing directly of pleasure and pain.

51. Diels (*Dox.* 504, n. 4; in *Vorsokr.* I, 219, he has become doubtful on this point;) understands that in ποιοῦσι there is a reference to Anaxagoras (named a few lines below) and to Empedocles. It seems less strained, however, to make this verb refer vaguely to any who hold this view, i.e., to Empedocles and those in agreement with him. " As a grammatical point, the subject to ποιοῦσι cannot be 'the views of Empedocles'. If Theophrastus had meant this he would have said ποιεῖ with Ἐμπεδοκλῆς as the implied subject. I should conjecture that the 'they' who are the subject are 'those who hold views like Empedocles's'', which would virtually mean the Italian and Sicilian medical schools. I hardly think Diels can be right in seeing a reference to Anaxagoras, who has not been named since § 1." (A. E. T.)

52. I had translated σύμφυτα "things cognate"; and upon this Professor Taylor writes: "τὰ σύμφυτα seems to mean things which are grown together, which coalesce in their growth. The only other usual meaning of the word, 'inbred', 'innate', is not appropriate here. For the sense 'cognate' Liddell and Scott only give two references. The first is Plato, *Phaedrus* 246 A, where the soul is compared to a σύμφυτος δύναμις ὑποπτέρου ζεύγους τε καὶ ἡνιόχου. Here the sense is, I think, *not* that the winged horses and the driver are 'cognate' but that they are 'grown together', make as it were *one* animal. (Cf. *Republic* 588 D, σύναπτε τοίνυν αὐτὰ εἰς ἓν τρία ὄντα, ὥστε πῃ συμπεφυκέναι ἀλλήλοις which, I think, makes the meaning of the word in the *Phaedrus* passage certain.) Stallbaum correctly renders the word in Latin by *concretus*, and Stewart, in his *Myths of Plato*, seems to mean the same, as he translates 'composite'.

Notes on the Translation and Text

And it is clearly right. The other passage is Plato, *Philebus* 16 C, where 'all things that are ever said to be' are said to have πέρας καὶ ἀπειρίαν ἐν αὑτοῖς σύμφυτον. The editors explain here that the word means 'innate', 'intrinsic', though I think the former sense 'grown together', '*fused* into one' would be quite possible, but the ἐν αὑτοῖς is perhaps in favour of the accepted view. The sense could not be 'cognate' as Limit and Unlimitedness are *not* cognate but opposed. Thus the evidence for σύμφυτος in the sense of 'cognate' vanishes, and we must regard it as created by the inadvertence of lexicographers. The real point is that if kindred things cause pleasure by *contact*, pleasure ought to be keenest where you have one thing actually coalescing in growth with another, because contact is then most complete. Thus, to take an illustration from Plato's theory of vision, vision takes place when two kindred things, the fire issuing from the eye and fire without us, are fused into one; therefore if pleasure is due to contact of like with like, the act of vision ought to be always intensely pleasurable. Theophrastus adds that universally *sensation* should also be keenest in the case of such coalescence, because according to Empedocles pleasure and sensation have the same cause—the contact of like with like. It would thus follow that the intensity of the sensation and the intensity of the pleasantness should go together, sensation should always be pleasant and the more intense sensation should be the more pleasant. That this is the argument is shown by the consideration he goes on to urge against it."

53. See § 10; and, later, § 23.

54. See § 8. Beare (p. 22), following more precisely the Greek wording, translates thus: "It is moreover a strange doctrine that some eyes", etc. But since it was a patent *fact*, even in ancient times, that eyes differ in this way, the absurdity must lie, not in stating this, but in the peculiar explanation offered. I have therefore interpreted the Greek as compactly intending this. "As to the words,

The Greek Physiological Psychology

the verb ἀποδίδωσι is understood from the beginning of § 16. 'His explanation of pleasure and pain is inconsistent. ... And odd, too, is his explanation of the fact that.'" (A. E. T.)

55. Instead of being supplemented, as Empedocles' theory assumes to be the case in the eye.

56. The supplement coming perhaps from the surrounding element. The white object is by day bathed in light, and this supplements and intensifies the object's action upon the eye; and *mutatis mutandis*, the dark object, by night.

57. Which is partly in agreement with Empedocles' own doctrine that superior vision by night is due to a greater proportion of fire in the interior of the eye. Cf. §8.

58. We have here not the usual word (χρῶμα) for colour, but a term (χρόα) that occasionally and earlier meant 'surface'; and I had, in order to suggest this ambiguity, translated it "surface or colour". Professor Taylor is convinced that it cannot mean 'surface' here. "In *Aristotle* the word *never* means anything but 'colour'; he notes in *De Sensu* c. 3 that the *Pythagoreans* used the word to mean 'surface'. This shows that it was not used in that sense in ordinary Attic, or he would not have needed to explain the meaning. In Ionic poetry it means 'skin', but I can find no evidence that it ever meant 'surface' except in the language of the Pythagoreans mentioned by Aristotle, who, of course, wrote Ionic. Theophrastus certainly uses the word here in the common Attic sense 'colour'. This is the more appropriate since his argument is that one and the same explanation accounts for the fact that some creatures' *eyes* see best at night, and that some colours (*colour* is according to him and Aristotle *the* specific object discerned by the eye) glow in the dark. Hence on every ground the alternative 'surface' must be wrong." (A. E. T.)

But since Theophrastus did not write the usual term for colour here, may it not have been his purpose, in avoid-

Notes on the Translation and Text

ing the more common and definite term, to avoid the implication that in looking at phosphorescent objects in the dark we saw their proper *colour* (χρῶμα)—a position which Aristotle himself explicitly denies (*De Anim.* 419ª 6)?

59. Beare (p. 23) understands this to refer to the apparent luminosity of *eyes* by night. Yet it seems well not to exclude the thought of phosphorescent objects, and accordingly I have made my translation more general.

60. Referring to the Empedoclean doctrine stated at the end of § 8, that the best eyes are those in which fire and water are present in equal quantity.

61. Or, "if either ⟨element⟩ in excess hinders vision."

62. That is, even under the most favourable conditions —where the fire and water of the eye are of equal quantity—the ocular fire would by day be so augmented by the external light that dark objects could not be seen; and by night the 'dark' element would be so increased that all light objects would become invisible. And consequently even such eyes would in the end have no advantage over eyes that had a preponderance of fire or of water; for these, too, have their peculiar virtues—the 'fiery' eyes for seeing dark objects, the 'watery' eyes for seeing things that are bright.

63. Or, "it is commonly held".

64. The meaning of this troublesome passage is variously given by others. Beare (p. 136) translates it: "But if wasting is a consequence of emanation from a substance (and Empedocles uses this very fact of the wasting of things as the most general proof of his theory of emanation) and if it is true that odours result from such emanation", etc. Philippson's version is: "Dein si interitus effluvio, quo signo utimur vulgarissimo, fit, atque accidit, ut odores effluvio fiant", etc. Wimmer, omitting after σημείῳ the comma and the words συμβαίνει δὲ, gives, "Dein si effluvium sequitur deminutio, idque ut certissimum affert argumentum quod odores quoque effluvio fiunt", etc. "The meaning is 'and

The Greek Physiological Psychology

he uses this as the most universal *presumption in favour of his theory.*' A σημεῖον in the technical logical language of Aristotle is anything which affords a *presumption* in favour of a given conclusion. (*Analyt. Pr.* II, c. 27.)" (A. E. T.)

65. Referring to the friendship or 'love', which with 'hate' is such an important factor in the Empedoclean philosophy. "'In the period of Love', i.e., the period of the world cycle in which 'Love'—the attraction of *unlike* elements toward each other—has the mastery and everything is being brought together in one compact spherical mass." (A. E. T.)

66. One would hardly expect such a concession; but Theophrastus possibly is thinking that the attractive force, even though dominant, might not utterly exclude repulsion, or 'hate', and some effluence sufficient to cause a faint or occasional perception might still occur.

67. Cf. Aristotle *De Sensu* 444.

68. Or "sick"; in either case there might be more rapid or more deep breathing.

69. Or "volatile".

70. Aristotle is explicit in his statement that Empedocles did so hold (*De Anima* 427ᵃ 21). The presence of γάρ here in Theophrastus makes the translation unsatisfactory. Various emendations have been suggested: Diels originally proposed εἴπερ instead of εἰ γάρ; Usener, εἴ γ' ἀπὸ; Schneider εἰ διὰ; etc. Diels finally returns to the reading given in the body of the text above.

71. Or, so far as the mere wording indicates, "all things"; and there is evidence that Empedocles held this more general view. See Fr. 110, 1. 10 (*Vorsokr.* I, 263); Fr. 103 (*Vorsokr.* I, 260).

72. As is the blood; and the fact, namely that the blood contained all the elements in perfect mixture, seemed to Empedocles the warrant for supposing that the blood was best constituted to know the rest of the world. See § 10.

Notes on the Translation and Text

73. Poppelreuter (*Zur Psychologie des Aristoteles, Theophrast, Strato*, 39) takes this clause as stating Theophrastus's own belief that the μορφή (in the sense of ἀρχή) of the organ explains its psychic capacity. I prefer to think that Theophrastus simply means that the structure of the organ would better account for special talent than would the blood in the organ; but without in the least committing himself to this 'structure' theory.

74. That is, that the form of the organ certainly affects the power to use the organ.

75. Keeping the emendation adopted in the *Dox*. In the *Vorsokr.* Diels returns to μόνον of the MSS.

76. The principle of the resonator seems here to be intended, suggested perhaps by listening to shells. Whether Alcmaeon's mode of explanation in this respect is wholly different from Empedocles', depends upon our interpretation of the troublesome word κώδωνα in § 9. If this means a bell in the ordinary sense, then Empedocles and Alcmaeon stand on quite different ground; but far less so if the word was intended to mean the bell of a trumpet, a transmitter and resonator. Beare (p. 93) has translated the present passage in a somewhat different way from mine.

77. Beare (p. 93 n.) takes κοίλῳ to mean "the external meatus with the apparatus in general by which the vibrations of the outer air are caught and conducted inwards toward the tympanum"; and he holds that κενόν, which he translates 'vacuum', apparently = ὁ ἀήρ, since Aristotle (419ᵇ 33) seems to regard the air as 'empty'. Philippson, in despair, suggests that τὼ κόχλω was originally written here, where now we have τῷ κοίλῳ. In the text above, the punctuation of the *Dox.* has been kept; in the *Vorsokr.* it is ἠχεῖν (φθέγγεσθαι δὲ τῷ κοίλῳ), κ.τ.λ.

78. This possibly means the water that bathes the eye; or it would perhaps be no great injustice to τοῦ πέριξ ὕδατος if we were to understand it to refer to the 'humours' enclosing the ocular 'fire'. Beare (p. 11)

The Greek Physiological Psychology

translates here: "the eyes see through the environing water". "The πέριξ ὕδωρ, I take it, is entirely outside the eye. It means the 'water' (or as we should call it the 'atmosphere') all around us." (A. E. T.)

79. Or "Vision is due to the gleaming and transparent character", etc.

"I think that in τῷ στίλβοντι καὶ διαφανεῖ, καὶ has the very common meaning of 'i.e.', 'that is to say'. Alcmaeon probably used only the word στίλβον, which in later Greek was mostly used of the 'gleaming' or 'glossy' look of such things as oil, though it was also, as Beare seems to forget, regular of the stars in the sense of 'twinkling'; hence Theophrastus explains the word by giving its technical Aristotelian equivalent, 'i.e., the diaphanous'. There is no reason to suppose, as Beare does, that *Alcmaeon* used the word διαφανεῖ." (A. E. T.)

One is tempted to read, and if necessary to emend, this passage so that Alcmaeon would be describing not only the eye-ball, but also certain *external* conditions important for vision—namely the 'gleaming' (i.e., light) and the 'transparent' (i.e., a medium, such as the air). That the recognition of the importance of light, of which Plato later made so much, would not be an anachronism is evident in the fact that Anaxagoras recognized it (§ 27). Plato's view, that there are *three* indispensable *external* factors in vision, would then be the result of a gradual and orderly gathering and development of suggestions given by several of the ablest of his predecessors.

80. Beare's objection (p. 13 n.) that a *purely* transparent substance does not *reflect* an image, has not prevented the use of 'transparent' instead of 'diaphanous' in translating the present passage. Transparent substances certainly reflect from their surfaces.

81. Retaining the pointing of the *Dox.* In the *Vorsokr.* the period after ὁμοίου becomes a comma.

82. The meaning seems to waver between the idea of a reflected *image*, such as we have in a mirror, and that of a

Notes on the Translation and Text

reflection without an image, as when the colour of a flower held close to a less perfect surface, like that of the cheek, is 'reflected' there.

83. Beare (p. 38) translates: "but this image is not reflected in a part of the pupil of like colour with the object, but in one of a different colour." This would imply that the pupil, for Anaxagoras, had different colours in the same eye, and that the object had to depend upon reaching some portion of the pupil where there was a colour suitable to reflect it. But this seems to me to violate the simple meaning of this and the final sentence of this section. Anaxagoras apparently is speaking of the general principle of reflection,—namely, that objects are always reflected in those of a colour 'opposite' to their own, and especially of 'weaker' colours. The visually effective portion of the eye, for him, is of the colour of *night* (§§ 37, 27); and there is nothing to indicate that he believed each pupil to be particoloured, with provision accordingly for reflecting in its different parts objects of different hue.

84. Beare takes this passage as referring not only to different parts of the pupil, as has been said in the preceding note, but also to Anaxagoras's doctrine that any colour contains every other, although one colour may be predominant. Only this *predominant* colour is reflected in the pupil, is his interpretation of this sentence, which he translates (p. 38): "But (whether by night or by day) the colour which predominates in the object seen is, when reflected, made to fall on the part of the eye which is of the opposite colour." I have taken what I venture to regard as a far simpler and more natural view of this passage: that Theophrastus is here stating what in §37 he restates as Anaxagoras's teaching, that *colours are reflected in one another*, but particularly the *strong* in the *weak*.

85. I.e., by opposition, or contrast.

86. I.e., according to Beare (p. 103) following Wachtler, the bone which encloses the *brain*. With this interpretation Professor Taylor agrees.

The Greek Physiological Psychology

87. Cf. § 17.

88. Namely, that perception is due to *opposition*.

89. Beare (p. 209) seems to take the words τοῦ χρόνου πλήθει as referring here to the effects of time *and age* in *dulling* sense. Theophrastus in this passage seems to me, however, to keep to *pain* rather than to the blunting of sensibility, and to have in mind the easily observed effect of persistent stimulation in which *mere time*, mere persistence, makes an otherwise moderate stimulation painful.

90. Professor Taylor here gives as the translation, "And we cannot *attend long* to the same things". I have thought it possible, however, that οὐ δύνασθαι ἐπιμένειν—the impossibility of 'staying' upon the same objects,—here indicated not so much the impossibility of keeping the attention long upon an object, as the impossibility of standing, or enduring, an unchanging object from the sheer *pain* of it, especially if it be intense. An impossibility in the field of attention would not, I feel, so well illustrate the universal presence of pain, with which this portion of the section is concerned.

91. With Beare (p. 108) I understand the meaning here to be, that such eyes see large objects and also see distant objects (μεγάλα τε καὶ πόρρωθεν); and not as Fairbanks takes it, large objects that are at the same time distant. And similarly of τῶν μικρῶν καὶ τῶν ἐγγύς, at the opening of § 30.

92. There is, of course, a decided difference between 'loud' sounds and 'distant' sounds, and between faint sounds and those near by; since distant sounds are often faint, and loud sounds come from objects at hand. And similarly of 'large' and 'distant' objects for sight: distant objects are small, relative to the eye; and, were the present theory consistent, should be visible only to the smaller animals. It is conceivable, however, that Anaxagoras thought of the distant object as sending a more scattered, a more expansive, stimulus, and consequently as coming to us somewhat after the manner of a large object. In the case of vision, but not of hearing, the more distant object

Notes on the Translation and Text

might have been supposed to require a larger organ, since a greater power out-streaming from the eye might be needed to reach to the greater distance.

93. I have retained τὸ πυκνὸν and αὐτὸ τὸ μανὸν of the MSS., and have rejected the emendations τὸν πυκνὸν and αὐτὸν τὸν μανὸν of the *Vorsokr*. This change by Diels, who has the closing words of §35 in mind, and has made the two passages conform, seems to be based on the assumption that Anaxagoras has only *air* in mind, whereas it seems to me possible that he thought of the air but also of some odorous substance *in* the air and distinguishable from it. In any event the thought of Anaxagoras is illogical, as Theophrastus points out in §35. His idea is less unreasonable, however, if it be that, *as the air rarefies, the odour becomes more dense* or thick, since in §35 such air is said to be more odorous (cf. also §30). A small animal, according to his theory, would then inhale only the air and would almost wholly lose the odour. But even so, the closing sentence of the section,—that large animals would perceive no subtile odour—hardly follows.

Upon my retention of the neuter forms, with the idea that Anaxagoras may possibly have thought of 'the dense' and 'the subtile' here as not wholly and always identical with the air, Professor Taylor thus passes sentence: "I venture to think that you are finding a nonexistent refinement of meaning in what is probably a mere transcriber's error".

94. Adopting, with Beare (p. 138 n.) Philippson's change of ἀέρος to ὀσμῆς.

95. See §29 and §2.

96. Adopting Usener's ἔστι for ἐκ.

97. Cf. *De Caus. Pl.* I, 16, 11: "She [i.e., Nature] is ever pressing on toward what is best."—'Η δ' ἀεὶ πρὸς τὸ βέλτιστον ὁρμᾷ.

98. The meaning is, that they each satisfy a natural need —namely, of acquaintance with truth or fact; and that

since they stand in this like relation to needs that, while distinguishable, yet have a common character, we should expect the two satisfactions to show a like relation to pleasure and pain.

Professor Taylor writes: "The meaning is 'For each bears the same relation to its own employment (or exercise)'. τὴν αὐτὴν χρείαν, if sound, would of course mean 'to the *same* employment', but this does not give the requisite sense. Diels gets it by *understanding* αὐτοῦ after τὴν αὐτὴν but I would suggest that the text should be emended to τὴν αὐτοῦ χρείαν. The meaning is, 'as thought is to its exercise, so is sensation to *its* exercise'. But the exercise of thought is pleasant, ergo, by analogy, the exercise of sensation should normally be pleasant. I do not see how craving for knowledge and craving for sense-stimulation can be called 'the same craving', and if they were the same, the analogy would surely lack one of its required four terms."

99. Or perhaps the meaning is specific—"excess ⟨of the stimulation⟩" which has just been mentioned as evidence that perception is painful.

100. Or perhaps merely "in a word"; so Beare. Cf. § 29.

101. Such an assertion, namely, as that sensory acuity is dependent upon size. Professor Taylor interprets the passage otherwise. "I think εἰ ἄρα καὶ δεῖ λέγειν οὕτως is not, as you make it, an indirect question, but a conditional clause. The whole will mean 'As I have said, there might be a doubt about *this* point [viz. whether it would follow from Anaxagoras's statements that large animals should have keener senses than small ones, or vice versa], even if it were right to maintain such a view (i.e., even if it were right to connect variations in sensibility with variations in size, there would be a doubt whether sensibility varied directly or inversely as size). [But, the suppressed thought is, it is wrong to connect sensibility with size at all.] For in analogous cases, etc.'" (A. E. T.)

Notes on the Translation and Text

102. That is to say, the actual external movements, distances, and sizes are not *accurately reproduced* in the image; for it would be idle to say that these external features produce nothing corresponding to them in the reflection. Theophrastus has just said that in the image the objects have a size, and he might well have said that in this image they also show movement and separation. By διάστημα I hardly believe that Theophrastus meant exclusively the 'third dimension', or what is now known in psychology as visual 'depth', of which Berkeley had so much to say, and which, it is true, is not represented even inadequately in the visual image. More probably he meant the intervals between objects in general, their separation from one another, as distinguished from their size.

103. As already noted, this seems to me a restatement of the thought in the last sentence of § 27, and to be an obstacle to Beare's rendering of that passage.

104. Because, according to Anaxagoras, sight is due to reflection; and since reflection here is reciprocal, there would on each side be all that is needed for vision. Yet because the 'weaker' colours reflect better, they especially would have visual power. Beare (p. 39) translates μέλαν as black *eye*, and understands the meaning of the passage to be that black eyes should see better; and, apparently, that Theophrastus is continuing the *exposition* of Anaxagoras's doctrine. I have understood it, rather, to be a *criticism*, showing to what absurdity the doctrine would lead, inasmuch as the colour would see me as really as I the colour. The passage seems to me to continue the idea presented at the close of the preceding section, where Theophrastus points out that, upon Anaxagoras's principle, water and polished metal and any other lifeless thing that *reflects* ought also to *see*. Here he but develops the same thought that since, for Anaxagoras, all colours reflect one another, they should all have the power to see.

105. And that, consequently, we see best by day, since vision depends upon opposition.

The Greek Physiological Psychology

106. And yet—to fill out his meaning—we *see* them. Beare (p. 39 n.) who feels that the passage as it stands in the text "makes no sense", has supplied ἀλλά or καίτοι before οὐκ ἔχει, and gives this translation: "we see black colours just as well as white, though the former do not contain light". One may well feel discouragement, but not despair, over the passage as it stands. For if we understand the term "lack light" to mean that they are not what we call *luminous* bodies, like the sun, or a blazing fire, then white objects are as devoid of light as are black objects; they have no *intrinsic* light. And since we see them when, to careless observation, there is no light bathing them, Anaxagoras's idea that light is a cause (or a *contributing* cause, § 27) of vision is refuted.

"I think the text may be defended, οὐκ ἔχει φῶς meaning simply 'are not themselves luminous'. I can see the white colour of this paper and the blue-black of the writing on it, but the light by which I see both is external to both: it is the light of the sun. But the structure of the sentence certainly suggests that a special point is being made of our ability to see black. Hence the proposal to insert καίτοι is very attractive, and I don't feel sure that Beare is not right." (A. E. T.)

107. There seems to be nothing for ὅσπερ ἐλέχθη to refer to save the opening sentence of § 36 (which reproduces with some change the statement in § 27), wherein the same expression κοινή ... δόξα appears in a general designation of Anaxagoras's account of vision. The statements that seeing is by reflection and that vision is of fire, seem thus to have served equally well to mark the "traditional view" as it lay in Theophrastus's mind, and which Anaxagoras is declared to have adopted "to a certain extent". So far as 'fire' is concerned, the nearest approach to a recognition of its importance by Anaxagoras seems to be found in his assertion that light is a cause or a contributing cause of visual reflection (§§ 27, 37). And Anaxagoras's failure to give greater importance to fire or to use

Notes on the Translation and Text

it in a more suitable way (since Theophrastus rejects the idea that light is absolutely necessary to vision) seems to be the ground here of a half-hearted criticism.

108. One hesitates to do violence to the text here, although the 'alone' contradicts what has just been said by Theophrastus regarding Anaxagoras. And furthermore Clidemus's claim to originality in assuming that the *transparency* of the eye is the cause of vision—unless the whole emphasis is to be laid upon the *exclusive* importance of transparency—would have to be shared with Alcmaeon, who explained vision by "what is gleaming,—that is to say, the transparent" (§ 26). The difficulty is avoidable either by dropping μόνος from the text (cf. *Dox.* 510, n. 4), or by emending it to μόνης, after the analogy of μόνου in § 20, line 5.

109. Or "suppleness", as Professor Taylor suggests.

110. Cf. Arist. *De Gen. et Corr.* 322^b 12, to which Diels refers.

111. "The word ἄθρους only means 'in a body', and implies nothing as to rarity or density." (A. E. T.) By Beare the word is translated "compact". The statement in the present section seems to me not too easy to reconcile with the statement in § 41, that smell is keenest in those who have *least* air; and in § 42, that what is true of vision is true of the other ⟨senses⟩, namely, that it is keenest when the air and the ducts are λεπταί.

112. The word φλεβία might be translated "blood-vessels and ducts".

113. The mere words here would permit one to read "the brain", but this seems less attractive. The massing or crowding of the cephalic air was said a few lines before to be important for its functioning; an opposite condition, rarefaction, is now said to be unfavourable. The brain itself could not so readily be conceived as too rarefied to perceive odour. Diels (*Vorsokr.* I, 419) suggests as a possible reading here: φλεβία λεπτά, τὸν δ' ἐν οἷς ⟨ἂν⟩ ἡ δ. ἀ. ᾗ οὐ μείγνυσθαι. In the text adopted by him, he places

an interrogation mark in square brackets after καὶ; in the *Dox.* he had suggested ὡς for καὶ.

114. The meaning here is obscure, and the text is probably corrupt. Perhaps the thought is, that the 'cephalic air' serves as an intermediary between odour and brain, which already by its lightness and fineness is almost adapted to receive odour. This 'air' which is like odour because of its density, is also enough like the brain in consistency to transmit odours to it, and thus the difference, otherwise too great, is bridged.

Beare (p. 140) believes that the MSS. text, which I have retained, cannot stand—and Professor Taylor agrees with him in this—because "Diogenes could not have said that the air or the brain is λεπτότατον in those whose sense of smell is defective, for according to him the greater the thinness of air in the brain, and the greater the fineness of its ducts, the more excellent is the faculty of smelling".

But I think there is no contradiction between the assertion of the MSS. here and the other evidence which we have as to Diogenes' theory of smell. At the opening of § 42 he says of vision, that it is keenest where the internal air and the ducts are λεπταί, and that this is true of the other senses. There is nothing in this to preclude the idea that the internal air might upon occasion become *too* attenuated for keen smelling; that is to say, it is far from justifying the assertion that according to Diogenes "the greater the thinness of air in the brain ... the more excellent is the faculty of smelling" (Beare, p. 140 n.). Specifically the conditions of such excellence are stated in § 41 to be (*a*) an exceptionally small quantity of cephalic air, and (*b*) exceptionally long narrow passages. And aside from Theophrastus, the ancient authorities are silent as to Diogenes' theory of smell.

115. I.e., the pupil.

116. The suggestion that for μακροτέρου of the MSS. we should read μικροτέρου, which Beare (p. 141) after Diels (*Vorsokr.* I, 420) adopts, does not appear to me happy. If

Notes on the Translation and Text

'small' refers to the diameter, as Beare takes it, nothing is added to στενοτέρου; if it refers to the length, it seems no more likely than its opposite to be regarded as an aid to keen smell. For it is possible that long narrow passages might have been regarded as distributing the inhalation more widely or thoroughly in the cephalic air. Professor Taylor, however, is inclined to think that the shorter passage would be considered as of greater aid to the needed mingling.

117. φλέβες can well mean the larger passages (in contrast with the πόροι of the sensory organs) not merely for the blood but for the air; and, in the case of the tongue, for blood, air, and even food (cf. §§ 41, 42, and esp. 43). In this particular passage the φλέβες might include even the more internal windings and passages of the ear, as well as the veins proper.

118. The text here is in a desperate state, and no one's emendations seem wholly satisfactory. I have adopted Philippson's substitution of καὶ τὸ περὶ for καθάπερ, and have rejected Diels' substitution (*Vorsokr.* I, 420), accepted by Beare (p. 105), of ὀσφρήσει for αἰσθήσει, because in the case of smell the one thing needful was that the passage to the seat of sense should *not* be short, but *long and narrow* (see above, § 41). The 'passage here is doubtless the meatus.

119. While black eyes are here set in contrast to bright objects (λαμπρά) and are declared to be keener by day, yet the exceedingly bright eye (λαμπρότατον) is declared a moment before to be keenest in general. But in describing the eye the term means lustrous and brilliantly reflecting, as is the case with dark eyes; whereas in describing objects here it seems to denote luminous or dazzling objects, which would naturally be well reflected in a dark eye.

120. Compare with this the evidence adduced in the Brihadâranyaka-Upanishad, 1, 5, 3, that intelligence (*Manas*) is necessary to the action of the senses.

The Greek Physiological Psychology

121. Beare (p. 169, n. 3; p. 170, n. 1) suggests that Theophrastus may have misunderstood the word ἡδονή, used by Diogenes and Anaxagoras and Heraclitus for mere taste or smell.

122. For the comma which Diels has after εἶναι, I have substituted a colon.

123. For light on this passage, see Arist. *Problemat.* 964ᵃ 4, to which Diels refers.

124. See the opening line of § 39.

125. "It should be indicated somehow that the word used for moisture ἰκμάς is Ionic and its presence shows that there is an echo of Diogenes's own words, just as there is in the *Clouds* of Aristophanes where Socrates is made to say that he hangs himself up in the basket to prevent the ἰκμάς from getting at his thought and spoiling it." (A. E. T.)

126. Philippson understands the subject here to be πνεῦμα; and, with a change of ἄφρον into ἀφρόν, translates the passage, "ipsum autem spumam esse". The meaning seems to be, rather, that the air which—if it could only permeate the body,—would make the bird intelligent, is used up in the digestive process. Compare with this the account below (§ 45) of the collecting of air in the chest, in young children.

127. This troublesome passage Philippson tries to unsnarl by transferring the closing clause οὐ γὰρ κ.τ.λ. (striking out ἀλλήλων) so that it follows upon ἄφρον εἶναι. Diels' index (*Dox.* p. 676ᵃ), when referring to this line, gives "(bestias) inter se intellegere nequire". In rendering the passage as it stands, one must feel that it is almost too discerning in so naïve a psychology to declare that vocal difficulties—instead of merely expressing or leaving unexpressed a mental inferiority already there—are an important *cause* of mental inferiority.

128. Beare (p. 259) believes that the thought is still upon children, and that the words here refer to *their* forgetfulness and lack of understanding. I have thought

Notes on the Translation and Text

that the meaning is more general, since the "proof" directly given is not peculiar to children.

129. Diels (*Dox.* 512, n. 24) understands *animalia* here. But I take it that Theophrastus has now dropped the subject of distinguishing men from animals and is passing on to the difficulty, created by Diogenes' doctrine, of distinguishing the function of different parts of the one body. This becomes clearer in the closing sentence of § 47. "As to the meaning of πάντα, I should have supposed that it means 'everything whatever', since nothing is quite impervious to air. But I don't think it *demonstrable* that either Diels's translation or yours is wrong." (A. E. T.)

130. Referring probably to the failure of the air to permeate the body.

131. See § 44.

132. Diels has a period after κενόν; and says: "post φρονεῖν Theophrasti refutatio intercidisse videtur".

133. In the *Vorsokr.* Diels without explanation reads μεστὰ for ἔτι of the MSS.,—the meaning then being, "provided the tissues are *full of* thick oily moisture". But it seems to me difficult to believe that thick oily moisture would have been regarded by Democritus as *furthering* the entrance of these tenuous air-prints.

134. In the lists that have come down to us, we do not find precisely this title, περὶ τῶν εἰδῶν, among Democritus's works; but we do find περὶ εἰδώλων and περὶ ἰδεῶν. (See *Vorsokr.* II, 20, 59, 60.)

135. For example, objects concealed in a mist. And possibly Theophrastus has in mind objects concealed by other bodies. If *air* can come from behind an opaque object, or around a corner,—he perhaps is thinking—why then do not the air-prints likewise?

136. Because cool air, being more compact, would better take an impression; and it ought better to preserve both the new impressions and the older impressions made in the day. The word ἔμψυχος may mean 'animate' (ἐν,

ψυχή) or 'cold' (ἐν, ψῦχος). The comparative in either case would, as Professor Taylor has pointed out to me, regularly be ἐμψυχότερος, and Wimmer's change of the MSS. ἐμψυχότερος to ἐμψυχρότερος, which Diels adopted in the *Dox.* but rejected in the *Vorsokr.*, is quite uncalled for. The word is therefore ambiguous in form, but here it seems to me clearly to mean 'cooler'. For Theophrastus is discussing the *preservation of air-prints* at night, and the presence of more 'soul-atoms' in the air would hardly contribute to this, whereas coolness would. Upon this point I have felt compelled to differ from the judgment expressed by Beare (p. 28 n.). "And—though this is not finally decisive,—ἔμψυχρος would be etymologically a false formation." (A. E. T.)

137. In view of the statement in § 57—ὥσπερ οὐ ταῖς ἀκοαῖς κ.τ.λ.—this sentence is puzzling. Beare (p. 101), seeing the conflict between the two, takes the statement in §57 to be due to an oversight by Theophrastus. But it seems to me probable that the assertion in §57 is correct, since it agrees with what has been said immediately before the present sentence in §55, that sound penetrates the entire body although the chief avenue for sound is the ear. It also is analogous to Democritus's treatment of *vision*, as set forth in §54, where visual perception is ascribed not to the eyes only but to the entire body. It would therefore seem probable that in the present sentence the text is corrupt, and that Theophrastus originally asserted something very different,—namely, that we perceive with the rest of the body, and *not* solely with the ears.

Dr. Taylor, however, does not believe that the text here is at fault. He makes the important suggestion that Democritus seems to be merely denying any rôle in hearing to currents of air which make their way into other parts of the body without going through the ears; for it is mentioned as a distinct point that 'sound' which has once entered by the ears is then distributed all over the body. "It would be possible to deny that sound which

Notes on the Translation and Text

got in by some other channel plays any part in sensation," he goes on to say, "and yet hold that sound which, having got in at the ears, has been transmitted to other parts does play the same sort of rôle which he seems to have assigned to reflections transmitted from the eye to the rest of the body. Whether this actually reproduces Democritus's thought I do not know, but it would make the whole theory consistent."

138. Upon the distinction between φωνή and ψόφος, Professor Taylor cites *De Anima* 420^{b}5–421^b as giving what both Aristotle and Theophrastus meant by these two terms, and writes: "When φωνή is contrasted with ψόφος it means pretty much 'tone' as contrasted with 'noise'." Yet here (as in the beginning of §6 and of §21) it seems hardly probable that such a contrast is intended, since almost the very idea expressed by φωνήν near the end of §55 and beyond the middle of §56 seems to be repeated a few lines from the beginning of §57, where now ψόφον is substituted. If we think of 'sound' as the general term, under which there are two species, 'noise' and 'tone', then it would seem that occasionally either φωνή or ψόφος is used by Theophrastus as a general term for all 'sounds', and yet again as a specific term for 'tone' and 'noise' respectively. Cf. notes 18, 222, and 238.

139. Compare with this the idea held by Democritus that for sight also the air is compressed and stamped, and the importance which Diogenes ascribes to air in sense perception generally. The thought that the sharpness of the impressed form gave to us the distinctness of the speech we hear seems strengthened by what is said below in §56.

140. Beare (p. 100) takes this to be "the membranous covering of the inner surface of the concha", and not the tympanum, because 'density' in this would probably have been regarded as an obstruction to the entrance of the air.

141. "Democritus means, no doubt, the cavity of the

skull which, on his theory, would contain the 'internal air' (or? less likely, the pia and dura mater)." (A. E. T.)

142. Upon this passage, which I had been inclined to interpret after the manner of Mullach, who understands that the subject of action is 'Democritus' rather than 'the body' (see Beare 101, n.), Professor Taylor writes: "I do not think the subject to ποιεῖ is Δημόκριτος; I think it is τὸ σῶμα. I do not see how it could be any argument against Democritus' view that the whole body is affected in hearing to say that this is true of all the other psychical functions. If anything this would tend to confirm his theory. Clearly the meaning is 'For it [the whole body] does *that much* (τοῦτό γε) [i.e., 'is affected somehow' by the special sensory process] equally in all sensation, and not only in sensation but in all mental life'. The observation is a comment of Theophrastus' own. He means that there is a general 'bodily resonance' accompanying all mental processes, but this does not prove that the whole body is the organ of sight or hearing, etc. He adds the point that the resonance occurs 'not only in sensation but in the mental life (generally)', because he, like Aristotle, holds that there is one function of the soul which has no 'organ' or bodily process connected with it—viz. 'pure' thought. His argument is, even in 'pure thought' which depends on no organ and no *specific* 'neurosis' (as we should say) whatever, there is always an accompanying 'bodily thrill', ergo *a fortiori* you cannot argue that because such a 'thrill' accompanies hearing, the whole body is the organ of hearing. By taking ποιεῖ to mean '*Democritus* makes', you miss the whole point of the argument. Beare has got the point right in his free rendering (p. 101 of his book)."

143. "What Anaxagoras meant by 'aether' is 'fire'." (A. E. T.)

144. One might be tempted to translate the words as, rather, "Anaxagoras merely mentions the colours"; but

Notes on the Translation and Text

from other sources we know that this is hardly true. See, e.g., Sext. VII, 90 (*Vorsokr.* I, 409); Fr. 4 (*Vorsokr.* I, 401, 10 ff.); Schol. in Gregor. XXXVI 911 Migne (*Vorsokr.* I, 403, 21 f.). And for other evidence see Beare, 40. Possibly some statement of *what* Anaxagoras said, following directly upon the words περὶ αὐτῶν, has been lost from the text.

145. And yet Theophrastus later subjects each of these authors to a searching criticism. Probably his thought is, that he regards himself here as an expounder and critic of these authors, rather than as an independent expounder of the full truth about sensory objects.

I have kept ποτέρως of the MSS. and of the *Dox.*, which in the *Vorsokr.* is changed to ποτέρων.

Professor Taylor writes: "The sense seems to be 'it cannot be the subject of argument' (or? 'of the argument'). This, I should imagine, means either (*a*) 'cannot be a disputed question', because Plato is so clearly right (according to the doctrine of Aristotle and Theophrastus), or (*b*) 'is not the question we are now discussing' (as, in fact, it isn't). The former version seems to me closer to the actual words, the latter to fit the context better. I have consulted Professor Burnet. Neither of us can make any grammar of ποτέρων ἔχει τἀληθές if it is more than a misprint, and neither can find any parallel which would make it clear what οὐκ ἂν εἴη λόγος means. There is clearly *something* wrong with the text, but I do not think the error lies in ποτέρως."

146. Instead of being open to solid objection on the ground of confusion or inconsistency at this particular point, Democritus moves in the two directions taken generally by modern physical science. For he reduces what we are accustomed to call the 'secondary' qualities to effects in us, even as does Locke, while at least some of the 'primary' qualities (namely size, shape, and motion; but not weight) still have their seat in the external object. See Aët. I, 12, 6 (*Dox.* 311); I, 3, 18 (*Dox.* 285).

The Greek Physiological Psychology

147. In the *Vorsokr.* Diels has τὴν φύσιν [κρίσιν?] ἔχειν, influenced by Preller. See *Dox.* 516, n. 27. I have omitted the bracketed and queried κρίσιν. In the *Dox.* he had changed σταθμὸν of the MSS. to σταθμοῦ, and had suggested τινὰ φύσιν for τὴν φύσιν.

"The words mean that *something* (whatever we read as the subject of ἔχειν) has its standard or measure in the *bulk* of the atom. Diels evidently does not understand what φύσις could mean in this connection, so he suggests κρίσιν, 'our *judgment* would have the bulk of the atoms as its standard',—i.e., we should judge the bulkier also to be always the heavier. I think φύσις is right and the sense is 'the *atom* would have its standard (sc. of weight) in its bulk'. But that is because *I* think Burnet is right in holding that φύσις in the Pre-Socratics means 'real' or 'primary' *body*." (A. E. T.)

148. I.e., of the atomic complex; for there is no evidence that Democritus's theory admitted a change in the form of *the atom*. With this passage and what immediately follows, cf. § 65, where heating is described as a production of 'void' in the object; and also the account in the *Physic. Opinion.* of Theophrastus, Fr. 13 (*Dox.* 491).

149. That is, causes in us a more intense sensation.

150. Cf. the closing lines of § 67.

151. "I think you should explain in a note", writes Professor Taylor regarding this section and § 66, "that σχήματα all through this passage means just 'atoms'. Democritus also called them by the equivalent name ἰδέαι or εἴδη. This is important because both σχῆμα and εἶδος are terms from Pythagorean geometry, meaning originally 'regular figures'. The use of them proves the historic descent of atomism from the 'Italian' philosophies."

The reader will be aware, however, that Professor Taylor would not have the meaning 'atom' apply in the phrase τὸ σχῆμα μεταπῖπτον in § 63, where τὸ σχῆμα is used for the 'figure' in which the atoms are *combined*. Save for

Notes on the Translation and Text

this passage in § 63, I have translated the term σχῆμα by "figure"; and by the use of "shape" and "form", ordinarily for μορφή and εἶδος respectively, I have tried to indicate these changes of expression. But the transition from σχῆμα to μορφή in several of the passages that follow indicates that at least in Theophrastus's mind the expressions might upon occasion be interchanged, even for the "atom".

152. Cf. §§ 63 ff. for farther facts regarding Democritus's conception of heat and cold.

153. The meaning here is unsatisfactory; but the form of ἄλλους makes any other rendering seem forced.

154. I think it possible that, here and six lines below, the true word is ἰσοσκελῶν instead of οὐ σκαληνῶν, since ἰσοσκελῶν is used by Theophrastus in his exposition of Democritus's doctrine, in *De Caus. Pl.* 6, 1, 6.

155. As in the briny scum on liquids; but the thought may also include the coming of salt-crystals upon the surface of solid bodies.

156. Keeping περιπλάττεσθαι of the MSS., instead of Diels' emendation περιπαλάττεσθαι.

157. The combination of 'round' and 'angular', which is puzzling, was perhaps pictured as a form more or less globular, set with sharp, straight projections; this almost incompatible union arising from the desire to combine the extreme mobility associated with the sphere, with the roughness of what is angular; since a *biting* taste, as for example that of horse-radish, is at once volatile, penetrating, and hot. Beare here has: "small, spherical, and regular, but not scalene". "Regular", it would seem, must here be but a misprint or other slip for "angular", the Greek being γωνιοειδῆ. "If you think of such a figure as an icosahedron, I think you will see what 'round and angular' means." (A. E. T.)

158. "That is, it διαχεῖ. We have been told this already of 'the round', in dealing with sweetness (§ 65). It is here

added that the angular διαχεῖ as well as the round.' (A. E. T.)

159. Cf. the end of §63.

160. Cf. the close of §61 and §62.

161. Diels has thought it necessary to insert ⟨διορίσαι⟩ after τὰ ἄλλα. As for the meaning of τοῖς σχήμασιν here, it seems to me probable, in the light of §63, that it is used to cover both (*a*) the 'figures' of the particular atoms, and (*b*) the 'configurations' of the atomic aggregations.

162. "τὸ αὐτὸ refers to the sensation, τῶν αὐτῶν to its *cause*. The point is, that Democritus tries to establish a definite doctrine about the physical cause, say, of the sensation *sweet*; but to assume that there is just one such physical cause for it and that we can know what this cause is is inconsistent with the sceptical reflection which Theophrastus goes on to quote from Democritus. ἀλήθεια as usual in fifth or fourth century Greek means rather 'reality', 'the real state of the facts', than 'truth' in the subjective modern sense." (A. E. T.)

163. "κατὰ φύσιν γὰρ μᾶλλον only means that the better and healthier organism is more 'normal' than the inferior and diseased. Theophrastus' reason for saying this is, of course, that like Aristotle he means by the φύσις, or real character of a thing, that which the thing is when at its best." (A. E. T.)

164. "ἡ φύσις τοῦ πικροῦ is virtually identical in meaning with τὸ πικρόν." (A. E. T.) The repetition of φύσις at the close of the section, however, is evidently with reference back to φύσις here.

165. "κατ' ἀλήθειαν means 'as a real objective fact'." (A. E. T.)

166. The learned have given various interpretations of this passage. It has been taken to mean that 'the small' or 'the bitter' (μικροῦ of the MSS., emended to πικροῦ by Schneider, who is followed by Diels) or 'the dead' (νεκροῦ, by Philippson) possesses or possess some share of under-

Notes on the Translation and Text

standing. Diels in the *Dox.* translates it *nominatim autem de amaro nos habere notitiam convenientem.* The index to the *Dox.* cites the passage with the phrase: *de amaro judicium idoneum ferri posse.*

"πικροῦ must clearly be right as against μικροῦ (or the *absurd* νεκροῦ) because the whole point is that Theophrastus holds that Democritus said something which could be taken to mean, that our apprehension of some *sensible quality* is more or less 'intelligent', i.e., gives insight into objective fact, and that this is inconsistent with his more universal denial that secondary qualities are 'real'. The 'small' can't illustrate the point because *size* was really a primary character of atoms themselves according to Democritus, and thus with the reading μικροῦ you don't get the inconsistency on which Theophrastus wishes to insist." (A. E. T.) "I think it is clear why Democritus thought that our sensation of 'the sharp' has an element of objectivity. He meant that we actually seem to sense the contracting of the pores in the tongue and palate when we taste τὸ πικρὸν, and it is this contraction which is the real fact underlying the sensation." (A. E. T.)

167. "τῆς πικρᾶς οὐσίας is a mere paraphrase for τὸ πικρόν, like Plato's τὸ τοῦ σώματος εἶδος for the body simply." (A. E. T.)

168. "The allusion is to the famous passage in which Democritus says of various secondary qualities that they only exist νόμῳ. τὸ πικρὸν is one of those mentioned, νόμῳ γλυκὺ καὶ νόμῳ πικρόν. This, says Theophrastus, amounts to saying that bitterness is *purely* subjective, but if it corresponds, as Democritus says, to a specific atom it *can't* be purely subjective. The reference (Diels *Fragmente* Demokritos B 9) ought to be given in a note, or the reader may miss it." (A. E. T.)

169. For farther criticism by Theophrastus of Democritus's theory of tastes see *De Caus. Pl.* 6, 1, 6 ff.

170. Cf. §§ 61 and 62.

171. Literally, "have the same impulse of locomotion".

The Greek Physiological Psychology

"He seems to mean that if a heavy atom and a light one *only* differ in size and in no other way, both should have a tendency to move in *the same direction* (whereas Aristotle and Theophrastus held that 'light' things tend to move upwards, but 'heavy' things downwards. Compare the similar criticism in Aristotle *de Caelo* 303^b 4-8, referred to by Diels in his note to this passage in *Dox.* 520)." (A. E. T.)

172. "δύναμις in this section clearly means (as it does in various passages of the Hippocratean Corpus) the 'effect' produced on our organism by things—i.e., a sense-quality, in contrast with the cause of that quality, which, on Democritus' theory, is the size or shape, etc., of certain atoms. These qualities are called δυνάμεις because they are the ways in which things affect or work on us. (See my *Varia Socratica*, p. 231)." (A. E. T.)

173. The context makes it reasonably clear that he is forcing home his criticism that the sensory process is a reaction of organ to stimulus, and cannot be explained by the character of the stimulus alone, but only by the relation which this bears to the reagent, namely the sense-organ, whose special constitution also we must therefore take into our account. We are helped by the passage in the *De Odor.* 64, where Theophrastus says: Τί δή ποτε Δημόκριτος τοὺς μὲν χυμοὺς πρὸς τὴν γεῦσιν ἀποδίδωσι τὰς δ' ὀσμὰς καὶ τὰς χρόας οὐκ ὁμοίως πρὸς τὰς ὑποκειμένας αἰσθήσεις; ἔδει γὰρ ἐκ τῶν σχημάτων.

174. Taste is here regarded by Theophrastus as a species of touch, and he argues for a uniform treatment of all the senses in the common class. Diels says of τὰ περὶ γεῦσιν "non sana sunt", suggesting instead of the text as it stands, τὰ περὶ γεῦσιν δηλῶσαι. ταῦτα γὰρ [sc. τὰ διὰ τῆς ἁφῆς]—which seems to me well to fit the general movement of the argument here. And yet ταῦτα, instead of referring to the qualities given us by touch, may refer to those given by taste (τὰ περὶ γεῦσιν), and Theophrastus be really clamouring to have the distinction recognized

Notes on the Translation and Text

between the gustatory qualities as we actually experience them and the external 'juices' (χυλούς) which arouse such qualities within us.

175. Beare (p. 31) suggests that a quincuncial arrangement of atoms here is intended. Professor Taylor writes: "The whole clause means 'obliquely inclined in their position relative to one another and in their combination in pairs'. I can't say that the description is very clear even with Beare's note. If you draw the cross-section to which he refers you get this pattern repeated indefinitely. I see at once what is meant by the obliquity θέσει, but not so clearly what is the obliquity in their 'conjunction in pairs' unless all that is meant is that no atom has another immediately vertically above or below it in the diagram, but this merely repeats the sense of λοξῶν τῇ θέσει πρὸς ἄλληλα. 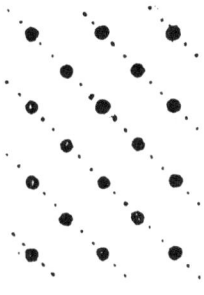 If the section of the atom were an ellipse instead of a circle, I could understand. For Democritus might mean that no two ellipses which are in the same 'row' of the diagram have a common axis, even though their centres lie on the same straight line. But I presume we have not sufficient evidence to *interpret* him in detail."

176. Beare's translation here is (p. 32), "owing to the intervention of the air". I had wondered whether the Greek might not mean "the retention of the air", in the sense of a retention *by* the air. But Professor Taylor does not think this interpretation possible; he believes the expression ἐναπόληψις means the 'intercepting' of small quantities of air between the atoms of the ἀπορροή.

177. This is the more obvious translation of συγκρίσεις, which Beare gives and which Professor Taylor is fairly sure is the meaning here. But there is to my mind something wrong in this region, and the context makes us expect a word that would permit one to translate it "components". For the present sentence in the trans-

The Greek Physiological Psychology

lation seems to me to give no satisfactory reason for the preceding sentence, as it pretends to do; since the preceding sentence asserts that the atoms causing "red" and the atoms causing "heat" are alike except in so far as those of "red" are *larger*. And then to *explain* this, we are told that "red" can be produced by atoms that are "*the same*" as those of heat but are gathered merely into larger "aggregations". This difficulty would of course be relieved by supposing that ὁμοίων here means "similar", in the sense that the atoms are alike merely in shape and are different in size. But the sense of συγκρίσεις near the end of § 76, where it seems to mean "increment" or "component", but which Diels apparently feels is not its meaning here, indicates a certain vagueness or variability in the use of that word.

Kranz (*Hermes*, vol. 47, p. 132 n.), for the reference to whom I am indebted to Professor Burnet through Dr. Taylor, makes the important suggestion that instead of μᾶλλον ἐρυθρὸν εἶναι we read μᾶλλον θερμὸν εἶναι, since the proof that this is also *red* does not begin until the next sentence. This emendation would meet the difficulty I have mentioned of properly relating the second sentence to the first sentence of this section.

178. The comparison expressed in μᾶλλον seems to me not to be of one degree of red with another, but of 'red' with 'hot'; difference in degree of redness is taken up a few lines below, when we come to ἐρυθρότερα. Beare's translation (p. 32), "for a hot thing is redder the larger the aggregations", etc., takes the thought otherwise. Kranz's emendation, stated in the preceding note, would give the meaning that merely larger *aggregations* of such particles would give *heat* rather than *redness*.

179. Or, "such ⟨aggregations⟩"?

180. Beare translates: "Coals of wood whether green or dry"; and I had translated the passage in the same sense, until Professor Taylor gave a far more satisfactory interpretation. "It is much more natural", he writes, "to

Notes on the Translation and Text

take ἤ here as comparative, 'than', especially as for 'whether green or dry' one would expect ξύλων εἴτε χλωρῶν εἴτε αὔων. αὖος by the way is an Ionic and definitely non-Attic word (the Attic for it is ξηρός). Hence it is probably quoted from Democritus." This I have accordingly indicated in the Greek text.

That there was clearly recognized in later times the problem why the flame from green wood is redder than the flame from dry wood, is shown in *De Igne* 31: Διὰ τοῦτο γὰρ καὶ ἡ τῶν χλωρῶν ἐρυθροτέρα φλὸξ ἢ τῶν ξηρῶν, κ.τ.λ.; and this supports, if support were needed, Professor Taylor's interpretation.

181. This, as an account of heat, is somewhat different from that found in § 65, where heat is attributed, not to subtilty of atomic constitution, but to the presence of empty space among the atoms. It would seem from these passages that Democritus's full explanation of heat involved both factors—the size of the atoms, and the amount of void.

182. The 'black' which Democritus was familiar with, doubtless in observing the mixture of pigments by artists, must have been a blue-black, to give the effect described here and later. "Democritus would also get his notion of black from strong shadows and from the look of objects at night—also blue-blacks." (A. E. T.) "μέλαν nicht nur reines schwarz, sondern jede dunkle Farbe bezeichnet, besonders Dunkelblau" (Kranz, *Hermes* 47, 135; he does not believe, however, that Democritus was guided, in his theory, by an actual mixing of pigments).

183. It seems to me likely that these are but the closing words of the account of some other mixtures, in which perhaps yellow more prominently figured; and I have accordingly ventured to indicate a hiatus in the Greek text.

Both Mullach and Burchard supposed some omission after πορφυροειδοῦς; while Prantl (p. 55) would transpose

the whole clause τὸ γὰρ θεῖον ... λαμπροῦ to a position immediately after ἐνῇ in the closing line of § 77.

Kranz, quoting Goethe upon the greenish hue of sulphur, seems to accept sulphur as properly exemplifying the mixture of golden green and purplish (*Hermes* vol. 47, p. 135).

184. See § 75.

185. Indigo is said to show a copper-violet lustre when rubbed. It is to this aspect that Democritus is perhaps attempting to do justice. No such 'sharpness' is ascribed to plain black. See § 74.

186. The text in the *Vorsokr.* is ἐὰν δὲ χλωρὸν ‹καὶ λευκὸν› μειχθῇ, φλογοειδὲς γίνεσθαι· τὸ γὰρ ἄσκιον καὶ μελανόχρων ἐξείργεσθαι. In the text of the *Dox.* an omission had been indicated before χλωρὸν; ‹καὶ λευκὸν› does not appear; and in the notes τῷ γὰρ ἀσκίῳ τὸ μ.ἐ. is suggested for τὸ γὰρ ἄσκιον καὶ μ.ἐ. I have adopted this suggestion; and for Schneider's addition of πλέον after χλωρὸν I have substituted πλέον τοῦ χλωροῦ, after the analogy of the expression τῶν δὲ πλέον near the close of this section. I have, in this, assumed that, in Democritus's theory, golden green is shadowless and that enough of it could 'expel', or compensate, the black in indigo. This seems to me a less violent solution than is obtained by Diels in introducing ‹καὶ λευκὸν›.

187. But in § 76, Democritus is reported as holding that red and white make golden, copper-colour, etc.! That the same combination can also be thought by the same writer to make *green* appears highly improbable; for it seems to me improbable, even apart from the mere inconsistency, that any one should derive green from a mingling of red and write. Yet in this Professor Taylor holds otherwise: "I think Democritus really meant to say that red and white make green, and that his reason may have been that he had seen a green after-image of red on a white background and supposed the effect to be due to a mixing of the original red (which by his theories should

Notes on the Translation and Text

be reflected from the background) with the white of the background." (A. E. T.)

188. The μέλαν which I had thought might be translated 'dark', is troublesome. The text as it stands seems to imply, as Professor Taylor points out, that some one is being contradicted who had maintained that white plus red yields black. "This is a strange theory, and I can't discover that any one *had* said so." (A. E. T.) Nor does Professor Burnet, whom he has consulted, know of any such theory. "He agrees with me that if this reading (that of the MS.) is sound, it can only mean 'white mixed with red does not give black, but gives a lustrous pale green', and that μέλαν χλωρόν would be an unheard-of phrase for dark green." (A. E. T.) Professor Taylor suggests that μέλαν may be the remains of μελανόχρων; "red and white make a bright, and not darkish, green". Kranz (see note 177), interpreting this passage, understands μέλαν as 'dark' and to mean a 'dark green': "Beinahe aber, heisst es weiter, ergebe auch *Rot* mit Weiss gemischt lichtes Gelbgrün (χλωρὸν εὐαγές) und nicht dunkles (μέλαν)". (*Hermes* 47, 136.) By the σχεδόν in this passage, Kranz understands that the bright yellow-green can not be produced perfectly (*nicht vollkommen*) by the mixture, but can be attained only approximately. Professor Taylor would prefer to translate it "in general" or "generally", as being the common Aristotelian usage.

189. Kranz (*Hermes* 47, 132) understands this to mean that the bright yellow-green of spring vegetation under the decomposing influence of the heat, passes gradually over into a darker green.

190. See § 73.

191. Or, "crenellated", as Professor Taylor suggests.

192. Keeping the reading of the *Dox.* In the *Vorsokr.* μιγνυμένας of the MSS. is restored, with the comment that it is "nicht verständlich".

193. Arist. *De Gen. Anim.* 785ᵃ 21, to which Diels, following Usener, here refers, does not clear up the meaning.

The Greek Physiological Psychology

Whether the thought is that some animals turn black if placed in shadow or if so turned that parts of their own surface cast shadows on other parts, is not clear from the statement. It is difficult to see what facts would justify either meaning.

194. Theophrastus's thought here being, that the *straightness* or *broken direction* of the minute passages in the object could not possibly be preserved in the atomic emanation which, according to Democritus's theory, is the immediate cause of the sensation, and which gives the sensation its peculiar quality.

195. And such an emanation from the 'void' would seem to be assumed in the explanation of green, of which a main constituent is 'the void' (§ 75). Professor Taylor believes that Theophrastus has in view more than Democritus's theory of green; since "the same difficulty really arises in any other case the moment you are asked to explain *why* the arrangement of pores in an efflux need be the same as that in the body from which it emanates". (A. E. T.)

196. "ἐπιπρόσθησις is strictly a technical term of astronomy, 'occultation'. This might be indicated by using that word here. The body causing the occultation was said to 'run up in front' (ἐπιπροσθεῖν) of the body occulted. I suppose it is a racing metaphor, to 'foul'." (A. E. T.)

197. And therefore black and white are not coördinate, as they seem to be represented in §§ 73 ff. Prantl (p. 181) understands this passage to be a statement of Theophrastus's own doctrine. But the Greek does not require such an interpretation, and the argument seems to move more justly without it.

198. See § 75.

199. This so far as I know is the earliest record of the particular pairing of *red and green* as *opposites*, analogous to the opposition of black and white—a view held to-day by Hering and others.

Notes on the Translation and Text

200. Or "primaries".
201. Or "the primaries".
202. Or "he", i.e., Democritus. But "if ὅδε means Democritus you get, 'if some one could decide which tastes are simple, Democritus would have more to say, i.e., there would be more in what Democritus says'. But why should there be more in what *Democritus* said, merely because *some one* knows which tastes are simple?" (A. E. T.)

203. It is interesting to notice that in the *Timaeus* Plato presents the subjects with which we are most concerned in the following order: (*a*) heat and cold; (*b*) hard and soft; (*c*) light and heavy; (*d*) rough and smooth; (*e*) pleasure and pain; (*f*) taste; (*g*) smell; (*h*) hearing; (*i*) colour. That this order is here preserved by Theophrastus without a single change—this, with the various verbal similarities, makes one almost see Theophrastus at work with the *Timaeus* spread before him.

204. *Timaeus* 61 D, E.

πρῶτον μὲν οὖν ᾗ πῦρ θερμὸν λέγομεν, ἴδωμεν ὧδε σκοποῦντες, τὴν διάκρισιν καὶ τομὴν αὐτοῦ περὶ τὸ σῶμα ἡμῶν γιγνομένην ἐννοηθέντες. ὅτι μὲν γὰρ ὀξύ τι τὸ πάθος, πάντες σχεδὸν αἰσθανόμεθα· τὴν δὲ λεπτότητα τῶν πλευρῶν καὶ γωνιῶν ὀξύτητα τῶν τε μορίων σμικρότητα καὶ τῆς φορᾶς τὸ τάχος, οἷς πᾶσι σφοδρὸν ὂν καὶ τομὸν ὀξέως τὸ προστυχὸν ἀεὶ τέμνει, λογιστέον ἀναμιμνῃσκομένοις τὴν τοῦ σχήματος αὐτοῦ γένεσιν, ὅτι μάλιστα ἐκείνη καὶ οὐκ ἄλλη φύσις διακρί-

THEOPHRASTUS § 83.

Πλάτων δὲ θερμὸν μὲν εἶναί φησι τὸ διακρῖνον δι' ὀξύτητα τῶν γονιῶν.

The Greek Physiological Psychology

νουσα ἡμῶν κατὰ σμικρά τε
τὰ σώματα κερματίζουσα τοῦτο
ὃ νῦν θερμὸν λέγομεν εἰκό-
τως τὸ πάθημα καὶ τοὔνομα
παρέσχεν.

It thus appears that of the *three* factors to which Plato attributes the cutting power of heat,—namely, (*a*) the small size of the particles of fire, (*b*) the sharpness of their angles, or edges, and (*c*) the swiftness of their motion —Theophrastus explicitly mentions but one. In § 87 Theophrastus repeats this inaccuracy.

205. *Timaeus* 62 A, B.

Theophrastus § 83.

τὰ γὰρ δὴ τῶν περὶ τὸ σῶμα ὑγρῶν μεγαλομερέστερα εἰσιόντα, τὰ σμικρότερα ἐξωθοῦντα, εἰς τὰς ἐκείνων οὐ δυνάμενα ἕδρας ἐνδῦναι, συνωθοῦντα ἡμῶν τὸ νοτερόν, ἐξ ἀνωμάλου κεκινημένου τε ἀκίνητον δι' ὁμαλότητα καὶ τὴν σύνωσιν ἀπεργαζόμενα πήγνυσιν· τὸ δὲ παρὰ φύσιν συναγόμενον μάχεται κατὰ φύσιν αὐτὸ ἑαυτὸ εἰς τοὐναντίον ἀπωθοῦν. τῇ δὴ μάχῃ καὶ τῷ σεισμῷ τούτῳ τρόμος καὶ ῥῖγος ἐτέθη, ψυχρόν τε τὸ πάθος ἅπαν τοῦτο καὶ τὸ δρῶν αὐτὸ ἔσχεν ὄνομα.

ψυχρὸν δὲ ὅταν δι' ὑγρότητα ἐκκρίνοντα τὰ ἐλάττω καὶ μὴ δυνάμενα εἰσιέναι τὰ μείζω κύκλῳ περιωθῇ· τῇ γὰρ μάχῃ τρόμον καὶ τὸ πάθει ῥῖγος εἶναι ὄνομα.

"There is a real but trifling inaccuracy in Theophrastus' statement that Plato calls the πάθος, or sensation, ῥῖγος, since Plato says that both τρόμος and ῥῖγος are names of the struggle between the particles and that the πάθος is

Notes on the Translation and Text

called ψυχρόν. Presumably he quotes from memory." (A. E. T.)

206. Theophrastus here makes almost a verbatim transcript of the passage in *Timaeus* 62.

Timaeus 62 B.	THEOPHRASTUS § 83.
σκληρὸν δέ, ὅσοις ἂν ἡμῶν ἡ σὰρξ ὑπείκῃ, μαλακὸν δέ, ὅσα ἂν τῇ σαρκί· πρὸς ἄλληλά τε οὕτως. ὑπείκει δὲ ὅσον ἐπὶ σμικροῦ βαίνει.	σκληρὸν ⟨δὲ⟩, ᾧ ἂν ἡ σὰρξ ὑπείκῃ, μαλακὸν δέ, ὃ ἂν τῇ σαρκί, καὶ πρὸς ἄλληλα ὁμοίως. ὑπείκειν δὲ τὸ μικρὰν ἔχον βάσιν.

207. Cf. §§ 88 f., and *Timaeus* 62 C–63 E, beginning, as does this passage of Theophrastus, with βαρὺ δὲ καὶ κοῦφον.

In summary Plato's theory is as follows. Heavy and light cannot be defined in terms of 'up' and 'down'; for the universe is a sphere, and up and down do not exist in any absolute sense. Any and every outlying part of the universe is, in a sense, 'opposite' to the centre of the universe, and any direction from the centre is either upward or downward, as we may choose to regard it. Nor can we define 'heavy' and 'light' in terms of mass simply, as though a greater mass were always heavier than a smaller. For while a greater mass of earth is always heavier than a smaller, here upon earth, yet a greater mass of fire is lighter. And in the region of fire the very opposite is true.

Leaving now these negative features and moving toward a positive definition, there is, then, a separate region in which each of the simpler substances belongs and to which it tends as to its kindred,—fire to the region of fire, earth to the region of earth—and thither it tends the more strongly the greater is its mass, and resists more strongly any effort to remove it thence. Imagine ourselves now in the region of fire: fire will be 'heavy', because it does not yield readily to our effort to remove it; and earth will

The Greek Physiological Psychology

be 'light' because it offers no resistance; and a greater mass of fire would, in a scale, weigh more than a small amount. But in the region we actually inhabit—that of earth,—earth is 'heavy' and fire is 'light'. Heavy and light, then, are not properties absolute and intrinsic; whether a given kind of body shall be regarded as the one or the other depends on the region in which we take our stand.

208. It is true that Plato says that any one can easily understand them; nevertheless he offers an explanation. See *Timaeus* 63 E–64 A, where roughness is declared to be due to a combination of hardness and irregularity; smoothness, to uniformity and density.

209. *Timaeus* 64 C–E.

τὸ δὴ τῆς ἡδονῆς καὶ λύπης ὧδε δεῖ διανοεῖσθαι· τὸ μὲν παρὰ φύσιν καὶ βίαιον γιγνόμενον ἀθρόον παρ' ἡμῖν πάθος ἀλγεινόν, τὸ δ' εἰς φύσιν ἀπιὸν πάλιν ἀθρόον ἡδύ, τὸ δὲ ἠρέμα καὶ κατὰ σμικρὸν ἀναίσθητον, τὸ δ' ἐναντίον τούτοις ἐναντίως. τὸ δὲ μετ' εὐπετείας γιγνόμενον ἅπαν αἰσθητὸν μὲν ὅτι μάλιστα, λύπης δὲ καὶ ἡδονῆς οὐ μετέχον, οἷον τὰ περὶ τὴν ὄψιν αὐτὴν παθήματα, ... βία γὰρ τὸ πάμπαν οὐκ ἔνι τῇ διακρίσει τε αὐτῆς καὶ συγκρίσει.

Theophrastus § 84.

ἡδὺ δὲ καὶ λυπηρόν, τὸ μὲν εἰς φύσιν ἀθρόον πάθος, τὸ δὲ παρὰ φύσιν καὶ βίᾳ [λυπηρόν], τὰ δὲ μέσα καὶ ἀναίσθητα ἀνὰ λόγον. διὸ καὶ κατὰ τὸ ὁρᾶν οὐκ εἶναι λύπην οὐδ' ἡδονὴν τῇ διακρίσει καὶ συγκρίσει.

To this should be added *Timaeus* 64 A–B, 65 A–B, and also *Timaeus* 81 E, *Philebus* 31 D, 32 E, 42 C–D, 52 C for the chief passages on the more physiological aspects of pleasure and pain.

Notes on the Translation and Text

210. Plato's own account to be compared with this of Theophrastus will be found chiefly in *Timaeus* 59 E-60 B, 60 D-E, and 65 C-66 C.

211. Cf. *Timaeus* 59 E-60 B.

212. Plato himself, however, does not say that there are only four kinds, but rather that only four have *received names*; there are many more, he holds, but they are nameless (*Timaeus* 60 A).

213. Cf. *Timaeus* 65 C-66 C.

Beare (p. 171) gives as a translation here: "while among the affections (πάθεσι) which water undergoes, he places the earthy taste (τὸν γεώδη χυμόν)"—an interpretation which I find difficult to follow, inasmuch as Theophrastus himself does not force it upon us, for he does not say what kind of 'affections' these are; and Plato does not mention an earthy flavour as among the 'affections' of *water*. He has two earthy savours as forms of *earth* (cf. *Timaeus* 60 B, γῆς δὲ εἴδη; and 60 D-E); and when treating of the affections of the *tongue*, he speaks of earthy particles (γήϊνα μέρη, *Timaeus* 65 D). It is probable that Theophrastus had this latter passage in mind; but possibly he intended to refer to the former passage, and instead of ἐν δὲ τοῖς πάθεσι he may have written something like ἐν δὲ τοῖς περὶ γῆς.

214. Here Theophrastus is inexact. For in Plato (*Timaeus* 60 D-E), the earthy taste is in fact two earthy tastes, alkali and salt; and these are given by Plato, not in his account of the organic 'affections' of taste, but in his account of the gustatory 'objects'. It is true that in explaining the affections of taste, Plato (*Timaeus* 65 C-E) speaks of earthy particles which enter the 'veins' and contract and dry them; and, again, of the bitter action of alkali; and this statement, rather than the passage that gave more direct heed to alkali and salt, Theophrastus may have had in mind. It is not improbable that he entirely overlooked the account of alkali and salt.

215. Wimmer marks a break in the text after χυμόν

The Greek Physiological Psychology

Beare translates the phrase thus: "And it is by these particles", with reference in a foot-note to the γήϊνα μέρη of *Timaeus* 65 D. I have taken ταῦτα as referring, vaguely, to the preceding words for the four 'saps' and for the one 'earthy flavour'. It is, however, a rough and careless statement; for it would not be true that Plato, even as reported by Theophrastus, held that each and every savour always coagulated and compacted the organic juices.

216. The text here is uncertain. Instead of χυμούς of the MSS., where Philippson (followed by Beare, 171) reads πόρους, I have read χυλούς. The words συνάγοντα τοὺς χυλοὺς καὶ συγκρίνοντα,—if we understand χυλοὺς to be the fluids contained in the φλέβια,—represent fairly well Plato's συνάγει τὰ φλέβια καὶ ἀποξηραίνει of *Timaeus* 65 D. Yet this particular sentence in Theophrastus is unsatisfactory because in Plato, and in Theophrastus's own account a few lines below, the sweet taste may relax and not contract the tissues.

217. Or "sour", as Professor Taylor here would translate πικρόν.

218. Cf. Beare's translation: "Those particles which are warmed by the heat of the mouth." Theophrastus does not say by what they are heated; and Plato has the pungent not only heated by the mouth, but also *heating* it, as though the pungent had a heat of its own. The less explicit phrase, "filled with heat", therefore seems preferable, since it provides also for this apparently intrinsic fieriness in peppery savours.

219. Cf. *Timaeus* 66 C, where these opposite effects of sweetness are set forth,—its power to relax when there is an unnatural contraction in the tongue, and to contract when there is an unnatural expansion there.

220. The passage upon which Theophrastus must have based his account is found in *Timaeus* 66 D–67 A, of which the following is Mr. Archer-Hind's translation:

"As regards the faculty of the nostrils no classification can be made. For smells are of a half-formed nature: and

Notes on the Translation and Text

no class of figure has the adaptation requisite for producing any smell, but our veins in this part are formed too narrow for earth and water, and too wide for fire and air: for which cause no one ever perceived any smell of these bodies; but smells arise from substances which are being either liquefied or decomposed or dissolved or evaporated: for when water is changing into air and air into water, odours arise in the intermediate condition; and all odours are vapour or mist, mist being the conversion of air into water, and vapour the conversion of water into air; whence all smells are subtler than water and coarser than air. This is proved when any obstacle is placed before the passages of respiration, and then one forcibly inhales the air: for then no smell filters through with it, but the air bereft of all scent alone follows the inhalation. For this reason the complex varieties of odour are unnamed, and are ranked in classes neither numerous nor simple: only two conspicuous kinds are in fact here distinguished, pleasant and unpleasant. The latter roughens and irritates all the cavity of the body that is between the head and the navel; the former soothes this same region and restores it with contentment to its own natural condition."

221. Or "odorous matter", as Professor Taylor suggests.

222. To the word φωνὴν I have given a meaning less restricted than is ascribed to it by Beare (p. 108), who translates it "vocal sound". Beare's rendering would be in keeping, however, with what seems to me a somewhat strained interpretation of the opening of § 91. "In this discussion of Plato's language, the word seems to mean 'tone', since what is said is only strictly applicable to tones as opposed to mere noises, though Plato's own remarks about 'rougher' and 'smoother' sounds (*Timaeus* 67 B) show that *he* was also thinking of noises." (A. E. T.) See also notes 18, 138, and 238.

223. The chief passages in the *Timaeus* with which Theophrastus's account may be compared are here given in Mr. Archer-Hind's translation:

The Greek Physiological Psychology

"Let us in general terms define sound (φωνήν) as a stroke transmitted through the ears by the air and passed through the brain and the blood to the soul; while the motion produced by it, beginning in the head and ending in the region of the liver, is hearing. A rapid motion produces a shrill sound, a slower one a deeper, a regular vibration gives an even and smooth sound, and the opposite a harsh one; if the movement is large, the sound is loud; if otherwise, it is slight." (67 B–C.)

"In the same direction are we to look for the explanation ... of sounds too, which from their swiftness and slowness seem to us shrill or deep, sometimes having no harmony in their movements owing to the irregularity of the vibrations they produce in us, sometimes being harmonious through regularity. For the slower sounds overtake the motions of the first and swifter sounds, when these are already beginning to die away and have become assimilated to the motions which the slower on their arrival impart to them: and on overtaking them they do not produce discord by the intrusion of an alien movement, but adding the commencement of a slower motion, which corresponds to that of the swifter now that the latter is beginning to cease, they form one harmonious sensation by the blending of shrill and deep." (80 A–B.)

224. Cf. § 5, where a somewhat fuller account is given of the *physiological* process of hearing; whereas this passage explains difference of pitch, which is there neglected. The corresponding texts of Plato and of Theophrastus are as follows:

Timaeus 67 B.	Theophrastus § 85.
Τρίτον δὲ αἰσθητικὸν ἐν ἡμῖν μέρος ἐπισκοποῦσιν τὸ περὶ τὴν ἀκοήν, δι᾽ ἃς αἰτίας τὰ περὶ αὐτὸ συμβαίνει παθήματα, λεκτέον. ὅλως μὲν οὖν	φωνὴν δὲ εἶναι πληγὴν ὑπὸ ἀέρος ἐγκεφάλου καὶ αἵματος δι᾽ ὤτων μέχρι ψυχῆς· ὀξεῖαν δὲ καὶ βαρεῖαν τὴν ταχεῖαν καὶ βραδεῖαν·

Notes on the Translation and Text

φωνὴν θῶμεν τὴν δι' ὤτων ὑπ'
ἀέρος ἐγκεφάλου τε καὶ αἵματος μέχρι ψυχῆς πληγὴν διαδιδομένην, τὴν δὲ ὑπ' αὐτῆς
κίνησιν, ἀπὸ τῆς κεφαλῆς μὲν
ἀρχομένην, τελευτῶσαν δὲ
περὶ τὴν τοῦ ἥπατος ἕδραν,
ἀκοήν· ὅση δ' αὐτῆς ταχεῖα,
ὀξεῖαν, ὅση δὲ βραδυτέρα,
βαρυτέραν· τὴν δὲ ὁμοίαν
ὁμαλήν τε καὶ λείαν, τὴν δὲ
ἐναντίαν τραχεῖαν· μεγάλην
δὲ τὴν πολλήν, ὅση δὲ ἐναντία,
σμικράν.

Timaeus 80 A, B.

... καὶ ὅσοι φθόγγοι ταχεῖς
τε καὶ βραδεῖς ὀξεῖς τε καὶ
βαρεῖς φαίνονται, τοτὲ μὲν
ἀνάρμοστοι φερόμενοι δι' ἀνομοιότητα τῆς ἐν ἡμῖν ὑπ'
αὐτῶν κινήσεως, τοτὲ δὲ σύμφωνοι δι' ὁμοιότητα. τὰς γὰρ
τῶν προτέρων καὶ θαττόνων
οἱ βραδύτεροι κινήσεις ἀποπαυομένας ἤδη τε εἰς ὅμοιον
ἐληλυθυίας, αἷς ὕστερον αὐτοὶ
προσφερόμενοι κινοῦσιν ἐκείνας, καταλαμβάνουσιν, καταλαμβάνοντες δὲ οὐκ ἄλλην
ἐπεμβάλλοντες ἀνετάραξαν
κίνησιν, ἀλλ' ἀρχὴν βραδυτέρας φορᾶς κατὰ τὴν τῆς
θάττονος, ἀποληγούσης δέ,
ὁμοιότητα προσάψαντες μίαν
ἐξ ὀξείας καὶ βαρείας συνεκεράσαντο πάθην.

συμφωνεῖν δ' ὅταν ἡ ἀρχὴ
τῆς βραδείας ὁμοία ᾖ τῇ
τελευτῇ τῆς ταχείας.

The Greek Physiological Psychology

Certain doubts of syntax in this account by Plato (cf. Archer-Hind, 246 n.; and Beare, 106 f.) should be considered in the light of Theophrastus's rendering, which seems to me to support the construction adopted by Beare (pp. 106-108) and by Mr. Archer-Hind in his *note*, although (as Professor Beare points out) not in his translation.

225. The vagueness of the original, in using the term ὁμοία, I have not tried to overcome in the translation. As to the more precise nature of this resemblance scholars have had much difficulty. I feel that Plato meant something other than identity in speed of translation. Besides this, he seems to have had in mind an agreement in the 'roughness' or 'smoothness' of the tones—what we call their timbre or 'clang-tint'. Professor Taylor feels that in this I am wrong: "Plato *seems* to be thinking of (1) rate of transmission of sound, (2) 'correspondence' of rates of vibration, and the 'conformity' seems to me to refer specifically to the latter."

226. Cf. § 5.

227. *Timaeus* 67 D, E.	Theophrastus § 86.
... τὰ δὲ μείζω καὶ ἐλάττω, τὰ μὲν συγκρίνοντα, τὰ δὲ διακρίνοντα αὐτήν, τοῖς περὶ τὴν σάρκα θερμοῖς καὶ ψυχροῖς καὶ τοῖς περὶ τὴν γλῶτταν στρυφνοῖς, καὶ ὅσα θερμαντικὰ ὄντα δριμέα ἐκαλέσαμεν, ἀδελφὰ εἶναι, ... τὸ μὲν διακριτικὸν τῆς ὄψεως λευκόν, τὸ δ' ἐναντίον αὐτοῦ μέλαν, ...	λευκὸν μὲν τὸ διακριτικόν, μέλαν δὲ τὸ συγκριτικὸν ἀνὰ λόγον [δὲ] τοῖς περὶ τὴν σάρκα θερμοῖς καὶ ψυχροῖς καὶ τοῖς περὶ τὴν γλῶσσαν στρυφνοῖς καὶ δριμέσι· ...

Theophrastus obtains further material from the portion of the *Timaeus* following the passage just quoted.

228. An omission has here been indicated, for I must believe that Plato's account of *red*, the fourth primary colour,

Notes on the Translation and Text

which should occur at this point, has been lost from Theophrastus's account by some clerical blunder. Otherwise the statement immediately following is quite misleading; for it would say that Plato derived the compound colours from three simple colours, whereas Plato himself says that they are derived from four.

229. For the shortcomings of this criticism see n. 204.

230. That is, what yields in the direction in which the pressure is exerted, and in such a way as to form a depression. The particles thus keep a certain stable relation to their fellows, and do not, as in the case of fluids, scatter in various directions. Cf. Aristotle's description of 'the hard' and 'the soft' in *Meteorol.* IV, 4, 382ª 11, to which Diels refers. Professor Taylor would render the passage in Theophrastus thus: "But none of these statements is acceptable, nor, more generally, is it held that soft is what offers no resistance, but that it is what gives way in the direction of its depth without shifting its position."

231. Upon this section Professor Taylor has written out a translation and full commentary, which I give entire.

"Translation. 'Further he has defined heavy and light not universally but for the ⟨special⟩ case of earthy bodies. For it is generally held that of them the heavy is difficult, the light easy, to remove to a foreign region. But fire and air are held to be, and actually are, light in virtue of their motion to their proper regions. Hence it will not be true that what contains fewer homogeneous parts is heavy and what contains more light. Fire is, indeed, lighter the more there is of it, but if the fire is placed 'above' both statements will be applicable, if it be placed here, neither. It is the same with the case of earth, for the greater volume will descend more rapidly from 'above'. Thus earth and fire are not absolutely heavy and light respectively, but each with reference to the region. And earth does not behave alike 'here' and 'there' (reading with Diels's note ἐνταῦθα κἀκεῖ for ἐνταῦθα καὶ which gives no good sense,) but in opposite ways. For here it is that which contains fewer,

but there that which contains more of the homogeneous parts, which is lighter.'

"Commentary. This must be carefully compared with Aristotle *de Caelo* IV, c. 2, which criticizes the *Timaeus* passage in much the same way, and explains what are meant by τὰ ὁμογενῆ. The *main* point of the criticism is that Plato's definitions (that is called heavy which it is hard to detach from the matter with which it is surrounded, that light which is easily detachable) make heavy and light purely relative to the standpoint of the observer. As Plato himself explains, *we* call air light because it readily escapes from the surface of the earth and stones heavy because it takes an effort to throw them into the air and they fall back again. But an observer placed in the atmosphere high above the earth's surface would for a similar reason call stones light because it requires no effort to expel a stone from that region, and air heavy because you couldn't easily expel it. Aristotle and Theophrastus object to this that, in their opinion, light and heavy are 'absolute terms'. Light=what tends to mount, heavy=what tends to sink. I.e., their whole criticism turns on their belief that up and down are objectively fixed directions in absolute space.

"Now for the details.

"*Plato . . . bodies.* As the word γεώδη shows, this is a direct echo of Plato's language in *Timaeus*, p. 63. The meaning is that Plato bases his definition on a consideration of what we mean when we call stones and rocks heavy. He points out that a heavy 'earthy body' is one which it is hard to remove from the earth's surface, a light one one which can be easily 'raised against gravity' as we say. Then he bases his whole theory of the purely relative sense of these terms on the consideration that for exactly the same reasons an air-dweller might call air heavy and stones light: this is a correct account of Plato's reasoning, and ἀφώρικε cannot mean that his *definition* is acceptable even for stones, because Aristotle and Theophrastus would say that what you mean by calling stones heavy is not

Notes on the Translation and Text

that they are hard to move from the earth's surface but that they naturally move *down*. (Aristotle makes this quite clear in *de Caelo* IV, 2.) The statement which Plato makes about heavy and light earthy bodies they admit to be true, but they do not regard it as a correct *definition*.

"*But fire . . . regions.* This means that Plato is wrong in giving a definition according to which it would follow that from an assumed position (e.g., a position in the upper air, or among the heavenly bodies) air or fire would be correctly described as *heavy*, because not readily to be expelled to a different region. It is true that fire or air would be as hard to expel from its region as earth from its, but according to Aristotle and Theophrastus, for all that, fire and air are *light* because they tend to move *up* away from 'the centre', there is *no* standpoint with reference to which they can be called heavy.

"*Hence it will not . . . light.* τὰ ὁμογενῆ, as is clear from the use of the word in *de Caelo* IV, 2, means the homogeneous particles of which a body is composed, and specially with reference to the theories of the *Timaeus*, the triangles out of which Timaeus builds up the corpuscles of the popularly recognized 'elements'. It might seem tempting at first to exchange the places of πλεῖον and ἔλαττον as Philippson does, but the existing text really gives a better sense. The meaning is, I think, seen from a similar use of the example of fire in *de Caelo* IV, 2, 308ᵇ 15 (ὥστ' οὐ δι' ὀλιγότητα τῶν τριγώνων ἐξ ὧν συνεστάναι φασὶν ἕκαστον αὐτῶν, τὸ πῦρ ἄνω φέρεσθαι πέφυκεν· τό τε γὰρ πλεῖον ἧττον ἂν ἐφέρετο καὶ βαρύτερον ἂν ἦν ἐκ πλειόνων ὂν τριγώνων. νῦν δὲ φαίνεται τοὐναντίον· ὅσῳ γὰρ ἂν ᾖ πλεῖον, κουφότερόν ἐστι καὶ ἄνω φέρεται θᾶττον). Theophrastus means that according to Plato's account of the matter it would be possible in some cases for a smaller bulk to be heavier than a larger bulk of the same composition, and (remember that on the Aristotelian theory of an absolute up and down this proposition is not an immediate inference from

The Greek Physiological Psychology

the former,) for a larger bulk to be lighter than a smaller bulk of the same composition. This is in fact probably true. If Plato held with Aristotle and Theophrastus that a big stone falls faster than a small one, then it follows from *his* definition in the *Timaeus* that from the standpoint of an observer in the upper air the small stone would be 'heavier' and the large one 'lighter'. (Aristotle and Theophrastus maintain, as against this, that light does not mean 'not so heavy' as something else, but that heavy and light are positive contraries like black and white. (This point is expressly stressed in the chapter of the *de Caelo*.)

"*Fire is, indeed . . . neither.* This is meant, I think, to rebut a possible argument against the last statement. It might be said that since the upward rush of a volume of flame is the more violent the greater the volume, this does show that a lesser bulk of fire *is* heavier than a larger bulk. Aristotle's and Theophrastus's reply to this is that it is true that the larger volume of flame is lighter, but that this is no argument for Plato's view of the purely relative character of weight and lightness. The two λόγοι spoken of seem to me not to be, as Diels says, those of τὸ πλεῖον and τὸ ἔλαττον but those of τὸ βαρύ and τὸ κοῦφον. In fact they are the two definitions (*a*) the heavy is that which is most difficult to remove into a foreign region, (*b*) the light is that which is most easy to remove into a foreign region. Plato says that in the region of fire, a big mass or volume of fire would be more difficult to shift into the region of air than a small one. This shift would appear to an observer in that region to be 'up,' (cf. *Timaeus* 63 C, ῥώμῃ γὰρ μιᾷ δυοῖν ἅμα μετεωριζομένοιν κ.τ.λ.), and the observer would say the bigger volume of fire is harder to 'raise' and is therefore *heavy*. This statement is also explicitly traversed in *de Caelo* IV, 2, 308ᵇ 20. (καὶ ἄνωθεν δὲ κάτω τὸ ὀλίγον οἰσθήσεται θᾶττον πῦρ, τὸ δὲ πολὺ βραδύτερον.) Thus, as Theophrastus says, with Plato's account of heavy and light the two statements given above are true 'when fire

Notes on the Translation and Text

is placed above'—i.e., if you look at the theory from the point of view of the region of fire. But 'here', looking at things from the point of view of earth, a great volume of flame 'rises' (takes the direction *we* call *up*) more readily, with a greater rush, than a lesser, so that Plato's two statements are exactly reversed. From our point of view, the more of the pyramids which constitute flame there are in the flame the *lighter* it is (with Plato's definition). Thus the result of the whole consideration so far is that, according to your supposed position as observer, you must hold, if you follow Plato, both that the bigger volume of flame is heavier and that it is lighter. [Of course Aristotle and Theophrastus themselves, believing as they do in an absolute up and down and consequently in a *positive* contrariety between heavy and light, hold that—without the introduction of any reference to relative standpoints—a big volume of flame *is* lighter, a big volume of earth heavier, than a small one.]

"*It is the same . . . from above.* This is another example intended to show that Plato's statements about light and heavy are either both true or both false, according to the observer's standpoint. We call a big stone heavy and a small one light, according to Plato, because we can *raise* the small stone more readily. But since Aristotle assumes it will be granted that a big stone drops from the air more rapidly than a small one, an air-dweller would, on Plato's theory, have to regard this movement as an *ascent* (as in Plato's own example the fire is said to 'rise' into the region of air) and call the small stone the heavier of the two. [Since Aristotle and Theophrastus hold that though one stone may be heavier than another, *no* stone at all is light, and *no* air or fire heavy, they regard these examples, which are of course obvious applications of Plato's principle, as a *reductio ad absurdum*.] So in *de Caelo* IV, 2, 308^b 24–26 Aristotle treats it as an absurd consequence of Plato's theories that according to him a volume of air may be heavier than a volume of

water, whereas according to Aristotle himself any volume of water *must* be heavier than *any* volume of air. (ἔσται —i.e., if Plato is right,—τι πλῆθος ἀέρος ὃ βαρύτερον ὕδατος ἔσται. συμβαίνει δὲ πᾶν τοὐναντίον· ἀεί τε γὰρ ὁ πλείων ἀὴρ ἄνω φέρεται μᾶλλον, κ.τ.λ.)

"*Thus earth ... region.* This is, of course, simply a correct summary of Plato's position, but it is clearly meant to be regarded as an evident absurdity.

"*And earth ... ways.* This is again a correct account of what Plato holds, but is meant to be felt as a paradox because it contradicts the δόξα (shared by Aristotle and Theophrastus) that earth is heavy ἁπλῶς.

"*For here ... lighter.* This still refers to 'earth'. Here the volume of stone which contains more 'cubes' than another is *heavier* (by Plato's definition), since it is harder to raise. But if we watched two stones falling from a point of observation in the upper air, since, as is assumed, the one with more cubical corpuscles would come to the ground first, and from our observation-point this would be a *rise*, we should call the stone of lesser bulk the heavier.

"The main point to be clear on is that from the Aristotelian point of view you must not say that one stone is light and another heavy at all, but only that the one is not so heavy as the other. Earth and water are always heavy, no matter where you are supposed to be looking from, and the greater their volume the greater their weight. Fire is always light, and the greater its volume the greater its levity. To get a companion-picture we might imagine a gas of negative weight."

232. Interchanging the position of ἔλαττον and πλεῖον, with Philippson. The sentence thus becomes intelligible, as Theophrastus's denial of what he believed to be Plato's doctrine. But Plato himself was speaking of a substance with reference to its *own place*; i.e., of earth with respect to the place of earth, of fire with respect to the place of fire. Theophrastus, as Diels points out, here follows the direction of criticism suggested by Aristotle in the *De*

Notes on the Translation and Text

Caelo IV, 2, where the *Timaeus* is cited. It is difficult for me to feel, with Professor Taylor (see p. 215) and with Diels, that this passage in Aristotle makes it desirable to keep the reading of the MSS. Such a reading seems to me to obscure if not to oppose what I take to be Theophrastus's trend of thought. For this reason it seemed necessary either to adopt Philippson's transposition of ἔλαττον and πλεῖον, or to strike out οὐκ after διόπερ.

233. The 'two statements' Professor Taylor believes to be these: (*a*) the heavy is that which is most difficult to remove into a foreign region; (*b*) the light is that which is most easy to remove into a foreign region. See note 231. But may it be that the two propositions are the ones stated by Theophrastus in the present section: (*a*) that "a heavy object is one that is borne to an alien place with difficulty; a light one with ease": and (*b*) that "the body with more of kindred substance is heavy; the one with less, light"?

234. And consequently would *there* be *lighter*, according to Plato.

235. This entire passage has evidently been mishandled by the scribes. I have substituted κἀκεῖ for καὶ, following Diels' surmise.

236. Plato expressly held that there were more than four varieties, but that four had *received names*: "Most forms of water, which are intermingled with one another, filtered through the plants of the earth, are called by the class name of *saps*; but owing to their intermixture they are all of diverse natures and the great multitude of them are accordingly unnamed: four kinds however which are of a fiery nature, being more conspicuous ['most transparent', Beare, 173], have obtained names" (*Timaeus* 59 E–60 A, tr. of Mr. Archer-Hind).

Theophrastus himself, on the other hand, held that there were either eight or seven varieties. See pp. 44 f.

237. The 'pores' here mentioned led Philippson to substitute in § 84, line 8, πόρους for χυμούς of the MSS.

The Greek Physiological Psychology

238. See §§ 6, 55, and 85, with the appended notes on the meaning of φωνή. Yet such is the shifting use of this word, that in the next sentence here in § 91 φωνή is distinguished from ψόφος.

239. Cf. §§ 5 and 86. Theophrastus here does great violence to Plato's doctrine. In Plato's theory of vision there is no fitting of particles of the object into the passages of sense; nor does his thought that there is likeness between the visual current and the external daylight, and that the visual current transmits *motions* (κινήσεις) from the object to the soul, approach to Empedocles' doctrine that particles of the object fit into the 'pores' of the eye.

240. For the Empedoclean doctrine see §§ 7 ff. The meaning of this fragmentary sentence has been completed according to the suggestion of Diels that after ἐστίν either ταὐτό or ἴσον has been dropped.

241. "I am sure the text is either mutilated or corrupt or both, but I think any attempt to ascertain what Theophrastus really meant to say in the sentence must be very problematical. ? ἄτοπον δὲ τὸ μόνῃ ταύτῃ κ.τ.λ. or τὸ μόνον ⟨ταύτῃ⟩ ταύτην ἀποδιδόναι ⟨τὴν αἰτίαν⟩ τῶν ἀ., 'to assign this *cause* only to this one sensation'. Or better, perhaps, with the same sense ἀ. δ. τὸ μόνῃ ταύτῃ ⟨τοῦτ'⟩ ἀποδιδόναι τῶν ἀ., τοῦτο meaning 'the fitting of particles into the organ'. Your translation presupposes some such text and I strongly suspect that μόνῃ ταύτῃ at least is right. Perhaps τὸ μόνῃ ταύτῃ would be sufficient to give the sense 'to assign ⟨this peculiarity⟩ to this one sense'." (A. E. T.)

242. The text here is patently corrupt; and I have tried, in the light of Plato's own words in the *Timaeus* 68 B–D, and of Theophrastus's account in § 86, to give what probably was intended. "The last sentence is, of course, corrupt, but I think there should be some indication of what you take the real reading to have been like, especially as you don't seem to be quite of the same mind

Notes on the Translation and Text

as Diels about the sense. Diels's suggestions give the sense 'And it is equally impossible to deny altogether that the other colours are mixtures and to assign the causes ⟨of these mixtures⟩; some argument and warrant is needed [sc., I suppose, for the refusal to give a detailed account of the proportions constituting these mixtures]'. I have a feeling that Diels's suggestions don't *quite* hit the mark. I don't like the construction of ἐνδέχεται with the two clauses οὔτε ... οὔτε. It is of course permissible enough, but strikes me as a little too much of a literary 'grace' for the style of the whole composition. But ἀναιρεῖν for ἀφαιρεῖν, and τὰς αἰτίας both impress me as probably right." (A. E. T.)

In view of the difficulties involved, I shall perhaps be pardoned for leaving to specialists in Greek the problem of restoring at this point the original text.

INDEX

ENGLISH

Aëtius, 162, 166, 191

Air, psychic importance of, 58, 100 ff.

Air-prints, Democritus's doctrine of, 110 f.; criticism by Theophrastus, 29, 61, 62 ff., 110 ff.

Alcmaeon, on sensation and sense perception, 88 ff., 155, 157; sight, 88 ff., 161, 162, 175 f.; hearing, 88 f., 175; smell, 88 f.; taste, 88 f.; touch, 90 f.; brain, 88 f.; intellectual processes, 88 f.; Theophrastus's method with, 51, 52

Anaxagoras, on sensation and sense perception, 66 f., 90 ff., 92 ff., 98 f., 157, 180; sight, 90 f., 92 f., 96 ff., 118 f., 161 f., 176 f., 182 ff., 190 f.; hearing, 90 f., 92 f., 178 f.; smell, 90 f., 92 f., 96 f.; taste, 90 f.; touch, 90 f.; pleasure and pain, 90 f., 92 ff., 170, 178, 180; intellectual processes, 94 f., 100 f.; air and ether, 118 f., 190; Theophrastus's criticisms and method with, 50, 51, 53, 54, 56, 58, 59, 62, 92 ff.

Animals, psychic life of; Alcmaeon on, 88 f.; Anaxagoras on, 92 f., 94 f.; Diogenes on, 102 f., 104 f., 108 f.; Empedocles on, 72 f., 80 f.; Theophrastus on, 40 f., 49, 58, 62, 98 f.

Archer-Hind, 208 ff., 212, 219

Aristophanes, 186

Aristotle, 15, 21, 23, 26, 27, 29, 30, 31, 33, 34, 46, 52, 55, 61, 156, 161, 164, 168, 172, 174, 175, 186, 190, 191, 194, 196, 201, 213, 214 ff., 218

Atoms, in Democritus's theory, 121 ff., 192 ff.; Theophrastus's criticism of, 56

Beare, 5, 6, 11, 29, 30, 156, 161, 163, 164, 165, 166, 167, 171, 173, 175, 176, 177, 178, 179, 180, 181, 182, 184, 185, 186, 188, 189, 190, 193, 197, 198, 207, 208, 209, 212, 219

Birds, psychic life of; Diogenes on, 104 f.; Theophrastus's criticism of Diogenes, 108 f.

Blood, psychic importance of; Diogenes on, 102 ff., 106 f.; Empedocles on, 74 f., 88 f., 174; Theophrastus on, 24, 59, 86 ff., 175

Brain, importance of; Alcmaeon on, 88 f.; Anaxagoras on, 90 f., 177; Democritus on, 114 f.; Diogenes on, 100 f., 183, 184

Breathing, psychic connections of; Anaxagoras on, 90 f.; Diogenes on, 104 ff., 106 f.; Empedocles on, 72 f.; Theophrastus on, 39 f., 50, 59, 84 f.

Burchard, 199

Burnet, 5, 11, 158, 164, 166, 167, 168, 191, 192, 198, 201

Chaignet, 6, 18

Children, psychology of; Diogenes on, 104 ff., 186

Clapp, 6

Clidemus, on sensation and sense perception, 155; sight, 98 f., 161 f., 183; hearing, 98 f., 100 f.; smell, 98 ff.; taste, 100 f.; judgment, 100 f.; Theophrastus's method with, 51

Colour, see *Sight*

Democritus, on sensation and sense perception, 19, 108 f., 118 ff., 156,

Index

157, 191, 192; sight, 29, 108 ff., 122 f., 136 ff., 161, 187 f., 189, 197 ff.; hearing, 114 ff., 188 f., 189 f.; smell, 140 f.; taste, 122 ff., 140 f., 193 ff.; touch, 120 f., 130 f.; intellectual processes, 116 f.; criticism by Theophrastus, 110 ff., 116 f., 126 ff., 136 ff.; Theophrastus's method with, 51-62

Diels, 6, 11, 158, 159, 163, 164, 166, 167, 168, 170, 174, 175, 179, 180, 183, 184, 185, 186, 187, 192, 193, 194, 196, 200, 201, 213, 216, 218, 219, 220, 221

Diogenes of Apollonia, on sensation and sense perception, 100 f., 106 f., 155, 156, 157, 189; sight, 100 f., 102 f., 106 f., 161 f., 185; hearing, 100 f., 102 f., 106 f., 185; smell, 100 f., 102 f., 106 f., 183 ff.; taste, 100 f.; touch, 100 f.; pleasure and pain, 102 f., 106 f.; memory, 106 f.; intellectual processes, 104 f., 106 f., 186; criticism by Theophrastus, 106 ff.; Theophrastus's method with, 51, 52, 58

Diogenes Laërtius, 27, 43, 54

Dizziness, Theophrastus on, 30 f., 46 f.

Ear, see *Hearing*
Echo, Democritus on, 63
Effluences; Empedocles on, 72 f., 164, 169, 173; Theophrastus on, 21, 57, 61, 82 ff.; assumed in "likeness" theory of perception, 66 f.
Emotion, Theophrastus on, 35; see *Pleasure and Pain* and *Temperament*
Empedocles, on sensation and sense perception, 66 f., 70 f., 74 f., 96 f., 148 f., 157, 164, 169, 171; sight, 70 ff., 78 f., 80 ff., 118 f., 161, 163, 164 ff., 172 f., 220; hearing, 72 f., 82 f., 84 f., 166 f., 175; smell, 72 f., 84 ff., 174; taste, 73 ff., 82 f.; touch, 73 ff., 82 f.; pleasure and pain, 74 f., 78 ff., 86 f., 170, 171; intellectual processes, 74 f., 80 f., 86 f.; temperament, 74 f.; talent, 74 ff., 86 ff.;

Theophrastus's criticism of, 39 f., 76 ff.; Theophrastus's method with, 51-54, 57-61
Eye, see *Sight*

Fairbanks, 159, 163 f., 178
Fish, compared with birds, 104 f.

Goethe, on colour, 200

Hard and soft, see *Touch*
Harmony, see *Hearing*
Hearing and sound; Alcmaeon on, 88 f., 175; Anaxagoras on, 90 f., 92 f., 178 f.; Clidemus on, 98 f., 100 f.; Democritus on, 114 ff., 188 f., 189 f.; Diogenes on, 100 f., 102 f., 106 f., 185; Empedocles on, 72 f., 82 f., 84 f., 166 f., 175; Heraclides on, 34; Plato on, 68 ff., 70 f., 144 f., 162 f., 209 ff.; Theophrastus on, 22, 23, 25, 33-35, 36; a group of investigators on, 118 f.
Heavy and light, see *Touch*
Heraclitus, on sensation and sense perception, 66 f., 156
Hering, 202
Hindu doctrine of sense and intellect, 185
Hot and cold, see *Touch*

Intellectual processes; Alcmaeon on, 88 f.; Anaxagoras on, 94 f., 100 f., 180; Clidemus on, 100 f.; Democritus on, 116 f.; Diogenes on, 104 f., 106 f., 186; Empedocles on, 74 f., 80 f., 86 f.; Parmenides on, 68 f., 158 f.; Theophrastus on, 15, 19, 59, 108 f., 190

Judgment, see *Intellectual processes*

Karsten, 159, 163
Kranz, 198, 199, 200, 201

Light, see *Sight*
Linforth, 7
Locke, 191

224

Index

Memory; Diogenes on, 106 f.; Parmenides on, 68 f.; Theophrastus on, 108 f.
Menestor on tastes, 44
Mirroring, Theophrastus on, 30
Mullach, 190, 199
Music, Theophrastus on, 25, 35, 50; see *Hearing*

Nose and nostrils, see *Smell*

Odour, see *Smell*

Pain, see *Pleasure and Pain*
Parmenides, on sensation and sense perception, 66 f., 68 f., 157; Theophrastus's method with, 51, 52
Perception, see *Sensation, Sense perception*
Philippson, 11, 159, 167, 169, 173, 175, 179, 185, 186, 194, 208, 218 f.
Plants, Diogenes on lack of thought in, 104 f., 108 f.
Plato, on sensation and sense perception, 66 f., 68 ff., 118 ff., 156, 157, 159 f., 191; sight, 28, 31, 68 ff., 142 f., 144 f., 148 ff., 160, 161, 171, 176, 212 f., 220; hearing, 34, 144 f., 148 f., 162 f., 209 ff.; smell, 38, 70 f., 144 f., 148 f., 160, 208 f.; taste, 70 f., 142 ff., 148 f., 160, 207 f., 219; touch, 70 f., 142 f., 146 f., 160, 203 ff., 213 ff.; pleasure and pain, 142 f., 206; Theophrastus's criticism of, 44, 50, 146 ff.; Theophrastus's method with, 51-55, 57, 60-61
Pleasure and pain; Anaxagoras on, 56, 59, 90 f., 92 ff., 178, 180; Diogenes on, 102 f., 106 f.; Empedocles on, 74 f., 78 ff., 86 f., 170, 171; Plato on, 142 f., 206; Theophrastus on, 22, 35, 38, 42, 48-50, 52
Poppelreuter, 18, 24, 175
"Pores," Empedocles' doctrine of, 70 ff., 148 f., 164, 169, 220
Prantl, 11, 18, 28 f., 199, 202
Priscianus, 11, 21-29, 31, 33, 34, 40, 45, 46
Pythagorean theory, 161, 172, 192

Reasoning, see *Intellectual processes*
Reflection, optical, Theophrastus on, 29 f.; see *Sight*
Rough and smooth, see *Touch*

Savours, see *Taste*
Schneider, 167, 174, 194, 200
Sensation; Anaxagoras on, 180; Empedocles on, 171; Parmenides on, 158 f.; Theophrastus on, 25, 190; Hindu doctrine of, 185; organic sensations, Theophrastus on, 46 f.; see *Sense perception, Sight, Hearing, Smell*, etc.
Sense organs, Theophrastus, on, 20, 21, 22, 23, 24, 29 ff., 34, 39 f., 45, 55; see *Sense perception, Sight, Hearing*, etc.
Sense perception; Alcmaeon on, 88 f., 157; Anaxagoras on, 90 ff., 92 ff., 98 ff., 157, 180; Democritus on, 108 f., 118 ff., 157, 192; Diogenes on, 100 f., 106 f., 157, 189; Empedocles on, 70 f., 74 f., 76 ff., 96 f., 148 f., 157, 164, 169; Parmenides on, 68 f., 157; Plato on, 118 ff., 156, 157, 159 f., 191; Theophrastus on, 18-26, 30, 48 ff., 52, 53; Theophrastus's classification of theories of, 66 f.; see *Sight, Hearing*, etc.
Siebeck, 6, 18
Sight; Alcmaeon on, 88 f., 161, 162, 175 f.; Anaxagoras on, 90 f., 92 f., 96 ff., 102 ff., 118 f., 161 f., 176 f., 190 f.; Clidemus on, 98 f., 161 f., 183; Democritus on, 56 f., 108 ff., 122 f., 132 ff., 136 ff., 161, 187 f., 189, 197 ff.; Diogenes on, 100 f., 102 f., 106 f., 161 f., 185; Empedocles on, 70 ff., 78 f., 80 ff., 118 f., 161, 164 ff., 172 f., 220; Plato on, 28, 68 ff., 142 f., 144 f., 148 ff., 160, 161, 171, 176, 212 f., 220; Pythagorean doctrine of, 161; Theophrastus on, 25, 26, 27-32, 57, 61, 62 ff., 183, 202; various investigators on, 118 f.; Theophrastus's classification of theories of, 70 f.
Simplicius, 31

Index

Smell; Alcmaeon on, 88 f.; Anaxagoras on, 90 f., 92 f., 96 f.; Clidemus on, 98 ff.; Democritus on, 140 f.; Diogenes on, 100 f., 102 f., 106 f., 183 ff.; Empedocles on, 72 f., 84 ff.; Plato on, 70 f., 144 f., 148 f., 160, 208 f.; Theophrastus on, 21, 22, 23, 25, 33, 36-42, 49 f.; various investigators on, 118 f.

Sophocles, 167

Sound, see *Hearing*

Stallbaum, 170

Stewart, 170

Talent; Empedocles on, 74 ff., 86 ff.; Theophrastus on, 15, 175

Taste; Alcmaeon on, 88 f.; Anaxagoras on, 90 f.; Clidemus on, 100 f.; Democritus on, 122 ff., 140 f., 193 ff.; Diogenes on, 100 f.; Empedocles on, 73 ff., 82 f.; Plato on, 142 ff., 148 f., 160, 207 f., 219; Theophrastus on, 20, 23, 24, 25, 41, 42, 43-45, 49 f., 61 f.

Taylor, 7, 11, 158, 160, 161, 162 f., 163, 164, 165 f., 170, 172, 176, 177, 178, 179, 180, 182, 183, 184, 185, 188 f., 190, 191, 192, 194, 195, 196, 197, 198, 199, 200, 201, 202, 208, 209, 213 ff., 219, 220 f.

Temperament, Empedocles on, 74 f., 168; as topic of Theophrastus's *De Sensibus*, 15

Theophrastus; his own doctrine of sensation and sense perception, 18-26, 30, 52, 55, 155 f., 191; of sight, 27-32, 183, 202; of hearing, 33-35, 36; of smell, 33, 36-42; of taste, 41 f., 43-45; of touch, 46 f., 192, 196, 213 ff.; of organic sensations, 30 f., 46 f.; of pleasure and pain, 48-50; of memory, 108 f.; of intellectual processes, 108 f.; on nature and causation, 56, 179; his requirements of scientific theory, 56 ff.; his method of exposition and of criticism, 51-64, 159 f., 191, 204, 207, 208, 220; his use of Plato's *Timaeus*, 159, 203; scope and value of his *De Sensibus*, 15-17; text and translation of the *De Sensibus*, 66-151

Thinking, see *Intellectual processes*

Timaeus, Theophrastus's use of, 159, 203

Tongue, in diagnosis, 104 f.; see *Taste*

Tone, see *Hearing*

Touch; Alcmaeon on, 90 f.; Anaxagoras on, 90 f.; Democritus on, 120 f., 130 f.; Diogenes on, 100 f.; Empedocles on, 73 ff., 82 f.; Plato on, 70 f., 142 f., 146 f., 160, 203 ff., 213 ff.; Theophrastus on, 25, 46 f., 61, 213 ff.; as used in "difference" theory, 66 f.; various investigators on, 118 f.

Usener, 174, 179

Vision, see *Sight*

Wachtler, 177

Wimmer, 11, 173, 207

Zeller, 6, 11, 18, 24, 31, 34, 50, 158

Index

GREEK

ἀήρ, 166
ἄθρους, 183
αἴσθησις, 155
αἰσθητόν, 160, 163
ἀκοή, 160
ἀλήθεια, 194
ἀραιόν, 168
αὖος, 199

διάστημα, 181
διευτονεῖν, 163
δύναμις, 196

εἶδος, 192 f.
ἔμψυχος, 187 f.
ἐναπόληψις, 197
ἐπιπρόσθησις, 202

ἡδονή, 186

ἰκμάς, 186

κώδων, 166 f., 175

μέλαν, 199, 201
μορφή, 193

ὄψις, 160

πικρόν, 195, 208
πολυπλάγτων, 158

σημεῖον, 174
στίλβον 176
συγκρίσεις, 197 f.
συμμετρία, 158, 169
σύμφυτος, 170
σχῆμα, 33, 192

φλέβες, 185
φύσις, 192, 194
φωνή, 162, 189, 209, 220

χρόα, 172 f.
χρῶμα, 172 f.

ψόφος, 162, 189, 220

For Product Safety Concerns and Information please contact our EU representative GPSR@taylorandfrancis.com
Taylor & Francis Verlag GmbH, Kaufingerstraße 24, 80331 München, Germany

www.ingramcontent.com/pod-product-compliance
Lightning Source LLC
Chambersburg PA
CBHW061443300426

44114CB00014B/1810